SLAVES
AND FREEDMEN
IN
CIVIL WAR
LOUISIANA

SLAVES AND FREEDMEN IN CIVIL WAR LOUISIANA

C. PETER RIPLEY

Louisiana State University Press · Baton Rouge

Library of Congress Cataloging in Publication Data

Ripley, C   Peter, 1941–
    Slaves and freedmen in Civil War Louisiana.

    Bibliography: p.
    Includes index.
    1. Freedmen in Louisiana. 2. Slavery in the
United States—Louisiana. 3. Reconstruction—Louisiana.
4. Louisiana—Politics and government—Civil War, 1861–
1865. I. Title.
√ E185.93.L6R5   301.44′93′09763   75–18043
    ISBN 0–8071–0187–7

I gratefully acknowledge permission to reprint material which appeared in different form under the title "The Black Family in Transition: Louisiana, 1860–1865," in *Journal of Southern History*, XLI, No. 3 (August, 1975), 369–80.

For Calvin Patterson
For Jack West
For those people who continue to struggle for
human liberty and individual dignity

Contents

Tables

Acknowledgments

Before a study of this type is completed it becomes a group experience. The people who assisted in various ways are legion, and the mention of their names here cannot repay the debts, large and small, that I owe them. James P. Jones and Joe M. Richardson of Florida State University encouraged the project from the start. My debts to them are manifold and probably unpayable, but they cover such a span of time that I have become comfortable with them. I hope they have.

Numerous other individuals read the manuscript, shared their knowledge and insights, and endured my enthusiasm for the Louisiana experiment. Foremost are William W. Rogers of Florida State University, William I. Hair of Georgia State College, John B. Myers of Columbus College, John F. Zeugner of Worcester Polytechnic Institute, and Julie Jones and Lawrence Powell of Yale University. Daniel Crofts, of Trenton State College, read two drafts of the manuscript, forcing me to rethink some parts, to reorganize other parts, and to be more precise throughout, a painful but worthwhile experience. John W. Blassingame has shared his ideas and research on the black experience in Louisiana, as well as his enthusiasm, for a number of years. If I have been a burden to any of these friends, let me thank them for their tolerance, absolve them of responsibility for the flaws herein, and share with them what proves to be correct. David Ammerman, C. L., Tommy, Alice,

Murph, Mario, Bill, Mo, Mike, Mary, Joe, and Goombah provided so many essentials I could not list them.

The staffs of the Library of Congress, the National Archives, the Southern Historical Collection of the University of North Carolina, the New York Historical Society Library, the Historical Society of Pennsylvania, the Bowdoin College Library, the Tulane University Library, the New Orleans Public Library, and the Maine Historical Society Library were all helpful. Special thanks are due Cliff Johnson and the staff of the Amistad Research Center of Dillard University and John Price and Margaret Fisher of the Louisiana State University Archives.

I would also like to acknowledge the Woodrow Wilson Foundation for its financial assistance. Final thanks are for Martha— patient woman and good friend.

C. P. R.

New Haven, Connecticut
April, 1975

List of Abbreviations

AGO   Adjutant General Office, Record Group 94, National Archives, Washington, D.C.

AMA   American Missionary Association

ARC   Amistad Research Center, Dillard University, New Orleans, Louisiana

BRFAL   Bureau of Refugees, Freedmen and Abandoned Lands, Record Group 105, National Archives, Washington, D.C.

CBSA   Customs Bureau Special Agents, Record Group 36, National Archives, Washington, D.C.

CWSATD   Civil War Special Agents Treasury Department, Record Group 159, National Archives, Washington, D.C.

DGR(C)   Department of the Gulf Records (Confederate), Howard-Tilton Memorial Library, Tulane University, New Orleans, Louisiana

DGR(U)   Department of the Gulf Records (Union), Record Group 393, National Archives, Washington, D.C.

DU   Dillard University, New Orleans, Louisiana

HLHU   Houghton Library, Harvard University, Cambridge, Massachusetts

HSP   Historical Society of Pennsylvania, Philadelphia, Pennsylvania

IGO   Inspector General's Office, Record Group 159, National Archives, Washington, D.C.

LC   Library of Congress, Washington, D.C.

LSU   Louisiana State University Archives, Baton Rouge, Louisiana

MHSL   Maine Historical Society Library, Portland, Maine

NA   National Archives, Washington, D.C.

NYHSL   New York Historical Society Library, New York, New York

NYPL   New York Public Library, New York, New York

PJM   Police Jury Minutes

TU   Howard-Tilton Memorial Library, Tulane University, New Orleans, Louisiana

UNC   Southern Historical Collection, University of North Carolina, Chapel Hill, North Carolina

SLAVES
AND FREEDMEN
IN
CIVIL WAR
LOUISIANA

Introduction

Reconstruction came early to Louisiana. One year after the start of the Civil War a Federal army, commanded by Brigadier General Benjamin F. Butler, sailed into New Orleans and occupied the southern tip of the state. In the months that followed, Union forces spread into the rich plantation parishes of lower Louisiana. There, between the spring of 1862 and the spring of 1865, while the war continued in other parts of the South, black laborers and native white planters began adjusting to a new social and economic order.

Even from the start of the war, the old order—slavery—was shaken. Confederate war policies, particularly impressment of slave laborers, disrupted the plantation system, while recalcitrant slaves won new concessions from uneasy masters. In the year that all of Louisiana was Confederate, institutional slavery was being gradually but steadily eroded.

The presence of a Federal occupational army accelerated the disintegration of slavery, although that was not the intent of those who directed the military effort. Slaves from the occupied parishes and from the Confederate interior abandoned plantations and sought sanctuary in forts, camps, and picket stations. But frequently the treatment which slaves and runaways received from the Union army fell short of a liberator's embrace, for during the early months of occupation (the spring and summer of 1862) Union policy aimed to prop up slavery, not to aid its demise. Lin-

1

coln believed that before he could woo potentially loyal planters
back into the Union he would have to revive the plantation economy; and that required a stable labor force. The political need to
rejuvenate the plantations and fear of black violence initially caused
military commanders in Louisiana and politicians in Washington
to support the status quo of antebellum slavery in the occupied
area. Nevertheless, as the war continued and as an increasing
number of slaves and runaways came under Union control, the
old system could not be sustained.

After a year of occupation, Federal military officials in the state
adopted policies and programs to help shape a new social, economic, and political order. Under tutelage of the military, slaves
and runaways were educated, paid wages, recruited into the army,
and given access to military courts. Military officials established a
Bureau of Free Negro Labor, a Board of Negro Education, and an
Enrollment Commission. Manned almost exclusively by Federal
officers, these bureaus and agencies affected nearly every aspect of
black life during the wartime transition from slavery to freedom.
The Enrollment Commission recruited black troops in Louisiana;
the Board of Negro Education established the most extensive black
educational system to that time in the nation; the Bureau of Free
Negro Labor was generally responsible for seeing that blacks were
neither wanting nor idle and for mediating relations between planters and laborers. The bureau's foremost responsibility involved
implementing and supervising a contract wage system on plantations, but its actual responsibilities were much broader. Because
black Louisianians were primarily considered as laborers essential
to the Federal policy of reviving the plantation economy, the labor
bureau touched all facets of black life—education, justice, family
security, housing, rations, and clothing, as well as wages and contracts.

The agencies and programs of occupied Louisiana presaged Reconstruction throughout the postwar South. The policies and goals
of Louisiana's bureaus of Negro labor and education resemble
those of the Bureau of Refugees, Freedmen and Abandoned Lands,
a postwar national agency established to aid the freedmen in all
the states of the fallen Confederacy. In both wartime Louisiana

and in the Reconstruction South, native white planters and liberated slaves worked—with Federal guidance—to adjust to new social and economic realities. Lincoln used Louisiana as a testing ground for a Reconstruction policy which he hoped would have wider application after the war.

Just as Louisiana struggled with reunion during the war, so too did the entire South during the late 1860s and early 1870s. Indeed, the influences and the cast of characters at work in southern Louisiana during the war—native planters, freedmen, Federal bureaus, military commanders, revived plantations, Union politics—suggest a wartime Reconstruction experiment. And as William S. McFeely shrewdly proposed in *Yankee Stepfather*, the Louisiana experiment was probably as much a determinant of subsequent Federal Reconstruction policy as was the "Rehearsal for Reconstruction" in the Sea Islands of South Carolina so eloquently described by Willie Lee Rose.[1]

Many of the larger postwar issues vital to Louisiana's black population were determined by late 1865. Blacks did not own the land most had hoped for and many had fought for. Their economic future held little more than annual labor contracts, sharecropping, plantation stores, and debt peonage. Most rural blacks found themselves again working the land and living in segregated plantation cabins under the watchful eye of the white population. A substantial black educational system—which served 28 percent of all southern black children in school in the fall of 1865—would not survive another year. Louisiana's black political leaders believed that demands for franchise and political equality would never be realized through the state government and that their only recourse lay in the United States Congress and the Federal Reconstruction of the South. Despite these hopes, neither "radical Reconstruction" nor its benefits—citizenship and temporary civil rights—allowed black Louisianians to move much beyond the terms set by the wartime experiment.

---

1. William S. McFeely, *Yankee Stepfather: General O. O. Howard and the Freedmen* (New York, 1970), 337; Willie Lee Rose, *Rehearsal for Reconstruction: The Port Royal Experiment* (New York, 1964).

I

Confederate Slavery

∾

I know why the caged bird sings, ah me,
When his wing is bruised and his bosom sore,—
When he beats his bars and he would be free;
It is not a carol of joy or glee,
But a prayer that he sends from his heart's deep core,
But a plea, that upward to Heaven he flings—
I know why the caged bird sings!

    —Paul Laurence Dunbar

When Edmund Ruffin pulled the lanyard and sent a shot at Fort Sumter, he ultimately did more damage to the foundations of slavery than to the walls of that crumbling citadel. Only with quick, total victory could the South have saved her labor system. As the war continued from year to year, it brought de facto emancipation closer and closer. Institutional slavery was protected by state laws which legalized it and by court decisions which held slaves as sacrosanct as any private property. Yet historians generally acknowledge that more than laws and court decisions was necessary to sustain the peculiar institution. Rewards and incentives in any number of forms were common, as was corporal punishment from the perfunctory to the sadistic; the isolation of plantation life reinforced the system as did the monotony and routine of plantation labors; the threat of the auction block and the prospect of being owned by a new and possibly more severe master usually restrained slaves—as did some aspects of religion. But Eugene Genovese

5

argues that a paternalistic master-slave relationship, more than any other feature or behavioral pattern, sustained slavery from within.[1]

The dominion of master over slaves was not absolute. Slaves maintained a considerable degree of conscious autonomy. John W. Blassingame concludes that within the slave community—away from the immediate supervision of the overseer or owner—slaves turned to their distinctive culture, their families, and their religion as buffers against harsher realities. Nevertheless, Blassingame sees slave behavior "bound up with" any number of influences, including such sustaining qualities as the "nature of the antebellum plantation [and] the behavior of masters."[2]

Slaves responded in a wide variety of ways to plantation life, to masters, and to the legal and sustaining features of slave society. Many tried to avoid contact with whites by working inconspicuously and by challenging the plantation regimen only occasionally. The other extreme was the violent slave. In the Louisiana State Penitentiary on the eve of the Civil War, 100 of 330 inmates were slaves, 79 of whom were convicted of violent crimes against whites —29 of those for murder and 4 for poisoning. Those figures only hint at the violent response of slaves, in that they do not include similar cases which never left the plantation or the parish. Somewhere between inconspicuous laborers and murderers were slaves who went on "strike" by fleeing. As described by Ulrich B. Phillips, they were usually prompted by an immediate and specific grievance; they hid nearby, returning after a tenuous agreement was reached with the master.[3] Temporary runaways were common and many no doubt were "strikers" as Phillips contends. Yet the volun-

---

1. Kenneth Stampp, *The Peculiar Institution: Slavery in the Ante-Bellum South* (New York, 1956), 141–91; Eugene Genovese, *Roll, Jordan, Roll: The World the Slaves Made* (New York, 1974), 4–7.

2. John W. Blassingame, *The Slave Community: Plantation Life in the Ante-Bellum South* (New York, 1972), 75–76, 103, 154.

3. *Report of the Board of Control of the Louisiana Penitentiary to the General Assembly* [January, 1860] (Baton Rouge, 1859), 39–51; Ulrich Bonnell Phillips, *American Negro Slavery: A Survey of the Supply, Employment, and Control of Negro Labor as Determined by the Plantation Regime* (Baton Rouge, 1966), 303–304; see also Blassingame, *Slave Community*, 133–53, 184–216, for a complete discussion of slave responses and personalities.

tary return of most "strikers" was less a matter of believing that they had concluded successful labor-relation negotiations, as Phillips suggests, than of knowing that they had little chance of complete escape.

Running away was a less viable response to bondage than is often acknowledged, and slaves seem to have shown greater wisdom regarding it (and mass revolt, for that matter) than have many observers who question why there was not more of both. A major reason is that chances for success were virtually nonexistent in the Deep South states. And Louisiana was one of the deepest. There was the patrol, the pass system, the dogs, and the need for food. Many slaves would not leave their families behind, and fleeing with them appreciably lessened the already minute chance for success. In parts of Louisiana the only routes for even temporary escape led through bayous and swamps, which were hazardous because of deadly wildlife and bloodsucking insects, and because few bondsmen could swim; most slaves were deliberately prevented from acquiring that skill, and, because of that disadvantage, the dogs often found the runaways at the river's edge.

A more fundamental question is—where could a runaway slave go to reach freedom from Louisiana? There was no place close enough to offer reasonable hope.[4] Most slaves had seen the results of abortive escape attempts—a whipping or the stocks for the fortunate, maiming by the dogs or death for the unfortunate. Masters assembled slaves to watch the punishment, for it provided a gory lesson on the futility of running. The obstacles, the hazards, the concern for family, the lack of a relatively close free area, and the cost of failure discouraged those attempting to escape Louisiana slavery.

Essentially the same factors pertained to mass revolts and insurrections. The controls, the isolation, the lack of communication, and the cost of failure made the idea a desperate one. Even if initially successful, few escaped the better armed and better mounted

---

4. See, for example, Solomon Northrup, *Twelve Years a Slave*, ed. Sue Eakin and Joseph Logsdon (Baton Rouge, 1968), 99–104, 182–85, for an intelligent discussion on this subject by a former slave from Louisiana.

white population, for freedom was too far away. Every region had its Nat Turner, either in reality or in folklore, and part of the traditional retelling included the ultimate failure—the hanging, the burning, the whipping, and the imprisonment of participants.[5] Knowledge of the past and an understanding of the system within which they lived convinced most slaves that revolt, like running, was usually futile.

The parish patrol, one of the more overt sustaining features of slave society, frequently served to enforce the master-slave relationship, particularly off the plantation. From the winter of the secession crisis through the outbreak of war, planters turned their attention to the patrols. Where the night riders were already operating, their size, frequency of rounds, and responsibility were increased. In many parishes they had to be revived; in others they were organized for the first time.[6] Whether new or old, patrols were needed, claimed one planted, because of "convulsive movements" in the country which "breed discontent and [which] will tend inevitably to open revolt in the absence of proper restraints."[7]

To provide the proper restraints, parishes were divided into wards and canvassed by patrols made up of at least five men drawn from the white population between the ages of fifteen and fifty. Participation was compulsory, and captains were authorized to call on all citizens if necessary. In some parishes directors or captains had to be slave owners or sons of slave owners. During each canvass all slave quarters in the ward were visited if not searched. Refusal by a master or overseer to allow access to the cabins was punishable by fines from fifty to five hundred dollars per offense. In Pointe Coupee parish all slave cabins were numbered and the number of occupants posted in a conspicuous place to aid the patrol.[8]

5. *Ibid.*, 188–90.

6. Iberville Parish PJM, July 23, 1859, January 14, September 2, 1861; Franklin Parish PJM, June 5, 1861; St. Charles Parish PJM, December 19, 1860, May 19, 1862; Alexandria *Constitutional*, May 25, 1861; Greensburg *Imperial*, February 16, 1861.

7. Franklin Parish PJM, June 3, 1861; Clara Solomon Diary (LSU), July 5, 1861; A. Heise to Mr. Bowman, July 5, 1862, in Bowman Family Papers, LSU.

8. Pointe Coupee PJM, May 1, 1861; West Baton Rouge *Sugar Planter*, July 6, 1861; Bienville Parish PJM, January 7, 1862; Caldwell Parish PJM, Jan-

While patrols also served as home militias, their major function was to control the "service population." In the weeks following the outbreak of war, police juries enhanced the patrols' authority by passing new local ordinances which supplemented the master and the *Code Noir* in controlling slaves. According to these laws slaves could not go out without a pass, assemble outside the plantation, hold balls or dances on the plantation unless supervised, gamble, watch gambling, loiter, drink alcohol, own or possess a horse "with or without . . . consent," tan leather or make shoes, "buy, sell or trade on [their] own account," or own a boat, dog, or weapon of any kind.[9] Whites and free blacks cooperating with a slave in any violation received fines or prison terms. Offending bondsmen received the lash. In theory and practice the entire black population was under the complete control of the patrols. Normally, only in capital cases did they need additional authority to inflict punishment.[10]

Despite stronger slave codes and revived parish patrols which supplemented the legal and sustaining features of slavery, the Civil War in Louisiana undermined the institution. The supportive influences could not offset the impact of Confederate hiring and impressment of slave laborers, of disruption and dislocation produced by refugee masters, of an increase in runaways and slave violence, of Federal raids, of Union capture of New Orleans, and of the presence of a blue-clad occupational army in southern Louisiana after April, 1862.

The Confederate government used slave labor as a means of releasing whites for military duty. For every black hired or im-

---

uary 10, 1861; Pointe Coupee *Democrat*, June 8, 1861; Opelousas *Patriot*, June 15, 1861.

9. See Joe Gray Taylor, *Negro Slavery in Louisiana* (Baton Rouge, 1963), Chap. 9; V. Alton Moody, *Slavery on Louisiana Sugar Plantations* (New Orleans, 1924), for information on the *Code Noir*; Lafayette Parish PJM, June 3, June 22, 1861; West Feliciana Parish PJM, June 5, 1860; Bienville Parish PJM, June 6, 1864; Caddo Parish PJM, June 4, 1861; Iberville Parish PJM, June 4, 1861; West Baton Rouge Parish PJM, April 26, 1861; Pass for Ceazar, April 19, 1863, in Ann E. Spears Papers, LSU.

10. Resolutions of the Executive Committee of Trinity Vigillant Association [1861], in Moses and St. John Richardson Liddell Papers, LSU.

pressed, a white could be armed and placed in uniform. Slaves built fortifications and worked on railroads, in salt works, coal mines, hospitals, saw mills, and in virtually every area of military and industrial activity.[11] The percentage of an owner's slaves eligible for impressment varied, but because of the early and continued Union threat in Louisiana, Confederate military authorities had wide discretionary powers in the matter. As early as the fall of 1862 the Confederate acting secretary of war wrote the commander at Port Hudson, Louisiana, that he should use all the resources at his command to defend his post. And even though planters were reluctant to furnish slaves to build fortifications, they could be called on "to contribute such a number of their slaves as may be needed for the purpose."[12] Two years later, in that part of Louisiana which was still Confederate all slaves and free blacks between eighteen and fifty years old were registered by the Bureau of Conscription and subject to call as laborers. Usually no more than one-seventh to one-fifth of the able-bodied hands were summoned, although state law provided that one-half the able-bodied males (ages eighteen through fifty) could be impressed.[13] Early in the war there were probably few states in the Confederacy where military hiring of slaves was used more widely than in Louisiana.

For slaves, working for the military was often a more difficult life than laboring on the plantation. Houses for impressed laborers at Fort Beauregard at Harrisburg, Louisiana, were sixty to seventy

11. E. Surget to George Logan, March 21, 1863, in George Logan Papers, UNC; George W. Deitzler to John A. Rawlins, February 3, 1861, *The War of the Rebellion: A Compilation of the Official Records of the Union and Confederate Armies* (Washington, D.C., 1880–1901), Ser. I, Vol. XXIV, Pt. 1, p. 15; hereinafter cited as *Official Records*. Unless otherwise indicated, all citations are to Series I. Walter Guion to Bessie E. Guion, January 24, 1862, in Guion Family Papers, UNC; A. J. H. Duganne, *Camps and Prisons: Twenty Months in the Department of the Gulf* (New York, 1865), 183; Shreveport *News*, July 19, 1864; Receipt, undated, in William Hale Papers, LSU; see also Joe Gray Taylor, "Slavery in Louisiana During the Civil War," *Louisiana History*, VIII, 27–33.

12. J. A. Campbell to W. N. R. Beall, October 23, 1862, *Official Records*, XV, 841–42.

13. Shreveport *News*, August 2, 1864; *Acts Passed by the Twenty-Seventh Legislature of the State of Louisiana in Extra Session at Opelousas, December, 1862–January, 1863* (Natchitoches, 1864), 10–11.

feet long, with no ventilation except one door. There were no sanitation facilities, no opportunities for bathing, no issuance of clean clothes, and no medical facilities. An irate surgeon wrote that "at present each negro had a space of *eleven inches wide and six feet long to his share*. If this state of things is continued half of these negroes will die of camp fever." And it does not appear that the surgeon was an alarmist, for a daily average of 10 percent of the slaves there were too ill to work.[14] The health situation at Harrisburg was not unusual, for "scores" of laborers returning from Port Hudson in early 1863 were described as mostly "sick and numbers of them have died of pnewmonia [*sic*]."[15]

Planters complained about the quality and quantity of the food, clothing, sanitary conditions and health treatment given their slaves in government employ. But they were even more concerned about physical abuse of their slaves hired by the army. Military authorities were repeatedly cautioned by superiors not to mistreat black laborers; soldiers were threatened with "severe penalties" for "maltreating, or beating . . . the slaves"—but with mixed success. In at least one instance planters refused to meet a call for one-third of their eligible laborers unless the military met certain conditions: planters would supply overseers to work the slaves and the military would assign a ward in the hospital for the slaves who would be attended by a planter-supplied doctor. Planters were demanding fair and humane treatment for their slaves, which, according to the planters, they had not been getting.[16] Shortly after this incident the Louisiana legislature authorized owners whose slaves were impressed by the state or the Confederate States to provide overseers and "all things affecting their [slaves'] health and comfort." At the

14. Payne Madison to George Logan, March 16, 1862, P. M. McKelvy to George Logan, January 23, 1863, Weekly Report of Soldiers, Men and Negroes Working on Fortification at Harrisburg, Louisiana, February 15, 1863, all in Logan Papers, UNC.

15. Your Brother to Dear Albert, February 17, 1863, in Cummings-Black Family Papers, TU.

16. General Order No. 3, Fort Beauregard, December 25, 1862, Petition and Resolutions of Planters of Morehouse Parish, March 2, 1863, H. M. Polk to George Logan, March 11, 1863, all in Logan Papers, UNC.

same time the legislature appropriated $500,000 "to pay for the hire or loss loss of slaves . . . by death or otherwise while employed . . . in the state."[17]

Civil authorities as well as the military hired slaves for building fortifications. Several parishes made a combined effort to defend the Red River area. The executive committee of that project was mindful of complaints against the military when it assured planters that their slaves would be well cared for. Transportation, food, shelter, medicine, and doctors were provided, and the committee personally guaranteed that "no slave shall be overtaxed or improperly treated." The civilians offered owners $25 per month per slave, $7 more than the army, and they, like the military, promised compensation for slaves lost through negligence.[18]

Throughout the war considerable competition existed for labor in Confederate Louisiana which added to the demands made of slaves. There was the normal, omnipresent plantation work. In addition, slaves were subject to call for labor on roads and levees in peacetime, and as the war dragged on and did more damage, that demand increased. But despite payment to planters of $1.50 and $2.00 a day per slave, levee and road inspectors had difficulty hiring a sufficient number of hands.[19] To these civilian needs were added the requests of various bureaus, agencies, and departments of the Confederacy. The Engineering Corps, the Quartermaster Department, the Transportation Department, the Ordinance Department, and the Cotton Bureau all wanted slave labor, and all made slave requisitions.[20]

17. *Acts Passed by the Sixth Legislature of the State of Louisiana at Its Extra Session Held in the City of Shreveport on the 4th of May, 1863* (Shreveport, 1863), 17–19.
18. Natchitoches *Union*, November 27, December 4, 1862; Avoyelles Parish PJM, November 24, December 20, 1862; Caddo Parish PJM, May 5, 1862; Bienville Parish PJM, January [?], 1863.
19. Franklin Parish PJM, June 4, 1861; Caldwell Parish PJM, January 10, 1861; Pointe Coupee Parish PJM, August 4, 1862; Avoyelles Parish PJM, September 1, 1862.
20. See, for examples, Logan Papers, UNC; Thomas D. Miller Papers, LSU; Shreveport *News*, July 1, 1864, "Wanted—200 able-bodied men to work in Ordinance Department."

Despite civilian and military needs, planters were reluctant to have their slaves labor off the plantation. Even prior to the war many owners had to be threatened with fines before they would send bondsmen for levee or road work. The same was true during the war. But poor treatment and unfinished work on the plantation explain only part of the planters' reluctance. Planters realized the destructive effect that hiring and impressment practices had on the labor system. The sustaining qualities of isolation, dull routine, and monotonous plantation labors were threatened by moving about, changing jobs, and communication with other slaves. When sheriffs or squads of Confederate soldiers appeared on plantations and impressed workers, the effect was not lost on the slaves. Protests and objections by owners, when ultimately overruled, further eroded the master-slave relationship and the institution.

The disruptive influence of the war and Confederate policies on the stability of slavery is reflected by the increased acts of insubordination, resistance, and violence by slaves. For the most part those acts took the forms traditional to slavery: slowdowns became more common; runaways tended to offer greater resistance; house servants became "bolder," and many found themselves in the fields. Incidences of arson, murder, and insurrection rose also.[21] The state legislative appropriation for "paiement aux proprietaires d'esclaves convaincus de crimes"—including "crimes" such as murder, arson, or revolt, either successful or attempted—more than doubled the first year of the war.[22]

21. See, for examples, John W. Meims to Major Liddell, June 8, 1861, in Liddell Papers, LSU; Kate Stone Diary (LSU), June 19, 29, 1861; Alexandria *Constitutional*, May 11, 1861; Alexander F. Pugh Diary (MS in Alexander F. Pugh Papers, LSU), August 26, 1861; Statement of 5th Judicial District, Parish of Iberville, December 21, 1861, in Letters Received, Provost Marshal, Iberville, DGR(U); *Report of the Board of Control of the Louisiana Penitentiary to the General Assembly, November, 1861* (Baton Rouge, 1861), 21–23.

22. *Annual Report of the Auditor of Public Accounts to the Legislature of the State of Louisiana, January, 1860* (Baton Rouge, 1860), 5; *Rapport Annuel de l'Auditeur des Comptes Publics, a le Legislature l'Etat de la Louisiane, Janvier, 1861* (Baton Rouge, 1861), 6; *Annual Report of the Auditor of Public Accounts to the General Assembly of the State of Louisiana [January, 1862]* (Baton Rouge, 1861), 6. Unfortunately no figures exist past January, 1862.

The arrival of a Federal army in southern Louisiana in April, 1862, accelerated the deterioration of institutional slavery and generated an increase in the number of runaways and in the amount of slave violence and insubordination in Confederate Louisiana. Securing the New Orleans area, Union forces made excursions into the interior of the state and extended their control. In order to escape the invaders many planters fled deeper into Louisiana, to Texas, or to Mississippi, abandoning homes, crops, and many times part of their labor force. They uprooted their families and left their way of life, in part, because they were aware that the presence of a hostile occupational army—even one dedicated to upholding slavery—would weaken the master-slave relationship and the institution. For those who fled when the military situation dictated, a single exodus was often not enough. One planter, perhaps typical, decided to leave his place and go to northern Louisiana "whenever it was apparent that the enemy are approaching," and planned that when northern Louisiana "becomes unsafe I will move further." Many who initially left Louisiana crossed into Mississippi, where they were forced to move again by a Federal threat there equal to the one in their own state. During one period the whole movement was described as a "panic," and for a time civilian traffic between the two states was stopped.[23] The movement of slaves to Texas was far more common than to Mississippi. A British traveler on the Louisiana-Texas border in the spring of 1863 wrote, "The road today was alive with negroes who are being run to Texas out of Banks' way. We must have seen hundreds of them." By early 1865, a resident of Bayou Boeuf, an area of large slaveholders, acknowledged that "most if not all of these families have removed their negroes to Texas."[24] The correspondence, diaries, and journals of those who either "ran" their slaves to Texas or offered hospitality

23. Henry Miller to his sister, July 20, 1863, in William W. King Papers, LSU; Your bro[ther] to Albert, April 28, 1863, in Cummings-Black Family Papers, TU; Louise to Frank, May [5 or 6], 1863, in Benjamin F. Cheatham Papers, UNC; Sarah L. Wadley Diary (UNC), October 25, 1863.
24. Arthur J. Fremantle, *Three Months in the Southern States* (New York, 1864), 85; George W. Guess to Mrs. S. H. Cockrell, February 9, 1865, in George W. Guess Papers, LSU.

to the refugees give an impression of a mass migration involving hundreds of whites and thousands of blacks. An even greater number made one or more moves to plantations of friends or relatives within the state.[25] The movement was so widespread that the already overtaxed Confederate forces in Louisiana were instructed "to render every assistance to planters removing their negroes, and to promote such action where negroes [are] at all liable to fall into the hands of the enemy."[26]

Yet, those masters who became refugees helped to undermine the master-slave relationship and the institution, for masters' and slaves' "running" was an experience which radically changed the determinants of that relationship. Planter paternalism often gave way to economic necessity as black wives and children were left behind and more valuable males went with masters. Isolation of slaves, much prized in the police jury regulations,[27] gave way to bondsmen mingling when traveling and when stopping at plantations. The dull routine of plantation life was replaced by dislocation and disruption in an exciting, if not panicked, wartime atmosphere. The master fleeing for his existence was not the same master who had ruled with whip and weapon when necessary. The aura of power and authority so central to his role in the slave system ebbed away as the plantation house was left behind; so too did the essence of the master-slave relationship.

25. In addition to previous citations see also Louise Ellen Power Diary (UNC), December 29, 1862, May 24, 1863; Bayside Plantation Journal (UNC), November 2, December 24, 31, 1861; Mrs. M. C. Meade to Theodore Stark, May 25, 1863, in Theodore O. Stark Papers, UNC; S. Harding Diary (LSU), July 29, 1863; Wadley Diary (UNC), October 27, 1864; Thomas Miller to his sister, March 1, 1865, in King Papers, LSU; Plantation Journal (MS in Palfrey Family Papers, LSU), November 12, 1862, April 14, 1863; R. Taylor to J. C. Pemberton, November 10, 1862, *Official Records*, XV, 859; "History of Evan Plantation" (MS in Henry McCall Papers, TU), 13–14; D. E. Haynes, *A Thrilling Narrative of the Suffering of Union Refugees and the Massacre of the Martyrs of Liberty of Western Louisiana* (Washington, D.C., 1866), 12.

26. E. Surget to S. S. Anderson, September 29, 1863, *Official Records*, Vol. XXVI, Pt. 2, p. 286.

27. See, for example, Opelousas *Patriot*, May 25, 1861, for an indication of how important isolation and noncommunication among slaves was considered. The paper reported that "a number of negroes have been seen gathering together to listen to the news which was read to them by one of their number." Readers were cautioned about letting newspapers fall into slaves' possession.

Many planters did not flee; they remained at home in hopes of a Confederate victory, or awaited Federal occupation with cautious optimism. But they too witnessed the day-to-day destruction of their labor system and their way of life. This was true even in the parishes other than those initially controlled by Union forces, for Union lines provided a realistic destination for potential runaways. Although it is difficult to determine precise numbers, runaways apparently increased with the outbreak of war; after the fall of New Orleans they unquestionably increased. Once slaves had a destination, they left—singly, in groups, and often as families—whenever they had the opportunity. A member of one of the larger planter families in Louisiana wrote in frustration: "I have feared for a long while that the negro would prove "unreliable whenever an opportunity presented itself of their obtaining their freedom."[28]

Once Louisiana bondsmen had a realistic destination, such as Union-occupied parishes, not even the strict controls placed on black laborers in Confederate employment deterred them. In 1864, twenty slaves working on one rebel fortification left by boat; and although only seven managed to escape, the attempt by such a large number while under armed guard was a bold one. Others working in less well-supervised jobs had greater opportunity, though it is doubtful that any who wished to escape had better success than those assigned to the Cotton Bureau agent in Alexandria, Louisiana. On one occasion eight of the ten slaves assigned to the agent escaped. Two months later the same agent, after constant complaints of having insufficient help, was sent ten more black laborers; one escaped the first night and six more the next day.[29] Slaves no doubt understood that a flurry of activity to work on fortifications or to confiscate cotton meant the probable approach of a Federal army. Particularly in parts of Louisiana farthest from the occupied parishes, chances of escape were greater if Union troops could be met.

28. William T. Gay to Ned, December 3, 1862, in Edward Gay Family Papers, LSU.
29. Thomas D. Miller to R. W. Sanders, July 23, 1864, Miller to W. C. Black, July 27, 1864, Miller to G. Soule, September 27, September 29, 1864, all in Miller Papers, LSU.

Newspapers and plantation journals increasingly mentioned runaways through 1861, but from the spring and summer of 1862 through the end of the war they were a constant matter of attention. The diary entries of a large slaveholder in the Lafouche area suggest the dislocation, disruption, and desertion which followed the occupation of New Orleans. There are seven references from the four-month period from July to November, 1862:

July 7, 1862, "James Pugh's estate lost 10 negroes last night."

July 8, 1862, "There has been a perfect stampede of the negroes on some places in this vicinity."

October 28, 1862, "The negroes are in a very bad way in the neighborhood and I fear will all go off."

October 30, 1862, "Found our negroes completely demoralized some gone and some preparing to go. I fear we shall lose them all."

October 31, 1862, "The negroes . . . run off. It looks probable that they will all go."

November 2, 1862, "Our negroes . . . are still leaving, some every night. The plantation will probably be completely cleaned out in a week."

November 5, 1862, "This morning there was a rebellion among the negroes at Mrs. G. Pugh."[30]

This account is exceptional only for the frequency of its entries. Literally thousands of bondsmen escaped from the interior and made their way to Union lines.

The mass escapes which took place in the Pelican State after April, 1862, provide striking testimony about slavery and about

30. Alexander F. Pugh Diary (MS in Alexander F. Pugh Papers, LSU). See also, for examples, Plantation Journal (MS in August LeBlanc Family Papers, LSU); Plantation Journal, 1861–1863 (MS in Phanor Prudhomme Papers, UNC), "portes avec les yankees"; Bayside Plantation Journal (MS in Bayside Plantation Papers, UNC), May 1, 3, 4, 11, 1863; Plantation Journal, 1863 (MS in Andrew McCollam Papers, UNC), "Negroes that have left the place"; seventy-six of one hundred and one.left as families. Okar to Gustave, June 26, 1863, in Gustave Lauve Papers, LSU, "The negroes have all left their owners in this parish"; L. Martin to W. R. Beall, September 21, 1862, in DGR (C), "most of the slaves have fled to the Yankees."

the thinking of those in bondage. Clearly, most slaves were realistically hesitant to make futile attempts for freedom; but given a reasonable hope for success, they left in droves. Nor can their successful escapes be credited to planter resignation or to a laxity of controls. Quite the contrary occurred.

With the arrival of Federal troops in southern Louisiana, the already oppressive controls in the Confederate interior were supplemented and tightened. Patrols were increased both in size and in the frequency of their rounds. Some parishes hired permanent guards who worked from dark to sunrise daily; others created river patrols to block that avenue of escape. At Baton Rouge skiffs were anchored on the Mississippi River above and below the city, each manned by two men with shot guns to "prevent . . . the absconding of the slave population." Towns responded with vigilance committees "to act as guardians of the public safety," and owners allowing slaves to live in cities without immediate white supervision were threatened with fines. Parishes appropriated funds to hire managers for plantations lacking sufficient white males to maintain order, and resourceful whites went to work as "Negro hunters" for the rewards. At Lake Washington owners had insubordinate slaves sent to work under Confederate guards. The new controls and the dislocation of the slave population necessitated the appointment of state agents to handle captured runaways.[31]

The greater restraints were predictable responses to increased acts of black violence (both real and imagined) after the spring of 1862. In the state capital "every sound in the distance [was] translated into some message of slaughter and carnage." Slaves in Madison Parish gave owners "a great deal of trouble" by killing

31. St. Charles Parish PJM, May 19, 1862; West Baton Rouge Parish PJM, June 21, 1862; Natchitoches *Union*, May 15, 29, 1862; Phelps to R. S. Davis, July 31, 1863, *Official Records*, XV, 535; Charles S. Crowe to C. L. Stevenson, March 31, 1863, *Official Records*, Vol. XXIV, Pt. 3, p. 701; Shreveport *News*, September 13, 1864; Bienville Parish PJM, April 16, 1863; *Annual Message of Governor Henry Watkins Allen to the Legislature of the State of Louisiana, January, 1865* (Shreveport, 1865), 8; Shreveport *News*, July 19, August 23, 1864. On August 23, 1864, the state agent at Shreveport had 129 runaways under his care.

several overseers and wounding other whites (one resident claimed he could recall twenty such cases). In Tangipahoa Parish slaves were discovered with a cache of horses and guns, thus prematurely starting an abortive revolt in which several blacks were killed. Confederate soldiers were dispatched to a plantation outside Cheneyville in southern Rapides Parish to take arms, ammunition, and horses from blacks who had acquired them in the confusion following a Federal raid. On Saint Louis Plantation in Iberville Parish a slave attacked the local sheriff who reluctantly agreed to release the offender after lamenting the poor effect it would have "at times like these." The sheriff added, "I cannot forbear telling you that during my struggles [with the one slave] your other negroes (although they did not assist) called on him to throw the white man in the ditch then kill him! If you wish come and see my marks."[32] White apprehension of blacks increased as Federal troops approached, and those fears explain, in part, the intensified controls, but it is clear that those fears were founded in fact and experience.

Many slaves never attempted to depart for Union lines. The new wave of repression, or concern for their families, or loyalty kept them at home. But they had only to wait for the arrival of Federal troops in their locale for liberation. In 1863 and 1864 large-scale Union military movements cut across the state from New Orleans to within miles of Shreveport. Lesser excursions designed to bring undefended territory under Union control or to collect cotton, sugar, mules, horses, wagons, and slaves were numerous.

Wherever the troops went they disrupted the labor system by their presence. The "Teche Expedition" in the spring of 1863 was one of the most disruptive, with Federal troops crossing and recrossing no less than eight parishes, some of which were rich in

32. Baton Rouge *Daily News*, August 7, 1862; Franklin Parish PJM, June 16, 1862; C. I. S. to John Perkins, September 12, 1862, in John Perkins Papers, UNC; T. D. C. to her husband, November 19, 1863, in R. J. Causey Papers, LSU; Special Order Number 162, June 23, 1862, Head Quarters, District of Western Louisiana, in H. D. Ogden Papers, TU; Jules Aucoir to Gay, April 27, 1862, in Gay Papers, LSU.

sugar and cotton plantations previously untouched by the war.[33] Wherever they went, the soldiers were greeted by cheering slaves who materially aided the military effort. On countless occasions bondsmen furnished information about hidden horses, mules, sugar, cotton, or rebel strength and activities. Equal assistance was given to individual Union soldiers who were wounded, hungry, or ill.[34]

As the Teche Expedition progressed, slaves joined the advancing column. Many walked off the plantation as the army passed; others, hidden and restrained during the day, found their way to Federal camps at night; those who joined included "old men with canes, bare-headed and bare-footed, children, women in short dresses, with bandanas wrapped over wolly [*sic*] pates, and carrying infants in their arms. Big and little, black and yellow, old and young, cripple and infirm, all with bundles and all kinds of traps, come pouring in from every quarter, at every hour."[35]

The procession must have been an impressive sight. By the time the expedition turned homeward it stretched no less than five miles and included troops, horses, mules, cattle, fifty army wagons, over 400 plantation carts and wagons filled with household goods, and close to eight thousand slaves, who comprised an army of liberation by their example.[36] The black and white "Army of the Teche"

---

33. The parishes included Lafourche, Lafayette, Assumption, St. Mary, St. Landry, St. Martin, Iberville, Iberia, and Baton Rouge.

34. See, for examples, Harris H. Beecher, *Record of the 114th Regiment N. Y. S. V.* (Norwich, 1866), 139–40; Edward H. Sentell Diary (NYHSL), May 7, 1863; George Gilbert Smith, *Leaves from a Soldier's Diary* (Putnam, Conn., 1906), April, 1863, 46–47; William B. Stevens, *History of the 50th Regiment of Infantry, Massachusetts Volunteers Militia in the Late War of the Rebellion* (Boston, 1907), 70; J. F. Moors, *History of the Fifty-Second Regiment Massachusetts Volunteers* (Boston, 1893), 156; George H. Hepworth, *The Whip, Hoe and Sword; or the Gulf Department in '63* (Boston, 1864), 140–42; Josephine Clare, *Narrative of the Adventures and Experiences of Mrs. Josephine Clare* (Lancaster, Pa., 1865), 4–5; Benjamin F. Stevenson, *Letters from the War* (Cincinnati, 1884), 274–75.

35. Beecher, *Record of the 114th N.Y.*, 131.

36. Thomas E. Chickering, *Diary of Forty-First Regiment Infantry Massachusetts Volunteers* (Boston, 1863), 10; Beecher, *Record of the 114th N.Y.*, 184–86; Alexander F. Pugh Diary (MS in Alexander F. Pugh Papers, LSU), May 25, 1863. Estimates of the number of slaves involved varies. One observer claimed 5,000, another 6,000, but both a military and a planter source offered 8,000.

was but one of many like it during the war. Even the militarily abortive Red River campaign returned with thousands of liberated blacks.[37]

Those slaves who for one reason or another could not or would not join the liberators were, to use a common planter term, "completely demoralized" after a visit by the Federals. Planters in contested or Confederate parishes complained after "those [who] did not go with the army remained at home to do *much worse*." For days following a Federal visit audacious slaves "had a perfect jubilee" and acted as if they were "practically free," even coming and going as they pleased. In one night the slaves on a large plantation killed thirty-five hogs to share with visiting bondsmen. On another they captured a rebel soldier and placed him in the stocks until he escaped. "The recent trying scenes through which we have passed," wrote one planter after a Federal raid, "have convinced me that *no dependence* is to be *placed* on the *negro*—and that they are the greatest hypocrites and liers [*sic*] that God ever made."[38]

Obviously Federal raids into Confederate or contested parishes went a long way in destroying slavery. They were a vehicle for freedom for thousands of bondsmen who wished to leave the plantation, and the freedmen in turn became an integral part of the forces of liberation. For those who did not leave, slavery would never again be the same. The features which sustained the institu-

---

37. See, for example, Charles Barnard to Maggie, May 26, 1862, in Charles Barnard Papers, MHSL; [?] to Mide, July 28, 1862, in Louis A. Bringier Papers, LSU; Homer B. Sprague, *History of the 13th Infantry Regiment Connecticut Volunteers During the Great Rebellion* (Hartford, 1867), 79–80; Alexander F. Pugh Diary (MS in William F. Pugh Papers, LSU), October 26, 1862; Power Diary (UNC), May 25, 26, June 27, 1863; Kate to her brother, August 30, 1863, in Albert Batchelor Papers, LSU; G. A. Breaux Diary (TU), November 23, 1863; Wadley Diary (UNC), April 15, 1864.

38. John H. Ransdell to Thomas O. Moore, May 29, 1863, in Thomas O. Moore Papers, LSU; William J. Minor Diary (LSU), January 3, 1863; [?] to Albert, September 21, 1864, in Batchelor Papers, LSU; John Ransdell to the governor, May 26, 1863, in Moore Papers, LSU; O. S. Acklen to Ade, August 23, 1863, in Acklen Family Papers, TU. In contrast, for slaves who remained loyal, see Clara Compton Raymond Memoirs (UNC), 12; "The Federal Raid on Ashland" (MS in Rosella Kenner Brent Papers, LSU), 19, 24–25; Pricilla Bond Diary (LSU), June 29, 1862.

tion—isolation, routine, paternalism, patrols, controls, and the master-slave relationship—could not survive the raids.[39]

Slavery in the Union-occupied parishes was similarly affected by the presence of the Federal army. But an important distinction must be made between the Union area and the Confederate interior. The Confiscation Act passed by the U.S. Congress in July, 1862, freed slaves of masters in the Confederate part of the state; but this act of Congress, like the Emancipation Proclamation which came six months later, exempted slaves in areas already under Federal control.[40] Thus slaves in the Confederate interior were liberated, but slavery in occupied Louisiana was bolstered by exemptions in the congressional legislation and in the Emancipation Proclamation. Planters and military officials were assured by Congress and the president that slavery in the Union parishes was safe, or so went the theory. But the theory worked poorly in practice; for the blacks, to judge from their actions, apparently no longer considered themselves slaves. They understood what the war was going to do to the labor system and took full advantage of the situation.

Masters and overseers in Federal Louisiana often found it difficult to control their labor force without compensation of some form. Slaves, using strikes and slowdowns, restructured the Old South labor system and altered the master-slave relationship until it more closely resembled employer-employee. In early September, 1862, the owner of Magnolia Plantation in Plaquemines Parish promised a "handsome present" for his slaves if they would end their slowdown and remain on the plantation. The slaves accepted the offer, but less than a month later some of the hands, in a "quite impudent" manner, demanded a month's pay which was refused. The slaves responded with another slowdown and occasionally worked only half days for the ensuing week and a half. When this produced no results, all the women went on strike and refused to

39. See, for example, Stevens, *History of the 50th Mass.*, 104; Smith, *Soldier's Diary*, 50, for the reaction of slaves seeing masters and rebel soldiers fleeing before an advancing Union army.

40. See James G. Randall and David Donald, *The Civil War and Reconstruction* (Lexington, Mass., 1969), 372–73, for a discussion of the confiscation acts.

return to the fields despite a visit by a Federal officer who encouraged them to be more cooperative. After a week the men of Magnolia joined the women in their strike; their idle time was spent erecting a gallows in the quarters. Only a visit by the absentee owner with a promise of compensation once the crop was harvested and sold ended the strike. After their initial and major success it took only "grumbling" on the part of the blacks to get more and better food and new clothes. The overseer's journal entry of December 25, 1862, graphically expresses the new order of things: "[The] negroes went to work [this] morning but came home at Breakfast saying that never having had a chance to keep [Christmas Day] before they would avail themselves of the privalege [*sic*] now."[41] The timing of the slaves on the Magnolia plantation is also significant. Although Federal troops had been in the area for some months, the hands waited until the busiest period of the year before acting. During the fall sugar cane is cut, hauled, and processed, and the entire crop can be lost if too much time elapses between cutting and processing.

The events on Magnolia were repeated throughout the area under Union control in the fall and winter of 1862. Many slaves left plantations and went to Union forts where they remained, contrary to Federal regulations. Occasionally more overt action was taken by blacks—plantations were burned, police and patrols were fired upon, and in Saint Martin Parish Federal troops were needed to control a roving band of blacks who were looting and terrorizing the parish.[42] Strikes, slowdowns, walkouts, confrontations, and armed violence were strange occurrences in an area where slavery was presumably protected by Federal legislation.

41. Magnolia Plantation Journal (MS in Henry Clay Warmoth Papers, UNC), September 6, October 2, 4, 6, 7, 11, 14, 17, 18, 21, 22, 31, November 24, 26, December 25, 1862.
42. See, for example, Plantation Journals, 1862–1863 (MS in Minor Papers, LSU); E. E. Kittridge to N. P. Banks, December 18, 1862, in Letters Received, Bureau of Civil Affairs, DGR(U); Munsul White to William Kennedy, September 7, 1862, in George F. Shepley Papers, MHSL; Magnolia Plantation Journal, (MS in Warmoth Papers, UNC), August 12, 15, 16, 17, October 19, 21, 1862; Wadley Diary (UNC), May 26, 1863; Henry L. Wood to Colonel, April 28, 30, 1863, in Simon G. Jarrard Papers, LSU; S. W. Sawyer to James Bowen, June 3, 1863, in Letters Received, Provost Marshal General, DGR(U).

It must have been increasingly clear that laws and proclamations alone could not guarantee the survival of institutional slavery. That was particularly true when the sustaining features and behavioral patterns that reinforced slavery from within—routine, isolation, paternalism, the master-slave relationship among others —no longer functioned as they had in antebellum slave society. As the war progressed slavery crumbled throughout the state. In both Union and Confederate parishes, slaves, to varying degrees, confronted planters and overseers for wages and new freedoms and challenged old relationships. Runaways dotted the state and acts of insubordination and violence reached a new level. Except in the few northern parishes still under Confederate control at the end of the war, the traditional slave system in Louisiana had ceased being effective before the state legislature abolished the institution in 1864. Events of the war, actions by planters, policies of the Confederate States government, the presence of the Union army, and the actions of the slaves themselves altered and damaged the system to the extent that anything short of abolition would have been cumbersome and nugatory.

II

Slaves and Contraband

The running away of the Negroes is the only
argument that he thus far offers in favor of
his liberty and his rights. He has not yet
resorted to arms.

—John W. Phelps, June 19, 1862

A troubled relationship developed between the Federal government, its occupational forces in southern Louisiana, and runaway slaves who sought sanctuary in Union lines during the spring and summer of 1862. When Benjamin F. Butler arrived in New Orleans as commander of the Department of the Gulf in April, he attempted to pacify the white population by announcing that "all rights of property of whatever kind, will be held inviolate, subject only to the laws of the United States." Butler's proclamation was consistent with Federal policy, which at the time did not tamper with slavery. An exception was a March Confiscation Act which prohibited using military power to return runaways who came from outside Union lines; but the act did not free those slaves, nor did it apply to slaves of masters inside Union lines.[1] But shortly after occupation, every Federal post, camp, and fort was overflowing with run-

1. Benjamin F. Butler, *Butler's Book: Autobiography and Personal Reminiscences of Major General Benjamin F. Butler* (Boston, 1892), 308; Randall and Donald, *The Civil War and Reconstruction*, 372–73.

aways; many were employed, but jobs did not exist for all. Difficulties arose because those who came from plantations inside the lines were not protected by the March Confiscation Act. Their owners complained to Butler about a confused and disrupted "servile population" and traveled to military posts and camps to claim their property. The persistence of Louisiana's runaway slaves necessitated arbitration between three divergent sets of aspirations and needs: those of Louisiana's bondsmen, of Federal policy makers, and of loyal planters.

Butler, a prewar Massachusetts Democratic politician and successful lawyer, held active military commands proportionate to his considerable political influence. Before the war ended, he became one of the most hated Yankees in the South. Nicknamed "the Beast," his reputation started in New Orleans, where he recruited black troops, executed a civilian for hauling down the United States flag, and referred to the city's anti-Union female population as "women of the street." Nevertheless, upon assuming command in Louisiana, Butler approached the slavery question cautiously.

Butler was clearly troubled by the friction between the slaves, planters, and the military in Louisiana. He had authority through congressional legislation to confiscate slaves of disloyal masters who aided the Confederate military. Because those slaves were involved in the war effort, they were treated like any other captured enemy contraband such as confiscated cotton. By using the contraband concept, some slaves—for purely military reasons—could be removed from their masters' control without attacking slavery per se. (The term contraband came to mean slaves of rebel masters who were allowed into Union lines and were employed or otherwise protected by the Federal military.) Additional congressional legislation which supplemented the March Confiscation Act also prohibited Butler from returning slaves who came from outside his lines. But what of slaves from the occupied parishes whose masters insisted upon their return? And what was he to do with those he could not usefully employ, who were frequently hungry, idle, or ill? In late May he confided to Secretary of War Edwin M. Stanton, "The question now pressing me is the state of the negro property here." He felt comfortable confiscating slaves who aided the Confederate effort. But slaves of loyal as well as disloyal masters came to his lines, and he believed confiscating all of them would be unfair to peaceful, loyal owners. Impressed by the dependence of Louisiana's economy upon slave labor, Butler felt wholesale confiscation would destroy the economy and unjustly injure owners who had crops growing. Moreover, it would be, he continued, "a physical impossibility to take all" of them. Should he, he asked the secretary of war, allow into his lines the first to run away—"the adventurous, the shiftless, and wicked to the exclusion of the good and quiet" who remained on the plantations? Then too there was the mundane matter of feeding the "vicious and unthrifty" types who, according to Butler, tended to be runaways. And, he asked, "if coming within our lines is equivalent to freedom . . . is it to be obtained only by the first to apply?"[2]

Influenced by these social and economic considerations, in late May, Butler directed that all runaways not employed by the military be sent out of Union lines, "leaving them subject to the ordinary laws of the community." Butler fully realized the consequences of the exclusion order. Indeed, the policy had been suggested to him by the president of the Jefferson Parish Police Jury. The parish official had complained that the refusal of military commanders to return runaways had a "demoralizing effect on the serving population." He acknowledged that congressional law prohibited their return but suggested that *"if all were excluded from Federal lines, then parish police officers could arrest and return runaways."*[3] The contraband policy of the Department of the Gulf for the spring and early summer of 1862 excluded from Union lines all runaways who could not be employed by the military. Blacks who had evaded masters, patrols, dogs, "negro hunters," and rebel troops to reach freedom were often disappointed: hundreds of escapees were returned to bondage by Butler's policy. But the tenacity of the slaves and the quasi-abolitionist tendencies of

2. Butler to Edwin M. Stanton, May 25, 1862, in Benjamin F. Butler Papers, LC.
3. M. Mithoff to Butler, May 20, 1862, *ibid.*

many of the soldiers in the occupying army made the policy difficult to enforce.

Not surprisingly, the fugitives paid little attention to the exclusion order—they kept arriving. Three weeks after the policy became effective, an officer on the Union line of defense reported a "large and constantly increasing number of blacks . . . congregated near the upper picket station." In hours the number doubled from 75 to 150. Males and females, young and old came singly and in groups from as far away as a hundred miles. They had no shelter, few clothes, and no food. Most had not eaten for days except for the few rations given them by individual soldiers. The officer requested additional instructions, noting that if the blacks did not receive assistance they would "surely starve." Despite the circumstances, policy was maintained and "the guard was instructed to permit none of them to enter the lines."[4]

Deprived of Federal protection and controlled by the "laws of the community," runaways remained subject to the traditional restraints of antebellum slave society, but those restraints proved inadequate once the institution began breaking down and once slaves had a destination. Occasionally groups of armed blacks attempted to force their way into New Orleans or Federal camps. In June over one hundred runaways armed with cane knives left plantations below New Orleans and moved toward the city. Municipal police attempted a mass arrest which resulted in several blacks being killed or wounded, but eleven escaped and were harbored by Federal troops. A similar incident occurred a few weeks later, and only Federal military reinforcements saved the police from being routed; there were casualties on both sides. Butler's contraband policy forced Federal pickets to play a role similar to parish patrols and consequently it initiated a series of events which alienated Louisiana blacks from their would-be liberators. Armed blacks attempting to gain freedom occasionally confronted Federals the same way they did parish patrols and local police.

4. Frank H. Peck to John W. Phelps, June 15, 1862, in Letters Received, DGR(U); see also Lt. Col. Bullock to Capt. Davis, July 12, 1862, *ibid.*

Pickets that tried to stop black infiltrators often found themselves under assault.[5]

But Federal troops, for the most part, did not scrupulously enforce Butler's order. Although few were abolitionists or even sympathetic to blacks, many resented the attitudes and actions of planters. They were offended by the enemy's arriving at camp, often brandishing weapons, whips, and leather straps, to demand the return of their human property. Many of the New England soldiers found the planters as a class repugnant. Whatever the reason, Federal soldiers frequently assisted runaways when given the opportunity. A Vermont soldier stationed at Algiers, Louisiana, wrote that his comrades were not unanimous about what to do, but most gave "every reasonable aid to any colored brother . . . groping [his] way to freedom," despite orders to the contrary. In some instances, soldiers physically drove off masters who were trying to force slaves to return with them. Troops stationed at the Federal Customhouse at New Orleans flagrantly and openly disobeyed the contraband policy. The night that the policy went into effect several blacks who "had been shot at, hunted with dogs, and . . . bore the marks of recent whipping" appeared and requested assistance before the police arrived. They were admitted and given passes and work papers fraudulently dated to exempt them from the exclusion order. Such instances were common, as was padding military labor reports with nonexistent jobs, thus allowing black "employees" to remain within Federal lines.[6]

Butler's subordinates did much to circumvent his contraband policy, but none did more than Brigadier General John Walcott Phelps, commander of Fort Parapet seven miles above New Orleans. Phelps was a West Point graduate who had left the army and then reenlisted with the outbreak of the war. An austere Ver-

5. Sprague, *History of the 13th Conn.*, 65; Journal of a Louisiana Rebel (NYHSL), Aug. 4, 1862; W. I. Allen to R. S. Davis, August 16, 1862, in Letters Received, DGR(U).

6. George H. Carpenter, *History of the Eight Regiment Vermont Volunteers* (Boston, 1866), 41–42; Sprague, *History of the 13th Conn.*, 61; Theodore D. Hales to Butler, July 12, 1862, in Benjamin F. Butler Papers, LC.

monter and an early champion of women's education, Phelps above
all else was an uncompromising abolitionist. Although hardly a
champion of black rights—he advocated colonization and later
opposed black suffrage—Phelps was determined that slavery and
the class which maintained itself by that exploitive system be destroyed. The most rapid and effective means of achieving that end
was, purely and simply, to free the slaves and arm them; nothing
less would do.[7]

Phelps was an unsettling influence in a troubled situation. In
the spring of 1862, Lincoln wanted no interference with slavery
aside from military necessity. He was concerned that tampering
with slavery would tilt the border states toward secession and
arouse conservative public opinion in the North. Moreover, throughout the war, Lincoln had one eye on reunion, and he hesitated to
antagonize potentially loyal whites in Louisiana, the state that was
to serve as a testing ground for his reconstruction policy. Always
the consummate politician, he did not commit himself on contraband policy until forced to. Butler was left vulnerable by presidential caution and by vague congressional acts that did not meet
the specific needs of the Louisiana situation. Whereas Butler had
been the first to apply the concept of contraband to runaway slaves
that came to his lines at Fortress Monroe, Virginia, in 1861, he
chose a more prudent course in Louisiana one year later.

Lincoln's and Butler's policies notwithstanding, Phelps would
have none of it. While other military commanders obeyed or
quietly skirted the exclusion order, Phelps challenged it directly.
Planters who went to Fort Parapet searching for runaways were
politely received but given no assistance. Rebuffed by Phelps, the
masters turned to higher military officials for redress, and Butler
was not one to let complaints go unnoticed.[8] He sent two of his

7. John W. Phelps to Charles Sumner, December 26, 28, 1862, in Charles
Sumner Papers, HLHU; John W. Phelps to D. C. Hyde, December 2, 1864,
John W. Phelps Papers, NYPL. For the Butler side of the controversy see James
Parton, *General Butler in New Orleans* (Boston, 1871), 495–516.
8. See, for examples, Polycorpe Fortier to Butler, May 22, 1862, June 4,
1862, M. Mithoff to Butler, May 28, 1862, V. Kruttschmidtt to G. F. Shepley,
June 9, 1862; Counsel of Prussia and Hanover to Shepley, June 9, 1862; A.
Lawson to Butler, July 15, 1862, all in Benjamin F. Butler Papers, LC.

aides to Parapet to reaffirm the exclusion order, to prevent "excesses," and to make a general report of the situation there. The report confirmed Phelps as being everything the planters said he was. He allowed soldiers to roam the countryside, to "insult planters, and [to] entice negroes away from their plantation." If a slave was punished "when he most deserved it" and Phelps became aware of it, he sent soldiers to bring the bondsman to the fort.[9] Clearly Phelps had not caught the spirit of Butler's statement concerning the protection of private property or of the exclusion order.

Butler cautioned Phelps, but with little success. The controversy later included Phelps's organizing black troops without authorization, but that was simply an aggravating factor and not the essence of the problem. From the outset Phelps had resisted the common military practice of using contraband slaves as fatigue labor. Precisely that issue would prompt his resignation from the army. Phelps declared that he was willing to prepare "Africans" for combat but "not willing to become [a] mere slave driver." Nor would he release blacks to the temporary custody of local whites to work on levees, even in a crisis situation that Butler described as "outside the question of returning negroes."[10] If Phelps's reasoning was uncompromising, it was also prophetic. He believed that the slave system was breaking down and that the time was opportune to destroy it by paying wages and organizing black troops. The use of contraband slaves as laborers made the United States government "appear . . . as a slave driver." On the particular matter of the levees Phelps concluded: "Hence, negroes who flee from their masters a hundred miles off and seek protection from the United States are what? Not formed into regiments to oppose the wicked rebellion and smite the oppression of their masters, but are set to work by United States authority to protect those masters against the threatening of nature."[11]

9. Butler to Capt. Haggerty, May 27, 1862, *Official Records*, XV, 445; Edward Page to Butler, May 28, 1862, in Benjamin F. Butler Papers, LC.
10. Butler to John W. Phelps, May 9, 10, 1862, *Official Records*, XV, 442–43; John W. Phelps to R. S. Davis, July 31, 1862, *ibid.*, 535; Edward Page to Butler, May 27, 1862, Butler to Phelps, May 10, 1862, both in Benjamin F. Butler Papers, LC.
11. John W. Phelps Diary (NYPL), May 22, 27, 1862.

For two weeks after he issued the exclusion order Butler continued to receive reports that Phelps ignored it. Phelps still allowed slaves, but not masters, to pass the pickets, and as many as fifty a day arrived at camp. Not content with aiding blacks, the Vermont general further antagonized planters by suggesting that news from Washington would arrive shortly, freeing all contrabands. In that atmosphere desperate planters appealed to the sympathetic ear of Butler's aide at Parapet: something must be done to provide labor to gather crops. The aide wrote his commander suggesting that such a move would generate a better attitude among the planters toward the Union. By late June, 1862, Butler's contraband policy was troubled from all sides.[12]

Increasingly, Bulter saw himself caught, unable to reconcile the economic needs of the planters and the conservative policies of the president with the breakdown of plantation discipline and the insubordinate actions of his own army. In June he plaintively wrote his friend Secretary of War Stanton that "the account of General Phelps is the negro side of the story," and, while expressing concern over the whole question, he did not see Phelps's action to be in accord with governmental policy. He concluded, "I am a soldier bound to carry out the wishes of my government. . . . I leave the whole question with the President." Butler was not to be absolved of responsibility that easily. Stanton replied that the matter had gone to the president, but until a decision was made, all were confident the situation would be handled with "skill and discretion" and without "serious embarrassment to the government or any difficulty with General Phelps."[13] Butler avoided embarrassment by not antagonizing Phelps.

Lincoln's response to the situation (as conveyed through Stanton) consisted of a vague reiteration of existing congressional statutes. The president believed that congressional acts prevented fugitive slaves from being returned to their masters, and they

12. Edward Page to Butler, June 6, 1862, Benjamin F. Butler Papers, Lawrence P. Joyce to his wife, June 14, 1862, in Lawrence P. Joyce Papers, MHSL; Edward Page to Butler, June 19, 1862, in Benjamin F. Butler Papers, LC.

13. Butler to Stanton, June 19, 1862, Stanton to Butler, June 29, 1862, both in Benjamin F. Butler Papers, LC.

authorized the Quartermaster and Commissary Departments to provide runaway slaves with the necessities of life; the acts further stipulated that able-bodied contrabands should work with adequate wages. Stanton, after outlining Lincoln's interpretation of how the congressional acts related to fugitive slaves, cautioned that the president was not issuing "a general rule in respect to slaves or slavery, but simply [trying] to provide for the particular case under the particular circumstances in which it is now presented."[14]

But if Lincoln was suggesting that Butler liberalize his contraband policy and use Federal resources to aid those blacks within Union lines, the effect was lost on Butler. Butler reiterated that he would follow administration dictates, but he wrote Secretary of the Treasury Salmon P. Chase, "I shall treat the negro with as much tenderness as possible, but I assure you it is quite impossible to free them here and now without a San [*sic*] Domingo. There is no doubt that an insurrection is only prevented by our bayonets." Butler apparently feared that a relaxation of his strict contraband policy —which would result in runaways' entering his lines—would end in violence. He wrote his wife, "We shall have a negro insurrection here I fancy."[15]

Butler dispatched two emissaries to Washington to meet administration officials on the contraband question. One was Military Governor George F. Shepley, a prominent Maine lawyer (Harvard Law School) and politician (Douglas Democrat) who owed his original commission and appointment as governor to his political friend from Massachusetts, Ben Butler. The second was Christian Roselius. German born, middle-aged and distinguished, Roselius was one of New Orleans' foremost lawyers and one of the state's most respected citizens. A Whig whose political service included

14. Stanton to Butler, July 3, 1862, *ibid.* Later that same month Lincoln authorized military commanders in Virginia, South Carolina, Georgia, Florida, Alabama, Mississippi, Louisiana, Texas, and Arkansas to seize and use as laborers as many slaves as necessary, "giving them reasonable wages for their labor." Executive Order, July 22, 1862, in Stanton Papers, LC.

15. Butler to Chase, July 10, 1862, Salmon P. Chase Papers, HSP; Butler to his wife, July 25, 1862, in Benjamin F. Butler, *Private and Official Correspondence of General Benjamin F. Butler During the Period of the Civil War* (5 vols.; Norwood, Mass., 1917), II, 109.

stints in the state legislature and as state attorney, he cast a negative vote at the secession convention. Soon to emerge as a leading Unionist, he nevertheless owned a large plantation in Carrollton, which was dangerously close to Phelps's camp. Of Roselius, Butler wrote, "He will be enabled [*sic*] to give you the precise state of things upon which I want the instruction of the government."[16]

Precisely what Butler desired is not clear. But his policies and correspondence suggest that with few exceptions he felt it unwise to tamper with slavery; the exceptions always directly concerned the war effort or disloyal masters. For reasons both social and economic he, apparently even more than Lincoln, was willing to use Federal troops and policy and local laws and restraints to maintain the status quo of slavery. He refused to allow runaways into his lines for a number of reasons, including a fear that he could not care for them or control them. Inside his lines he tried to keep blacks on plantations because the state was so economically dependent upon their labor and because they would be easier to control.[17]

In his continuing correspondence with officials in Washington, Butler's policy was challenged only by Salmon P. Chase, the highest-ranking friend of southern blacks in the administration. The secretary of the treasury cautioned Butler that Congress had authorized the president to order payment of wages to contraband slaves and to arm them if he desired. He pointed out that wages and arms were inconsistent with slavery and that northern public opinion was moving toward emancipation as a war measure. He also chided Butler for returning fugitives to masters willing to take the oath of allegiance. Finally, the friendly but firm letter suggested that Butler stop that practice and instead call on blacks to defend the Union. But Chase's opinions were, as usual, ahead of the administration's, and Butler was reluctant to adopt them as his own. More to his liking were the reports he received from Roselius and

16. Journal of a Louisiana Rebel (NYHSL), July 16, 1862; Butler to Lincoln, Butler to Stanton, both July 30, 1862, in Benjamin F. Butler Papers, LC.
17. Butler to Capt. Stafford, July 19, 1862, *Official Records*, XV, 526; Butler to Phelps, July 23, 1862, D. S. Parks to Butler, July 29, 1862, both in Benjamin F. Butler Papers, LC; New Orleans *Bee*, July 23, 1862.

Shepley. After meeting with Lincoln, Stanton, and Secretary of State Seward in early August, the military governor announced that he had received full discretion in "relation to the negro question [and will] continue the policy pursued by you [Butler] up to this time." Later that month Roselius reported that he too had talked with the president and cabinet members, and that Phelps would be recalled as a means of lessening Butler's problems.[18]

Again Butler did not receive detailed instructions. But he did receive vindication for the policy he had thus far followed, and he had administration approval to carry on. Apparently Lincoln, through Stanton, was willing to offer suggestions on the contraband problem and remove troublesome subordinates, but was unwilling to assume responsibility for issuing Butler explicit orders. Butler continued to welcome into his lines those fugitives he could employ; to them he gave rations but no wages, though payment of wages had been authorized by Congress. Nor is there any indication that he gave rations to runaways outside his lines, which he also had authority to do. "Loyal masters" had but to take the oath of allegiance to retrieve their runaway slaves. Throughout the spring and summer of 1862, military officials in the Department of the Gulf, supported by the Lincoln administration, tried to preserve the disintegrating social and economic order of plantation Louisiana.

Three events of late summer and early fall helped to resolve the conflict between Federal contraband policy and Louisiana's runaway slaves: the announcement of the Emancipation Proclamation in September had immediate impact, though not effective until January, 1863; a shortage of troops in the Department helped to smooth the way for acceptance of black soldiers; and a military expedition expanded Union lines around the Lafourche District, a rich plantation area which was home to thousands of bondsmen.

The Preliminary Emancipation Proclamation, as it applied to Louisiana, was a cautious document. It freed Louisiana slaves still

18. Chase to Butler, July 31, 1862, in Chase Papers, HSP; George F. Shepley to Butler, August 2, 1862, Roselius to Butler, August 20, 1862, both in Benjamin F. Butler Papers, LC.

outside Federal lines; but it exempted slaves whose masters resided in the occupied parishes and exempted slaves whose masters lived outside Union lines if they took an oath of allegiance to the United States Constitution by January, 1863. Nevertheless, it freed thousands of slaves and must have indicated to Butler the changing attitude of the administration toward slaves and slavery if only as a war measure.

The shortage of Federal troops in the Department was equally important in changing the status of fugitive blacks in Louisiana. From the time of his arrival Butler repeatedly and unsuccessfully wrote Washington asking for reinforcements. As he extended the line of defense and increased the need for troops, the resistance to arming New Orleans' considerable free-black population diminished.[19] A free-black militia, the Louisiana Native Guard, was mustered into service and recruitment stations were opened. At the recruitment tables the distinction between free and slave became blurred. Eager recruiters signed up slaves of loyal masters from the occupied parishes as well as blacks who fled disloyal masters in the interior. Finally those distinctions broke down; for once in uniform all were equally free, and this helped to destroy the various stages of limbo between bondage and freedom that Louisiana's black population—slave, runaway, or contraband—confronted in the spring and summer of 1862.[20]

In addition to the influences of the Emancipation Proclamation and the recruitment of black troops, the contraband crisis was broken by events emanating from the occupation of the Lafourche District of southwestern Louisiana.[21] Because the expedition extended Union lines, freedom was now closer to still more blacks from the interior. That, along with the Emancipation Proclamation,

---

19. See Chap. 6; see also Donald E. Everett, "Ben Butler and the Louisiana Native Guard, 1861–1862," *Journal of Southern History*, XXIV, 202–217.

20. George Denison to Salmon P. Chase, September 24, 1862, in Butler, *Butler Correspondence*, II, 328–29; Hans Louis Trefousse, *Ben Butler: The South Called Him Beast!* (New York, 1957), 131.

21. The Lafourche area is generally described as the parishes immediately north of New Orleans and west of the Mississippi River.

stimulated a new wave of runaways from Confederate Louisiana.[22] This complicated the contraband question because the new Union lines were too porous to keep out runaways, and the fugitives— many of whom were freed by the Emancipation Proclamation be- cause they belonged to rebel or refugee masters—overwhelmed military officials by their numbers. Shortly after establishing camps and picket stations, Federal officers reported as many as one thou- sand contrabands on hand with more on the way.[23]

What spurred Butler to change his contraband policy was the increased number of idle blacks and abandoned plantations under his control. The Lafourche District, one of the most beautiful and lush areas of the state, housed many of the South's largest and richest sugar plantations, which were worked by thousands of slaves. Some of the plantations were forsaken by owners and slaves; many more were deserted by owners; all had valuable crops standing in the fields. Moreover, many of the blacks in the La- fourche District were not contraband or runaways but freedmen. New arrivals from the Confederate interior were emancipated be- cause they belonged to rebel masters who would not come to Union lines and take the oath. Many slaves from within the district were freed because their masters had fled the area, and the remaining masters were considered disloyal by Butler.

In early November, Butler responded to the changed situation with General Order 91—an attempt to revive the plantation econ- omy, to harvest the crops for the profit of the government, and to deal with unemployed blacks. Planters from the Lafourche Dis- trict, with few exceptions, were declared disloyal, and their planta-

22. Assertions of this nature are difficult to document, but if slaves initially escaped to Union lines in the New Orleans area, then there is no reason to be- lieve they would respond differently to the presence of Union troops in the interior.

23. Thomas Cahill to Capt. Davis, September 9, 1862, T. W. Sherman to George Strong, September 25, 1862, George Hanks to H. E. Paine, October 10, 1862, all in Letters Received, DGR(U); Col. Holcomb to George Strong, Octo- ber 29, 1862, in Benjamin F. Butler Papers, LC; George Weitzel to George Strong, November 1, 1862, *Official Records*, XV, 170. One camp claimed 535 children and an unspecified number of adults.

tions were sequestered by the government. (Exempted were planters who could prove they had given no aid to the Confederacy since the occupation of New Orleans, a stringent guideline at best.)

The plantations, whether sequestered to the government or retained by loyal planters, were worked by black laborers for wages. A free labor program initiated a few weeks earlier in Plaquemines and St. Bernard parishes became effective in the Lafourche District. The program provided laborers with contracts to protect their wages; but Butler, continuing to resist the logic of events, included in each contract a stipulation that the agreements were outside the "questions of freedom or slavery." Nevertheless, he proposed to harvest an estimated million dollars worth of sugar for the profit of the government while experimenting with free labor.[24]

The contraband policy in the Department of the Gulf changed significantly with General Order 91 and the decision to revive the plantations. Previously Butler refused to allow most runaways into his lines because the government was unable to care for them; now responsibility for feedng and clothing black laborers fell to whoever worked the plantations. Butler also had been concerned about controlling blacks in Union lines; now plantation discipline offered some restraints, and General Order 91 provided guards and patrols to maintain order. Runaways who had sought contraband status and the protection of Union lines were rebuffed by Federal policy; but runaways and freedmen who could be employed for profit were welcomed.

The exclusion policy died quietly; it was never officially revised by general order or public statement from Butler or Lincoln, for the events of the war made it impossible to enforce. And as the plantation economy revived and labor was needed, runaways had no difficulty finding sanctuary in Union lines.

As slaves, runaways, and wage earners, Louisiana blacks had a difficult time during the months that Butler commanded the Department of the Gulf. They overwhelmed him with their numbers,

24. General Order No. 91, November 9, 1862, *Official Records*, XV, 592–95; Butler to Weitzel, November 2, 1862, in Benjamin F. Butler Papers, LC; Bell I. Wiley, *Southern Negroes, 1861–1865* (New Haven, 1938), 186–90.

and he reciprocated with the exclusion order. After months of indecision and confusion, the Preliminary Emancipation Proclamation, the need for black troops, and the occupation of the Lafourche District broke the crisis. Blacks, by their tenacity and refusal to accept the old order, had forced the issue.

III

"Free Labor—Free Men"

> The policy . . . from the first was to interest
> . . . every man in [the] Department in business, so
> that he might come to have a pecuniary interest in
> the stability and success of the Government of the
> United States.
>
> —Henry Clay Warmoth

As black Louisianians streamed to Federal lines they often brought with them little more than their families and their abilities as laborers. Union officials, no less than their Confederate counterparts, quickly realized the asset that a large laboring force could be to the military effort. While Butler's initial policy excluded hundreds of runaways, it allowed into Union lines those who could be usefully employed. Within a matter of months a more consistent black labor policy emerged in Louisiana, one which looked to restoring economic order while providing for and controlling the majority of the black population.

Much of the labor performed by contraband blacks, such as cooking, washing, mending, and supplying fresh vegetables, was for the convenience of white soldiers. Often cooks and laundresses were assigned to serve specific groups of men, as in the Thirteenth Connecticut, which had four black women per company to do the men's laundry. Normally the workers received only rations as compensation.[1]

1. Claudius W. Rider Diary (NYHSL), October 5, 1863; William Zackman to Bertha, July 20, 1862, in William Zackman Papers, LSU; Lawrence Van Al-

More pressing military labor was also allocated to black contrabands. Within the sweeping category of "general maintenance" every fort and camp had trees and brush to cut, latrines to dig, parapets and field works to construct, and wagons to drive, load, and unload. Increasingly, after the spring of 1862, that fatigue labor was done exclusively by blacks. The Union camp commander near Carrollton requested three thousand contrabands for construction work, and less ambitious requests were more common, for most officers were eager to spare their white troops fatigue duty so that time and energy could be used for drill.[2]

A third area of labor assigned to contrabands was repairing public works. Union occupation disrupted civil government in several parishes, and the military was forced to assume responsibility for maintaining levees. The need to keep them in good repair was recognized by the military, which knew sound levees were necessary to the resurrection of the plantation economy. The work on levees increased as wartime reconstruction continued, and greater numbers of contrabands aided in this work after purely military fatigue duties were assumed by black troops. As slaves, as contrabands, and as freedmen, black Louisianians in large numbers worked to maintain the levees, including ones on plantations.[3]

styne, *Diary of an Enlisted Man* (New Haven, Conn., 1910), 193; Charles B. Johnson, *Muskets and Medicine: Or Army Life in the Sixties* (Philadelphia, 1917), 190–91; William H. Wiegel to Butler, June 9, 1862, in Benjamin F. Butler Papers, LC.

2. S. B. Holabird to Irwin, January 7, 1863, in Letters Received, DGR(U). See also D. C. Houston to S. B. Holabird, January 5, 1863, and Register of Colored People Employed in Brashear City, July 3, 1864, both in Miscellaneous Records, Provost Marshal General, DGR(U); Edward Bacon, *Among the Cotton Thieves* (Detroit, 1867), 134; C. H. Bainey to E. J. Gay, May 12, 1864, Statement of Richard Shaw, August 24, 1864, both in Gay Family Papers, LSU; E. H. Sentell to his mother, January 24, 1863, in Sentell Family Papers, NYHSL; Edwin B. Lufkin, *The Story of the Maine Thirteenth* (Bridgton, Maine, 1898), 41; Neal Dow to G. C. Strong, October 13, 1862, in Benjamin F. Butler Papers, LC.

3. Butler to George F. Shepley, November 10, 1862, in George F. Shepley Papers, MHSL; Butler to Captain Page, May 27, 1862, in Benjamin F. Butler Papers, LC. W. O. Fiske to Major Grover, February 12, 1864, Letters Received, Provost Marshal Ascension; Bowen to Clark, December 16, 1863, Letters Received, Provost Marshal Orleans, both in DGR(U). W. R. Stickney to Henri Robinson, December 24, 1864, J. A. Musicot to C. H. Miller, December 15, 1864, W. E. Thrall to Henri Robinson, September 21, 1864, E. L. Wage to Henri Robinson, September 14, 1864, Alex Bailie to D. Ullman, December 9, 1864, all in Letters Received, Provost Marshal General, DGR(U).

Other duties were also assigned to contrabands, from cutting and hauling wood to working in hospitals. They built roads, railroads, and telegraph systems. Wherever menial and hard labor existed, Federal forces found a place for runaways.[4] Ironically, considering Butler's exclusion order, there was not always an ample supply of labor to fill the military needs at a given time and place. Occasionally Federal troops made raids into the interior to seize blacks for the specific purpose of using them as laborers. More common than raids was the practice of "arresting" supposedly "idle" or "vagrant" blacks and putting them to work. Butler authorized the practice, as did his replacement.[5]

But for the absence of corporal punishment, military treatment of contraband laborers was not unlike slavery. Although blacks were not bought and sold, they were impressed, moved about, and assigned jobs indiscriminately. Food, possibly less plentiful than it had been in bondage, consisted of a "contraband ration" which was roughly one-half the usual issue; laborers and some military officials complained that the reduced portions were insufficient to "sustain laboring men." Clothing was even more scarce. In slavery the men normally received two shirts, two pairs of pants, and one pair of shoes annually; but the military made no provision for issuing clothing even though commanders protested that the men worked in rags and without shoes. Eventually orders were issued which provided contraband laborers with food and clothing under certain conditions; but these were not relief measures, for without steady work contrabands received neither food nor clothing. Even

4. A. Dudley to Captain Davis, September 6, 1862, Rufus Brown to [?], August 15, 1862, both in Letters Received; C. Buckley to Colonel Holcourt, March 3, 1863, Letters Received, Provost Marshal Ascension, all in DGR(U). G. D. Shadhime to John Perkins, July 1, 1862, in Perkins Papers, UNC; A. A. to Butler, October 6, 1862, in Benjamin F. Butler Papers, LC; C. W. Greene to Mr. O'Brien, September 21, 1863, in E. A. Morse Papers, LSU.

5. Wadley Diary (UNC), July 14, 15, 1862; T. W. Sherman to Major General Strong, October 17, 1862 in Benjamin F. Butler Papers, LC. Henri Robinson to A. J. Masicot, December 11, 1864, Letters Received Provost Marshal Iberville; A. M. Fraur to Lieutenant Abbot, March 21, 1864, Letters Received, Provost Marshal St. Mary; W. H. Van Arnam to Starring, June 24, 1865, Letters Received, Provost Marshal General, all in DGR(U).

with work there were no guarantees; many labored a year or more without being issued clothes.[6]

The question of wages for black military laborers was apparently never seriously considered by Butler. After July, 1862, military commanders were authorized to pay contrabands if they wished, but Butler never did, despite pressure from subordinates. The commander at Fort St. Philip had a number of "very useful" contrabands who had worked regularly for three months and were in need of clothing and the necessities of life. He wanted to pay them some sort of wage but failed to receive the necessary authorization. For each slave working on levees the masters were paid $1.50 per day by the state; blacks working for the government without sanction of their masters were paid nothing by Butler's administration. Butler's replacement, who was more concerned about establishing a wage system, paid military laborers, but his pay scale was discriminatory: white laborers working for the military at Baton Rouge received approximately $39.00 a month ($1.50 per day), black laborers $10.00 a month, and black bricklayers $15.00 a month. Unskilled whites received far higher wages than skilled blacks in government employ.[7]

During the war years the major problem confronting Union officials in Louisiana was on plantations. The approach of Federal troops disrupted normal work routine for days. Slaves flocked to marching columns, forts, picket stations, and towns and cities. A portion of the labor supply was run to Texas or Mississippi just ahead of the blue-clad advance. Throughout the Union-controlled parishes plantations were abandoned by slaves, or masters, or both.

6. George Hanks to R. O. Ives, January 17, 1863, Letters Received, A. Grover to J. S. Clark, November 23, 1863, Letters Received, Provost Marshal Ascension; N. Kenyon to Thomas W. Conway, January 15, 1865, Letters Received, Provost Marshal Iberville, all in DGR(U). See General Order No. 6, January 8, 1863, *General Orders of the United States Army, Department of the Gulf, 1863–1864* (N.p., n.d.), in UNC, for Banks's contraband regulations.
7. Neal Dow to R. S. Davis, August 8, 1862, Letters Received, Provost Marshal General; Military Payroll of Laborers Employed on the Streets in Baton Rouge, January 5, 1865, Miscellaneous Records, Provost Marshal General, both in DGR(U).

Collapse of the plantations did not, however, correspond to Federal policy. Rather, important political considerations demanded a revival of the plantation economy. Lincoln wanted to use Louisiana as a testing ground for his reconstruction policy. But few local whites were apt to support the Union position while Louisiana was in the throes of economic chaos. Political reconstruction therefore had to be accompanied by economic recovery, and economic recovery meant restoration of the plantation economy. In turn, rejuvenation of plantations meant restoring order within the labor force. From the time of occupation it became increasingly clear that the old system of slavery was not the solution. Strikes, slowdowns, and desertions such as occurred on Magnolia Plantation confirmed that, as did the Emancipation Proclamation and the abolition of slavery by the state legislature in 1864. What was needed was a new order of things. But the new order had to be palatable to planters who would provide the leadership to bring the state back into the Union—but who believed that blacks would not work except under the lash. A final and lesser consideration to Union officials was what the laborers themselves wanted. They did not want the old order nor did they want a system approximating it; they preferred, and at times demanded, a wage system that was fair and free of restrictions.

In the Union parishes black laborers provided the initiative for the new system. Although still technically slaves during the first few months of occupation, they ran away and went on slowdowns and strikes. The refusal of blacks to stay and work peaceably on plantations frustrated planters and Union officials alike, who from April to October, 1862, attempted to maintain slavery and the plantation economy. After seven months masters and Union officials acknowledged the success of the slaves' tactics and came to an agreement. Planters from St. Bernard and Plaquemines parishes met with Butler's representatives and worked out the first slave-wage system in the state. Male laborers received ten dollars per month, less three dollars for clothes. Women and children under sixteen years of age received an unspecified lesser amount. Planters were required to provide food and medical attention. Twenty-six days of ten hours each constituted a working month; any daily extra hours accrued toward a full day; cruel or corporal punishment was forbidden; and refusal to work or insubordination could be reported to the provost marshal. After months of agitation, slaves in those two parishes were contracted wage earners.[8]

The agreement also included a provision for the government to "authorize or provide suitable guards and patrols to preserve order." The planters preferred creating home guards, in reality a euphemism for the slave patrol. After some discussion it was generally agreed that the planters would have their patrols with local provost marshals serving as mediators. Thus the treatment the new wage earners received was dependent to a large extent upon the disposition and attitude of the provost marshals.

Butler initiated a similar but more generous program on abandoned plantations in those parishes. Many had valuable cane and cotton standing that Butler wanted to harvest for the benefit of the government. The Charles A. Weed Factioning Company was authorized to manage these plantations and bring in the crops. Contraband blacks were used as laborers and paid one dollar for a ten-hour day, a much fairer stipend than planters were required to pay.[9]

The contract wage system used in St. Bernard and Plaquemines parishes was implemented in the Lafourche District after occupation. Thus, by late fall, 1862, Butler had most of the laborers in the Union parishes working on plantations—some for the profit of loyal planters, others for the profit of the government. After months of indecision and confusion, Butler was attempting to restore order by putting to work the contraband laborers in the Department and by reviving the plantation economy. Within a matter of weeks one planter reported that "the negroes are all at work gathering the cane and making it up in sugar." Butler was quick

8. Petition and Agreement Between Loyal Planters of St. Bernard and Plaquemines Parishes and Military Officials of the United States, October [?], 1862, in Shepley Papers, MHSL.
9. Special Order 441, October 13, 1862, in Benjamin F. Butler Papers, LC; see also Weed and Company papers in Rost Hermitage Plantation Papers, UNC.

to add that "the experiment of free labor . . . is succeeding admirably."[10]

Butler's experiment had all the ingredients necessary for economic success. Planters worked their own or confiscated plantations with Federal assistance. Blacks were returned to plantations at minimal wages and under strict controls. They were not allowed to leave without a written pass, and patrols collected transgressors and vagrants to ensure that all able-bodied blacks worked either on plantations or for the government. It was expressly forbidden to issue rations to the unemployed.[11]

Five weeks after issuing the order providing wages for blacks in the Lafourche District, Butler was replaced as commander of the Department of the Gulf by Major General Nathaniel P. Banks,[12] another Massachusetts politician (but a Republican this time) who had served with some distinction in the House of Representatives and as governor of his home state. Banks, like Butler, was "keenly ambitious" and owed his commission to his own political influence; both men were equally lacking in military ability. Banks was tall, handsome, gracious (if not cavalier), and sat a horse well. He showed few signs of the self-educated former mill worker who became one of the most enduring politicians of his time. His personality and style, if not his political party, seemed a conciliatory selection by Lincoln after "the Beast's" tenure as commander of the occupational forces. Aside from being Massachusetts politi-

10. General Order No. 91, Department of the Gulf, November 9, 1862, *Official Records*, XV, 592–93; United States Government, *8th Census Returns*, Table No. I; Lambert Remington to his father, November 26, 1862, in Ambert O. Remington Papers, TU. The Lafourche District was not specifically defined except as the parishes west of the Mississippi River excluding Jefferson and Plaquemines. Probably the parishes affected by Butler's order include Iberville, St. Charles, Terrebonne, Lafourche, Assumption, St. Mary, and Lafayette. That is a conservative estimate, which includes about 55,000 to 60,000 slaves.

11. General Order 14, Department of the Gulf, October 17, 1862, in Letters Received, DGR(U).

12. Butler's recall and replacement probably had little to do with black Louisianians directly. His biographers feel that troubles with foreign consuls and rumors of corruption surrounding his brother were major considerations. See Richard S. West, Jr., *Lincoln's Scapegoat General: A Life of Benjamin F. Butler 1818–1893* (Boston, 1965), Chap. 18; Trefousse, *Ben Butler: The South Called Him Beast!* Chap. 1.

cians, the two men had little in common. Unlike Butler, Banks was predictable and not prone to hasty decisions—slow, methodical, often procrastinating on major issues and always testing northern political attitudes before acting. If Butler had not been the ideal man to aid Louisiana blacks, neither was Banks. But the Emancipation Proclamation was effective as of January 1, 1863 and Lincoln was turning his attention to "loyal whites" in the Department. Louisiana reconstruction was underway and Butler, despised by local whites, was not one to woo planters back to the Union. As it turned out neither was Banks, but temporarily he was a welcome relief to Louisiana whites and he certainly did his best to accommodate planters.[13]

Banks assumed command of the Department in late December, 1862, and immediately made a public announcement dealing largely with the Emancipation Proclamation and the status and future of the black population. He endorsed compensation for slave property lost by loyal owners; and while he cautioned Union officers that congressional laws forbade the return of runaways, he also admonished subordinates not to encourage bondsmen to desert their masters. Gently, he "suggested to planters that some plan be adopted by which an equitable proportion of the proceeds of the crops . . . be set apart . . . for . . . compensation of labor." Banks concluded the announcement with a general discussion of the condition of slavery. He acknowledged that the institution existed "by consent and constitutional guaranty" but felt that the war "will inevitably bring it to an end." "If [slavery] is to be preserved war must cease."[14] Banks in effect advised masters that as far as possible his army was neutral on the slavery question, which he believed would be resolved in Washington, but that planters should reach an accommodation with their laborers and work to

13. See Fred H. Harrington, *Fighting Politician: Major General N. P. Banks* (Philadelphia, 1948), for a sound biography of Banks that stands up rather well considering the research done in the field since it was written. Harrington feels that what Banks did or did not do in Louisiana was dictated by reaction in the North.

14. Nathaniel P. Banks to the People of Louisiana, December 24, 1862, *Official Records*, XV, 619–20.

hasten an end to the war. Through that avenue alone could they hope to preserve the institution.

The new commanding general implemented his policies. Provost marshals in the parishes were told to employ all vagrants on levees and public works and to "avoid interfering in any manner with the relation of master and slave." They were neither to encourage slaves to abandon plantations nor to "compel by force or threats, fugitive slaves to return to their masters." However, those slaves who wished to return were to be given any necessary assistance. On the matter of confiscated property, Banks partially reversed the policy of his predecessor. A new Sequestration Commission was appointed which announced that "no further seizures of property will be made, except upon claims for debts due to the government." Appeals for release of properties already sequestered were entertained.[15] These were Banks's first steps in courting planters and reviving the economy.

No doubt encouraged by Banks's attitude and actions, planters in various parts of the occupied parishes formed committees to discuss the labor situation in the spring of 1863. The earliest and most influential group consisted of thirty-one planters from Lafourche and Terrebonne parishes who met at the St. Charles Hotel in New Orleans the first week in February. After caucusing privately and formulating their position, they invited Banks to join them. From the ensuing discussions emerged the basic features of the contract-labor system in wartime Louisiana.

Under the auspices of the Sequestration Commission the government agreed to "induce the slaves to return to the plantations where they belong," requiring them "to work diligently and faithfully . . . for one year, [and] to maintain respectful deportment to their employers, and perfect subordination to their duties." For their part planters agreed to "feed, clothe, and treat properly" the laborers. At the end of the year compensation was promised in the form of three dollars a month for semiskilled workers and two

15. Circular No. 2, February 2, 1863, in Letters Received, Provost Marshal St. James and St. John the Baptist, DGR(U); General Order No. 8, January 12, 1863, *Official Records*, XV, 643–44.

a month for able-bodied laborers or a one-twentieth share of the crop, whichever was greater. As was usual, all unemployed blacks were required to labor on public works without pay. As a concession for such obviously favorable provisions, the St. Charles group agreed to issue a circular to other planters endorsing and encouraging use of the contractual agreement. A provision added to the final contract forms stated that "acceptance of the contract does not imply the surrender of any right of property in the slave or other right of the owner."[16] As in Butler's earlier program, wages and contracts did not expressly free laborers, but both provided wedges toward emancipation.

The mechanics of the new system were implemented by various military bureaus and agencies. The Sequestration Commission was initially responsible for contracts on plantations run by native white owners. Abandoned plantations were controlled by the Quartermaster Department, which created the Plantation Bureau to lease and supervise the plantations for the profit of the government. George Hanks, thirty-year-old Hartford merchant and lieutenant with the Twelfth Connecticut, headed the Bureau of Negro Labor. Hanks and the agency were responsible for providing plantations with laborers as well as seeing that blacks were not idle or wanting. The labor bureau, more than any other, controlled and affected the lives of Louisiana's black population during the occupation period. The bureau used abandoned plantations as labor depots and home colonies. Bureau agents traveled throughout the parishes collecting "idle and vagrant" blacks and groups of contrabands who were gathered at provost marshals' offices, forts, and picket stations. The old, infirm, and ill were taken to home colonies; able-bodied workers, with their families, were taken to the labor depots and eventually to plantations, where they were given jobs, wages, cloth-

---

16. "Journal of the War," *De Bow's Review,* XXXVI, 100; E. G. Beckwith, Order of Head Quarters, United States Sequestration Commission, February 5, 1863, in Letters Received, Provost Marshal Orleans, DGR(U); Contract, February 5, 1863, in Gay Family Papers, LSU. See Pugh Diary (MS in Alexander F., Pugh Papers, LSU), February 18, 19, 1863, and Bayside Plantation Journal, II (UNC), April 22, 24, 1863, for other groups of planters meeting with Banks on the labor situation.

ing, and rations. Except for the authority of the Bureau of Negro Labor none of the agencies' responsibilities remained constant. Conflicts erupted between the Sequestration Commission and the Quartermaster Department; the Treasury Department was later involved. Not until June, 1865, did the Freedmen's Bureau consolidate all the activities under its auspices. In the meantime the contract system struggled along.

Banks sent one of his military aides, George Hepworth, as an independent agent throughout the department to explain the new system to blacks and whites. Hanks increased the bureau's work, collecting and dispersing laborers, for whom the demand steadily increased. E. G. Beckworth of the Sequestration Commission and Samuel W. Cozzens, head of the Quartermaster Department, both volunteer officers, worked to see that laborers on all plantations were under contract. Local provost marshals were authorized to enforce the various provisions.

In the early spring of 1863 the task confronting the military was formidable. "Idle" and unsupervised blacks were collected and taken to labor bureau depots and then sent to plantations under contract. On government plantations the system functioned smoothly, but on plantations run by local white owners or prewar overseers there were greater problems. Frequently, whites assumed the attitude that the laborers were still their property—not a surprising reaction, considering the ownership clause in the contracts. Many complained that "their negroes" were working for another man, or that not all of "their negroes" were returned to them. Some provost marshals quickly caught the spirit of the times and complained of blacks working for people "other than their owners." Few planters or military men understood or accepted what was happening. Most of the blacks, however, had a different view of themselves and their world, and those whites who continued to relate to them in the old manner had difficulties. A majority of the bondsmen considered themselves hired laborers, not slaves, and insisted upon being treated accordingly. They returned to the plantations with a different feeling and attitude and exhibited "a spirit of independence," no longer tolerating the old order, customs, rules, regulations, and language. Where the new feelings were not recognized or accepted, trouble followed. Frequently blacks banded together, made their own rules on hours and conduct, and continued working. Where this happened overseers and owners lost control and sought redress from the military. Black awareness of the labor shortage encouraged such activities. On an even greater number of plantations some or all of the laborers left their jobs; reports were widespread that blacks refused to work, confused freedom with idleness, and generally were unmanageable. Not infrequently it was the whites who were unmanageable, who blamed everyone but themselves for their problems. The only solution in their view was to coerce laborers to remain on plantations.[17]

Added to these labor difficulties was the almost immediate failure of the shares provision in the new contracts. Scarce currency and a lack of financial resources made shares more appealing than wages to a number of planters, a view not embraced by most laborers. For their part they contracted as wage earners, and, although contracts called for a yearly settlement of accounts, many expected monthly payments. On plantations where wages were not forthcoming, all or part of the labor force often left and returned to camps or labor depots. A hue and cry was raised by planters and military men about the need for coercion if blacks were to work steadily and become reliable employees. One provost marshal complained that black concepts of freedom did not include waiting a year for wages.[18] But the appropriate question remained, why should they have to wait a year when monthly wages were available on other plantations? Moreover, many bondsmen were no doubt reluctant to trust former slave owners with a year's earnings. The frauds and attempted frauds which later took place show that

17. Lansdale Cox to J. W. Rudyard, May 26, 1863, Letters Received, Provost Marshal Assumption; Silas W. Sawyer to Bowen, May 28, 1863, A. Robinson to Banks, February [?], 1863, James Kind to Bowen, June 3, 1863, John Elis to Bowen, June 11, 1863, all Letters Received, Provost Marshal General; Edward Page to H. L. Pierson, June 13, 1863, Miscellaneous Records, Provost Marshal General; L. O'Brien to Bowen, March 12, 1863, Letters Received all in DGR(U).
18. Edward Page to Bowen, February 16, 1863, in Letters Received, Provost Marshal General, DGR(U).

blacks exercised greater wisdom in this matter than did their military supervisors.

Despite problems, the new system made reasonable progress in the first half of 1863. By July, Hanks reported thirty-five plantations and over twelve thousand blacks under his control in the parishes of St. Charles, St. John the Baptist, Ascension, East Baton Rouge, and Iberville. A majority of the plantations were worked for the profit of the government, but a number were designated home colonies and used to care for old and infirm blacks who could not compete on the labor market. Sanitation conditions, crops, and plantations themselves were all reported as good despite setbacks because of Confederate raids during which young blacks were taken away, older men were mistreated, and crops and property were destroyed. Hanks armed and trained the laborers on some of the outlying places, such as Donaldsonville, where thirty blacks defended their new home against a rebel raid; they suffered casualties but repelled the advance and killed the ranking Confederate officer.[19]

On the abandoned and confiscated plantations supervised by the Quartermaster Department, Cozzens also reported wide use of the contract system. He had fifty-seven places: fourteen were rented, fourteen were worked by and for the government, two were returned to heirs, four were occupied by U.S. troops, and twenty-three were run by Hanks as labor depots, home colonies, or bureau offices. On all the working plantations the laborers were described as cooperative and peaceful. "I have found . . . that negroes when properly clothed and fed are willing, nay anxious to work under the agreement." Cozzens reported that many overseers felt that the men were working better than before. This is not surprising, for frequently blacks preferred government plantations to civilians'. Many claimed a willingness to labor for the government "without remuneration" if promised "they would not be whipped and separated from their families." But even on the places supervised by

19. George Hanks to Banks, June 30, July 12, 1863, George Hanks to M. M. Hawes, July 1, 27, 1863, all in Letters Received, Bureau of Civil Affairs, DGR(U).

the military, profit took precedence over consideration for laborers. Cozzens rented fourteen confiscated plantations because for one reason or another he did not believe they could be worked at a profit. When white lessees lost money, blacks most certainly suffered along with them.[20]

Progress on civilian-owned plantations was noticeable though not as rapid. Military agents sent throughout the parishes to supervise contracts found many planters unaware of the new system; but where it was fairly implemented results were good. George Hepworth, who, in the spring of 1863, made an extensive tour at Banks's request, reported that "wherever [laborers] are properly fed, clothed, and paid, there is no difficulty at all." Hepworth occasionally found cruel overseers and the telltale evidence of lacerated backs, and he concluded that "the overseer is the chief cause of trouble" and that "greater justice is done" where planters run their own estates. Planters closest to rebel lines tended to be less cooperative and less likely to embrace the contract system. Despite problems and difficulties, Treasury Secretary Salmon P. Chase's agent in Louisiana recorded as the prevailing view in March: "The hiring system will become general and acceptable."[21]

In the middle of the 1863 growing season a governmental conflict erupted over control of confiscated property, supervision of laborers, and care of aged and infirm blacks. The Treasury Department and the military were the chief antagonists in a largely political conflict emanating from Washington, with Louisiana blacks caught as part of the spoils. Secretary Chase appointed Benjamin F. Flanders Special Treasury Agent for Louisiana, Texas, and Mississippi. Among his other duties Flanders was authorized to collect and control abandoned property. Flanders, described as "a man of fine presence, with a clear, handsome Grecian face," was New England born and educated (Dartmouth College and law

20. S. W. Cozzens to Holabird, May 15, 1863, Frank Barclay to Banks, February 22, 1863, both in Letters Received, Bureau of Civil Affairs, DGR(U).
21. George Hepworth to Banks, March 5, April 9, June 15, 28, 1863, in Nathaniel P. Banks Papers, LC; E. R. Clark to General, May 3, 1863, in Letters Received, Provost Marshal General, DGR(U); Cuthburt Bullett to Chase, March 4, 1863, in Salmon P. Chase Papers, LC.

school). Before the war, Flanders moved to New Orleans where he successively taught school, edited a newspaper, and worked as a railroad superintendent.[22] A loyalist during the war and a founder of the Union Association in New Orleans, he was seemingly a natural choice for such a sensitive job. His politics were acceptable to the Lincoln administration, but he was less an interloper because of his prewar southern residency.

By the early fall of 1863, Flanders had contacted Banks and had assumed control of all abandoned and confiscated property in the Department, including fifty-two plantations, the majority of which were already rented or leased and working. The conflict arose over eighteen plantations run by Hanks's Bureau of Negro Labor, three of which were used as home colonies. Hanks had controlled those plantations since early 1863, when, having three thousand laborers "who either refuse to return to their owners, or have come from without our lines," he requested and received authorization to place them on abandoned plantations, pay them wages, and bring in the crops for the profit of the government. Some of the profits helped defray the cost of the bureau. The home colonies—the Infirm Farm in Donaldsonville, the Home Farm in Baton Rouge, and the Rost Colony in St. Charles Parish—had been established to provide for "the aged, decriped [*sic*] [and] infirm." The colonies were not massive undertakings compared to the thousands of black laborers supervised by the bureau, but they housed and cared for two to three thousand destitute or ill blacks who were no longer able to care for themselves. The remaining disputed places were used as labor depots, camps, and stations for the bureau. Nevertheless, Flanders protested that he did not believe he had the authority to use public money "for the maintenance of destitute and starving persons black or white." He concluded that the blacks would have to be removed from the plantations and cared for by the military. He claimed that he would again place them on abandoned plantations as they became available; no ex-

22. Chase to Flanders, May 13, 1863, Boston *Journal*, December 15, 1862, both in Benjamin F. Flanders Papers, LSU.

planation was given as to why the present plantations (previously abandoned) were not acceptable.[23]

Flanders' posture brought him heavy criticism. Hanks was troubled that the home farms would be abolished, and reported that the Treasury Department agents were turning older, less able members of laboring families off government plantations. Consequently, Hanks was reluctant to meet Flanders' requests for additional "able-bodied" workers. "I cannot consent to the separation of families or that able-bodied laborers shall be selected and the disabled, infirm, and children be turned adrift," concluded the labor superintendent.[24] Although Hanks was never friendly toward Flanders after the latter took control of the colonies, it does not appear that Hanks misrepresented the Treasury agent.

Banks protested to his superior, Chief of Staff Major General Henry W. Halleck. He recounted that upon his arrival in Louisiana he found thousands of idle and destitute blacks. After months of work and organizing, they were provided for—the able were working for wages and the less capable were largely providing for themselves on abandoned plantations under military control. Now that order was restored, he was being forced to relinquish control of the plantations to the Treasury Department, while remaining responsible for the old and infirm. Banks was uncharacteristically direct in dealing with the problem: "Does the support of the infirm and poor negroes go with the property to which they naturally belong or is it charged upon the army?" If the latter, then he requested instructions on the matter. Halleck took the question to Secretary of War Stanton, who wrote Banks "to make such orders and regulations as you deem necessary to remedy the suffering"; more specifically, Banks was authorized to retain or "assume con-

23. Flanders to Banks, September 17, 1863, Flanders to Chase, October 2, 1863, list of plantations transferred from Quartermaster Department to Treasury Department, undated, all in CBSA; The value of the fifty-two plantations was estimated at twenty million dollars as of 1860. George Hanks to James Tucker, April 17, 1863, Letters Received, Provost Marshal General; Hanks to Drake, July 11, 1864, Letters Received, Bureau of Civil Affairs, both in DGR(U).
24. George Hanks to I. S. Clark, October 16, 1863, in Banks Papers, LC.

trol over all such plantations, houses, funds, and sources of revenue as you deem most suitable for that purpose." As far as Stanton was concerned Flanders had no authority which superseded Banks's and "all civil authorities . . . must act in subordination to the General commanding."[25] Banks retained the home colonies under the auspices of the bureau of labor, but made a lasting enemy of Flanders. Throughout the remainder of the war the Treasury agent sniped at Banks and tried to usurp supervision of the state's labor forces. The Treasury Department maintained control of the bulk of the abandoned property, which included a large number of plantations.

Shortly after Banks reestablished his authority in the Department, new labor regulations were issued to coincide with the signing of contracts for 1864. Issued in January, 1864, General Order 23 was the most comprehensive statement yet on freedmen matters. It dealt with enlistment of black troops and with black education, but the bulk of it concerned labor and control of black workers. Flogging and cruel punishment was prohibited; wages ranged from three to eight dollars a month, with foremen and engineers receiving an additional two dollars per month; deductions from wages were allowed for feigned sickness, "indolence, insolence, disobedience to orders, and crime"; nine to ten hours constituted a work day, depending upon the season; planters were responsible for "just treatment, healthy rations, comfortable clothing, quarters, fuel, medical attendance and instruction for children"; half wages could be paid at the end of the growing season; a one-fourteenth share of the crop could be substituted for wages if both parties agreed; laborers were allowed to choose their employers but, once contracted, were bound for the year; chronic violators could be turned over to provost marshals to labor on public works without pay; for "the encouragement of independent industry" laborers were allowed plots of land (ranging from one-fourth to one acre) for private cultivation; use of overseers was discouraged.

25. Banks to Henry W. Halleck, October 15, 1863, *Official Records,* Vol. XXXVI, Pt. 1, pp. 764–65; Banks to Halleck, October 15, 1863, Halleck to Banks, October 26, 1863, both in Banks Papers, LC.

While Banks's plan outlined the mutual obligations of planters and laborers, it placed much tighter controls on the workers. "Plantation hands [were] not . . . allowed to pass from one place to another," to sell or buy clothing or whiskey, or possess arms or dangerous weapons "without authority." Wherever blacks would tolerate it, monthly payments were discouraged in preference to annual payment. A Free Labor Bank (later designated the Freedmen Bank) was established to encourage thrift. To protect the yearly earnings of laborers, crops could not be sold until arrangements were made for payment of wages. Plantation hands had first lien on all crops.[26]

The new regulations and the end of the first year's experiment as free laborers brought Louisiana blacks a few gains. Wages were raised and payments protected, but blacks frequently had problems collecting what was due them. Crops were sold, leaseholders abandoned plantations, and laborers were left penniless after a year's work. Union officials were no less guilty. The Sequestration Commission occasionally took its share of the crops from leased plantations, leaving the managers with resources insufficient to pay wages and issue rations for the following season. Some planters refused outright to pay until forced to by the military. One planter told Superintendent of Negro Labor George Hanks that "he would never pay a nigger a d——d cent while he could find a Confederate to carry a gun."[27] The new regulations tended to make such abuses more difficult to carry out, though attempts increased in 1864 and 1865.

---

26. General Order 23, February 3, 1864, *General Orders of the United States Army, Department of the Gulf, 1863–1864,* in UNC; Wiley, *Southern Negroes,* 210–21; John W. Blassingame, *Black New Orleans, 1860–1880* (Chicago, 1973), 49–77.

27. See, for examples, Charles Hartwell to John A. Roberts, February 14, 1863, in Felix Limongi Papers, LC. E. G. Beckwith to Bowen, April 22, 1863, L. N. Foster to Bowen, March 23, 1863, John S. Clark to Ulther Goodrich, January 22, 1863, George Hanks to Bowen, May 19, 1864, all Letter Received, Provost Marshal General; George Hanks to Major Grover, January 26, 1864, Letters Received, Provost Marshal Ascension; T. S. Burbaut to Banks, March 28, 1863, Letters Received, Bureau of Civil Affairs, all in DGR(U). Enoch Foster to Assistant Adjutant General, February 27, 1863, CXXXVII, Louisiana, BRFAL.

The privilege of cultivating patches of land for their own gain was converted to a right. First- and second-class hands with families were allocated one acre each. Normally a portion was used as a garden plot, but the more enterprising laborers grew cane or cotton as an additional source of income. Although garden plots were common in slavery, many planters denied that right to their free laborers. Even the Treasury Department prohibited the practice for a time.

In 1864 military officials cautioned planters against using overseers. It was, claimed Banks in General Order 23, the overseer who refused "to comprehend the condition of things," who represented "a relic of the past," and who was responsible for "most of of the embarrassments of the past year." It is difficult to judge how much effect Banks's warning had, but it is clear that actions by blacks contributed to the reaction by Union officials against that managerial class.

Increasingly, Federal regulations governing the labor force resembled a throwback to the slave codes and a preview of the black codes. Blacks under contract were not allowed to buy or sell certain items and were prohibited from possessing arms or "dangerous weapons." The most insidious aspect of the regulations was the prohibition of free travel of plantation workers. Only under "such regulations as may be established by the Provost Marshal of the parish" could blacks leave their place of employment. What eventually resulted was the reenforcement of the pass system—without written authority blacks could not leave the plantation. Although applicable in theory only to agricultural workers, the system was enforced indiscriminately, and in many areas personal liberties were sharply limited even after emancipation.

Throughout the new program there was a heavy responsibility placed on the local provost marshals. They were charged with mediating the day-to-day problems and, to a great extent, were responsible for seeing that both parties lived up to the agreements. But they, like the later Freedmen's Bureau agents, were susceptible to pressure from local whites and more often than not identified with planters at the expense of blacks. Not all were of that type;

some attempted to be fair, and a few tended to be problack; but the provost marshals generally sustained a very limited sort of freedom for the laborers in their district.

The most comprehensive labor system—General Order 23—was, for the most part, smoothly implemented in the parishes where contracts had been common in 1863. But greater problems and resistance were encountered in the areas using contracts for the first time in 1864. St. Mary Parish was a case in point, and planters there were quick to explain the differences to Banks. William Palfrey, successful and respected owner of three large plantations, spoke for the group. He explained that the lower parishes where the system was working had been spared the devastation of war. Buildings were intact; horses and mules were plentiful; seed cane abounded; blacks had remained on the plantations and labor was available. In contrast, St. Mary Parish, controlled alternately by Confederate and Union troops, suffered all the wartime destruction the lower parishes had not. Palfrey warned that under those conditions economic recovery would come only if planters were "allowed to go on without summary interference, permitted to make such arrangements as they can [and] such as present circumstances will permit with the negroes which remain." The planter constructed a scene of whites standing over piles of ashes and worrying about "their negroes" and economic recovery as much as Banks was. But what Palfrey desired was authorization to keep blacks working on plantations while planters committed themselves only "to make such arrangements as they can." Wages were out of the question; small shares were the best blacks could expect.[28]

Palfrey was skirting a problem which plagued the new labor system throughout the war and into Reconstruction. Federal policy makers failed to recognize that Louisiana was a large state, parts of which were more strongly Confederate than others. They failed to consider that the war had not done equal damage throughout and, most important, that the race and labor relations in southern Louisiana were tempered by the presence of a substantial Union

28. St. Mary Parish Planters Report to Banks, February 17, 1864, in Palfrey Family Papers, LSU.

force. For example, in Plaquemines Parish blacks had substantially modified the relationship with their masters/employers in the six months from occupation to implementation of the wage system. Many blacks received wages prior to Butler's first announcement. That was possible, in part, because of the moderating influence of Federal troops. In addition, locales such as Plaquemines Parish were relatively untouched by the war, as Palfrey claimed. The resources necessary for economic recovery were more readily available, and the population was not embittered from sustained fighting. The parish had been officially part of the Confederacy for only one year. Butler's early contraband policy and the exemptions in the Emancipation Proclamation also tended to be mollifying influences.

There is little wonder that planters in southern Louisiana embraced the contract system, given the presence of Union troops, the changed attitudes of blacks, the labor shortage, and their negligible losses as the defeated party in a civil war. But Union officials, in extending their influence and programs, paid little attention to these variables. They assumed that planters (and blacks) responded collectively despite varied circumstances. That clearly was not the case. Later events proved that, with some exceptions, whites adhered to Federal guidelines in direct proportion to the proximity of Union troops and the severity of enforcement. But policy continued to be shaped by events in southern Louisiana where Union officials observed the effects. At the end of the war the Freedmen's Bureau operated under the same fallacy. For example, policy for Shreveport, which was liberated in 1865, was dictated by events in New Orleans where Reconstruction had begun three years earlier.

Palfrey's pleas regarding the economic situation were legitimate and worthy of consideration. But also to be considered was the tendency of many planters in the interior to be more strongly Confederate and less inclined to deal fairly with blacks without the implied threat provided by the presence of Federal troops. Apparently in disregard of these problems, General Order 23 was implemented throughout the Union parishes, applying equally to civilian, military, and Treasury Department plantations.

The problems frustrating black laborers in 1864 were much the same as they had been during the first year of the "free labor" experiment. Planters violated contracts by charging blacks for rations and medical supplies, by issuing inadequate or substandard rations, or by charging them for rations issued on days when weather prohibited working. To curb abuses, circulars were issued emphasizing the terms of agreements and defining specifically what a weekly ration would consist of in the future: five pounds of pork or eight pounds of beef, ground corn, flour, beans or peas, sugar, vinegar, molasses, soap, and salt. Planters could sell laborers supplementary items but profits in excess of 10 percent were considered excessive and illegal.[29]

A major difficulty confronting black laborers under General Order 23 was the tendency of many employers to defraud them of wages. Contracts specified that workers would receive half their wages monthly, with the other half set aside as part of an accumulating amount to be paid at the end of the contract year. But, as it turned out, many received no monthly payment, and others were slated for shares, not wages, at the end of the season. Disbursement of the final payroll, in whatever form, was to be done under the auspices of the local provost marshal. By early fall Thomas W. Conway, a "business-like preacher," and Banks's appointee as the new superintendent of the Bureau of Negro Labor, proposed that planters not be allowed to take their produce to market until they deposited, in an escrow account, a sum equal to the wages owed their laborers. Authority for such sweeping control was not given, but Conway was empowered to place a lien on behalf of the laborers on the crop of any planter who did not pay his workers. Unfortunately Conway, bureau agents, and the already overtaxed and often unsympathetic provost marshals were responsible for enforcement.

Throughout the fall, responsible authorities spent considerable

29. G. W. Daley to George Hanks, May 12, 1864, in Letters Received, Provost Marshal Orleans, DGR(U); General Order 92, July 9, 1864, Circular, undated [1864], Circular, August 26, 1864, all in Letters Received, Provost Marshal St. Mary, all DGR(U).

time preventing fraud. White lessees of plantations were the most flagrant offenders because, owning no property, they were more mobile and less vulnerable to recourse if the initial deception succeeded. Occasionally it did. But Conway and some provost marshals tried diligently to identify potential offenders, often with good results. Incomplete figures of 1864's contracts show that the bureau seized over twenty thousand dollars in laborers' wages and saved hundreds from losing a year's earnings: cotton and cane crops were seized and sold, workers were paid, and the surplus funds were returned to employers.[30]

While the progress of black laborers was hampered by local whites, it was also disrupted by charges of fraud against military officials in the fall of 1864. Rumors abounded that George Hanks, the first superintendent of the Bureau of Negro Labor, and a number of provost marshals were accepting bribes and kickbacks from both planters and blacks. Reputedly some provost marshals, for certain fees, allowed blacks to leave their area and go to New Orleans. If true, some of the blacks involved may have been urban residents who were rounded up as vagrants and shipped to the countryside for plantation work. Hanks was charged generally with fraud and corruption and specifically with receiving money for placing laborers on plantations. The eager labor market and the increasing shortage of able-bodied males due to military recruitment created conditions where such fraud could have thrived. Hanks vociferously denied the charges but was relieved of duty

30. See, for example, CXXIX, Louisiana, BRFAL. This volume is a registry of complaints made to the provost marshal general. In 1864 a majority of the complaints were made by workers against planters who failed to pay wages; Thomas W. Conway, *Final Report of the Bureau of Negro Labor* (New Orleans, 1865), 5–7, 11. See also Conway to George Drake, September 29, 1864, Conway to Henri Robinson, September 26, 1864, A. S. Finley to Captain Lewis, October 3, 1864, all Letters Received, Provost Marshal General; William Evans to Captain Newton, October 15, 1864, Letters Received, Provost Marshal Ascension; N. Mitchell to Edward Bigelow, October 31, 1864, E. B. Ratcliff to Conway, December 27, 1864, Conway to Provost Marshal, Lafourche, November 5, 1864, Conway to Edward Bigelow, November 7, 1864, all Letters Received, Provost Marshal Lafourche; Conway to General Hurlbut, November 12, 1864, Conway to Drake, September 20, 29, 1864, both Letters Received, Bureau of Civil Affairs, all in DGR(U).

as head of the labor bureau. He repeatedly requested an investigation to clear up the matter, and one was ordered, but the findings were inconclusive. The fact that Hanks never produced the records of his office tends to leave him suspect. Whether justified or not, the charges damaged the credibility of the bureau and hurt the cause of black liberation because of the close association of the two.[31]

Probably more disruptive than the charges of corruption against the bureau of labor was Flanders' second foray into the affairs of black laborers. During the fall and winter of 1864–1865 Banks was away from the Department of the Gulf. In his absence General Stephen Hurlbut, who was left in charge, transferred the labor system to the Treasury Department. For a number of weeks Flanders made pronouncements on the subject, but paid little attention to the mechanics of implementation. His first set of regulations, never implemented, was essentially General Order 23 except for a much-needed increase in wages, but he took no substantial action until late November. In the interim Flanders received reports that lessees were abandoning many plantations, that seed cane had been sold on others, and that the cotton worm had all but ruined an even greater number. Compounding those problems was the continuing delay in making the contracts for 1865, which were, by late October, almost two months tardy. Both employers and laborers were uneasy. The prospects for a good agricultural year looked bleak. Flanders had what he wanted, control of the labor system; but he procrastinated, for lack of the ability or knowledge or both to make the system work.[32]

During the last week in October Flanders finally announced that he was ready to take control. He acknowledged the contracts made

31. George Bell to Stephen Hoyt, February 13, 1864, in George Bell Papers, TU; William Benedict to George Drake, May 10, 1864, Banks to George Hanks, July 27, 1864, Conway to George Drake, November 2, 1864, all in Letters Received, Bureau of Civil Affairs, DGR(U). George Hanks to Banks, August 10, 15, 1864, both in Banks Papers, LC; General Order 199, July 27, 1864, in CWSATD.
32. New Orleans *Tribune,* September 1, 1864; H. Stiles to B. F. Flanders, September 24, 1864; Thomas J. Henderson to Captain Stiles, October 10, 1864, both CWSATD; Conway to Banks, October 18, 1864, in Banks Papers, LC.

by the military for 1864 but encouraged military officials to con-
clude their business as soon as possible and to undertake no new
business unless requested by him. Conway was given until January
1, 1865, to settle the affairs of the labor bureau.[33]

For all his bravado Flanders was overwhelmed by the responsibilities. He had made no appointments, established no home
colonies, printed no contracts, secured no money to defray expenses, and generally had done nothing to ease the transition.
Conway reported that, during a meeting to discuss the transfer,
the Treasury agent "was almost crazy" and pelted him with questions about what needed to be done.[34] Conway opposed Flanders
and felt the transfer was an indication of a lack of faith in Banks,
whom he admired. Nevertheless, he made an effort to aid Flanders,
partly out of genuine concern for Louisiana blacks and partly out
of a personal desire to see the wage system prove successful. He
had worked hard for that. But the mechanics of the labor system
in Louisiana were much more complicated than issuing contracts
and seeing that they were enforced.

Rations for contrabands, medicine, agricultural tools, seed, and
provisions for the home colonies were provided from an amorphous
source called the military cotton fund. The fund probably was the
proceeds derived from the sale of cotton from the home colonies
and plantations run by the labor bureau. Clothing was purchased
through the Corps d'Afrique fund, which defies definition or de-
scription. Whatever their origins, both sources were military and
thus not available to Flanders, and Conway estimated that fifty
thousand dollars was needed "at once" so that the home colonies
could be worked. That was only the start. Additional home colonies were required, and personnel was needed to receive, process,
and relocate contrabands as they arrived at labor depots and mili-

33. B. F. Flanders to General Canby, October 21, 1864, in Letters Received,
Division of West Mississippi, DGR(U); New Orleans *Tribune*, October 30, 1864;
Conway to B. F. Flanders, October 25, 1864, in Letters Received, CWSATD.

34. Conway to Banks, November 2, 1864, Banks Papers, LC. Conway kept
Banks well informed of events in Louisiana during his absence, particularly those
relating to labor; see Correspondence, October and November 1864, in Banks
Papers, LC.

tary posts. Additional personnel was also needed to issue passes, to distribute letters sent by black soldiers to their families, to write, receive, and consolidate monthly reports, and to supervise payment of wages. As a final consideration, Conway noted that contracts for fifty thousand laborers on over one thousand plantations were already late and needed immediate attention.[35]

During the last week in November Flanders called a meeting with a group of planters to discuss management for the coming year. Wages and enforcement regulations were the main topics of discussion. Planters complained that losses from the previous year, the army worm, and generally poor economic conditions made higher wages unrealistic. They also insisted that some form of military compulsion was necessary, and while there was little or no talk of flogging, there was considerable support for armed troops administering military punishment which the radical black newspaper, the New Orleans *Tribune*, described as "nothing short of disguised slavery." The *Tribune* also questioned why one of the parties essential to the plantation economy was not present at the meetings.[36]

As it turned out, the question, although well taken, was academic. The new regulations were sent to Washington for approval, which they did not receive. Apparently planter pressure reached across the Potomac, convincing some that the higher wages and relaxed controls on laborers (the two provisions which distinguished Flanders' plan from General Order 23) were ill-advised. Hurlbut, who supervised the transfer under orders from Washington, agreed and may have been instrumental in stopping the new plan. He was as sympathetic as Banks towards the planters. Particularly opposed to higher wages, Hurlbut believed that an increase would prevent planters from hiring laborers for the ensuing year, and he shared his misgivings with officials in the Treasury Department.[37] There was some fear that planters would give up

35. Conway to B. F. Flanders, October 24, 1864, in CWSATD.
36. New Orleans *Tribune,* November 23, 24, 26, 1864.
37. George Harrington to Stephen Hurlbut, November 26, 1864, Letters Received, Bureau of Civil Affairs; Hurlbut to C. J. Christianson, January 16, 1865, Letters Received, Division of West Mississippi, both in DGR(U).

and not plant crops in 1865; if that fear turned out to be the case, the political ramifications would have been unacceptable to the Lincoln administration.

The decision to reject Flanders' leadership was reached some time in January, 1865, but the transfer back to Conway and the military bureau of labor was not completed until late February. By that time "the plantation work [was] sadly behind hand." Despite the higher wages and greater freedom with the Treasury plan, it is doubtful that the laborers would have realized any significant gains under Flanders' supervision. By the time Conway was back in control, work on the contracts was months behind. Regulations and contracts had to be printed and distributed, and signing of the contracts had to be supervised. Conway requested and received authorization to hire two assistants for each provost marshal to aid in the work. The cost was defrayed by assessing each planter who used contract labor a one-dollar fee.[38]

The regulations governing black workers in 1865 were essentially the same as the preceding years, though some changes were made. First-class male hands were paid one-half quarterly with full payment due on or before January 31, 1866. The repressive pass system was retained and reinforced: laborers who left their plantation without authorization would "forfeit all wages earned as the nature of abandonment and be otherwise punished as the nature of the case may require." Land for private cultivation was again provided for but with reservations. Blacks could raise no animals except poultry.[39] Disputes over ownership of animals, particularly hogs, prompted the new rule, and the issue was decided at the laborers' expense.

During the fall and winter months, while control over the laboring force was being disputed and when new contracts were being made, blacks were again confronted by employers who attempted to avoid payment of wages. The bureaucratic confusion and lack

38. B. F. Flanders to Hurlbut, February 24, 1865, Letters Received, Bureau of Civil Affairs; Conway to Hurlbut, February 28, 1865, Letters Received, Provost Marshal General, both in DGR(U).
39. New Orleans *Tribune*, March 14, 1865.

of definite authority only served to encourage such activities which were more plentiful than in the preceding year.[40] Again crops had to be seized and sold, and laborers were paid from the proceeds.

Uncollected wages was a particularly severe problem for plantation laborers taken into the army. Because of abrupt and shoddy recruitment techniques, many laborers were not given time to settle accounts with their employers before being marched away to recruitment depots. The bureau of labor assumed responsibility for collecting the wages and seeing that the soldiers received them. In such instances the fault lay more with military personnel than with planters, but the situation still created additional work for the harassed bureau agents, particularly in the fall and winter of 1864–1865.[41]

Shortly after Conway resumed control of the labor system, and planters and laborers signed contracts and settled into the work routine, the Bureau of Negro Labor was dissolved. In June, 1865, it was replaced by the Bureau of Refugees, Freedmen and Abandoned Lands, but that transition was singularly smooth and rapid. Conway became State Assistant Commissioner, and many of his subordinates from the labor bureau continued their duties as subassistant commissioners. The initial problems that many southern states faced with the end of the war—the establishment of the

40. See, for examples, Conway to E. Bigelow, January 4, April 7, 1865, Letters Received, Provost Marshal Lafourche; Conway to B. Boggs, January 7, 1865, C. L. Dunbar to W. Horton, March 20, 1865, both Letters Received, Provost Marshal St. Charles; Conway to G. Darling, February 2, 1865, Letters Received, Provost Marshal St. John the Baptist and St. James; H. Robinson to N. Kenyon, February 10, 1865, N. Kenyon to Miller, March 18, 1865, both Letters Received, Provost Marshal Iberville; C. Brooks to Conway, April 12, 1865, Letters Received, Provost Marshal Orleans, Plaquemines, and St. Bernard; E. L. Wage to D. W. Putman, March 1, 1865, Letters Received, Provost Marshal General, all in DGR(U). B. F. Cheney to S. Eldridge, April 27, 1865, Mississippi, BRFAL.

41. See, for examples, Conway to Edward Gay, December 21, 1864, miscellaneous document, December 28, 1864, both in Gay Family Papers, LSU; E. Bigelow to Conway, March 12, 1864, Letters Received, Provost Marshal Lafourche; Hanks to Darling, August 6, 1864, Conway to Darling, November 12, 1864, both Letters Received, Provost Marshal St. James and St. John the Baptist; Conway to Hurlbut, January 6, 1865, Letters Received, Bureau of Civil Affairs, all in DGR(U).

bureau, the rejuvenation of the plantation economy, and a new labor system—had been settled in a large part of Louisiana. The wartime policies and activities of the bureau of labor became the basis of the postwar Freedmen's Bureau. Economic reconstruction was almost three years old in parts of Louisiana when the war ended.

IV

"A Disagreeable Business"

Slavery is dead, but "free labor" lives,
and "free labor" is still to be killed.

—New Orleans *Tribune*

Banks's free-labor system drew attention and created controversy in Louisiana and in the North. Too radical for most planters, especially at first, it subsequently became the target of increasing black resentment. By 1865 critics of the Banks system could point to successful examples of less coercive labor systems which allowed for greater black autonomy and independence. As the war drew to a close and questions of the postwar economic order became paramount, the differing labor systems in Louisiana became part of the national debate over formulating Reconstruction policy.

When New Orleans' leading newspaper, the *Daily Picayune*, first became aware of the free-labor experiment, it ridiculed the idea, claiming it was absurd to think that free labor would work. Two favorite proslavery themes were stressed: "The two great staples of the South—cotton and sugar—can only be profitably raised by the negro, and by him, *ex necessitaterei*, in a condition of servitude."[1]

1. New Orleans *Daily Picayune*, July 9, 1862.

69

A large number of planters undoubtedly agreed with the *Picayune*. Years of thinking and rhetoric in defense of slavery had genuinely convinced them that blacks would work only if forced to. Some planters initially refused to make contracts and isolated themselves from the new economic realities with a belief that slavery would survive.[2] Others entered into agreements only when financial ruin became the alternative. Many used free labor cautiously, planting small crops or only corn the first season, even though they realized that a cash crop was necessary for economic recovery. Planters' letters and diaries are sprinkled with negative reactions: "[We] think the present system of labor will fail"; "I find it is useless to make any contracts"; "I have little faith in [free] negro labor"; "have made no arrangement with any of the negroes."[3]

Given those attitudes, it is not surprising that a survey taken by a Union official in February, 1865, showed that 65 percent of the planters in Orleans Parish still preferred the old system. Their preference probably had as much to do with race relations and the more independent posture of many blacks as with economics. There are indications that the new system was profitable from the start for those planters who used it wisely and fairly, or at least as profitable as slavery would have been under wartime conditions. Munsel White, a large and influential sugar planter in Plaquemines Parish, wrote that he made six thousand more gallons of syrup than he expected to the first year. His yield was smaller than in previous years, but so was his crop. Another planter on the Louisiana-Mississippi border, who acknowledged that his fate was tied to free labor, believed the system "profitable in dollars and cents." From Iberville Parish a small planter (twelve hands) reported,

2. L. S. Butler to Thomas W. Conway, July 10, 1865, in Letters Received, Assistant Commissioner, Louisiana, BRFAL.

3. H. W. Polk to John H. Bills, December 6, 1865, in H. W. Polk Papers, James L. Lobdell to Dear Sir, January 16, 1863, in Gay Family Papers, C. C. Eustis to his uncle, December 4, 1865, in William Minor and Family Papers, all LSU; William Thompson to his father, June 28, 1865, in Lewis Thompson Papers, UNC.

"The result so far has been a complete success." Similar reports were common.[4]

The positive response of those planters is reinforced by the initial reports of Freedmen's Bureau agents, particularly from the parishes reached by the Bureau of Negro Labor during the war. But where the bureau had not been active and where contracts were implemented for the first time in 1865, there was greater planter resentment and resistance. Planters complained of freedmen needing a "spell of freedom" before returning to work; but bureau agents reported that the planters themselves needed a period of conditioning before they could accept free labor and free men or could respond not as slaveholders but as employers. The contract system had never worked as well in the Confederate parishes as it did in the lower regions. A bureau agent in the interior, who constantly complained of uncooperative planters abusing and cheating blacks, finally wrote Conway in desperation: "Enforcement may not be necessary in the lower part of the state but here . . . it is."[5]

The inability to hire enough laborers was one aspect of the new system which irritated many planters. From the fall of 1863 to the end of the war there was a shortage of plantation workers in Louisiana, a condition aggravated by wartime dislocation and by recruitment of black troops. A few planters tried white labor, and there was talk of importing immigrants, but little came of either venture. Consequently, planters were forced to compete for the services of men they had once owned, men who were, as freedmen,

4. Deer Range Plantation Journal, III, December 30, 1863, in Munsel White Papers, UNC; A Louisiana Planter to the Editor of the New York *Herald*, October 30, 1864, in James Gordon Bennett Papers, LC; New Orleans *Tribune*, August 10, 1865; see also New Orleans *Times*, October 19, 1864; Whitlaw Reid Diary (LC), June 11, 1865.

5. For a succinct outline of the differences in acceptance of free labor in the Union and the old Confederate parishes in 1865, see W. R. Stickney Reports to Conway, July 2, 29, August 26, 27, 1865; D. H. Pease Report, October 31, 1865; Inspection Report of Plantation Bureau, January, February, March, 1866; William Dougherty to D. G. Fenno, November 7, 1865, all in Letters Received, Assistant Commissioner, Louisiana, BRFAL.

considered inferior, troublesome workers filled with a new spirit of independence. For many planters, having to delve in the common capitalist marketplace was offensive.[6] Slavery had been central to their existence, providing a life of comfort and leisure whether real or imagined. Emancipation and the new labor system required adjustments too drastic for some to accept. A planter from St. James Parish lamented, "I live surrounded by my former slaves, and sometimes for a little while I look upon the whole change as a dream." A woman claimed that it "hurt" her to have to pay wages to her former slaves. After reporting that laborers had parties until late in the night, another noted: "We have but little pleasure in our once quiet and happy home." Defeatism abounded: "I am in suspense, what my future is to be I have no idea." "I left home with few regrets . . . I could not stay with negroes." "There is little hope for the future." Comments concerning the loss of house servants also suggest that emancipation and free labor produced emotional as well as economic responses. A diarist remembered that a friend had lost all three of her servants, and she was found "in the suds"; another noted that a number of local plantations had only cooks left, saying, "What has become of all the house servants?" The situation and attitude was vividly described by one distraught Louisianian: "Some planters have not one servant left. Our wives and daughters have to take the pot and tubs; the men . . . take to the fields with plow and hoe." Alexander F. Pugh, one of the largest planters in the state, reacted perhaps

6. See, for examples, James L. Lobdell to Mr. Edward Gay, September 29, 1863, L. H. Clark to Mr. Gay, October 22, 1863, both in Gay Papers, LSU; J. D. Richardson to Dear General, December 4, 1865, St. John Liddell to James Conner, December 29, 1865, both in Liddell Papers, LSU. A. H. Jumper to W. D. Putnam, June 11, 1865, R. F. Braden to O. Remick, September 17, 1864, Bowen to Hanks, February 9, 1864, all Letters Received, Provost Marshal General; William Miller to Banks, July 22, 1863, J. W. Austin to Hanks, February 22, 1864, both Letters Received, Bureau of Civil Affairs; George Hanks to C. P. Stone, March 2, 1864, Letters Received, all in DGR(U). [?] to Dear Cousin, February 27, 1866, in McCollam Papers, UNC; Bayside Plantation Journal II (UNC), January 28, February 20, 1866; Hanks to James Tucker, May 27, 1864, in Banks Papers, LC; George Denison to Chase, February 12, April 13, 1863, Chase Papers, LC. Frank Morey to Fenno, September 2, October 1, 1865, in Letters Received, Assistant Commissioner, BRFAL.

typically to the new social and economic order: "Staid [*sic*] at home all day making out negro accounts. . . . —A disagreeable business."[7]

The New Orleans *Tribune*, organ of the prewar free-black leadership in Louisiana, criticized the Banks system on other grounds. Initially the *Tribune* reacted favorably to General Order 23 and Banks's labor system. The program was "much admired" and the general's motives were described as "praiseworthy and patriotic in intention." By the end of the first growing season the journal's attitude changed. In the fall of 1864 the *Tribune* acknowledged that some regulations had been necessary to restore economic order and to ease the transition from slave to free labor, but it rejected Banks's system as a "total failure" for two reasons. First was the realization that the tight controls over laborers were not temporary, as it was first assumed they would be. Second was the purely capitalist approach on the leasing and working of plantations. The *Tribune*, apparently led to believe that while blacks labored for low wages efforts would be made to "elevate them," found instead "greedy adventurers" anxious to exploit and cheat the underpaid freedmen.[8]

Rejecting Banks's plan, the *Tribune* took a radical turn to the left and suggested that "the old plantation system should have been summarily abolished, the plantations divided into five acre plots,

7. *De Bow's Review* (March, 1867), 332; Patrick O'Hare to Conway, October 11, 1865, Letters Received, Assistant Commissioner, Louisiana, BRFAL. Sophia Gay to Dear Children, December 6, 1863, in Gay Papers, LSU; Mary E. Rivers Diary (UNC), August 23, November 1, 1865, February 2, 1866; M. Gillis to St. John R. Liddell, October 6, 1865, in Liddell Papers, LSU; Lee to My Dear Lady, August 4, 1865, Gibson-Humphreys Family Papers, UNC; Okar to Dear Gustave, June 26, 1863, Lauve Papers, LSU; Alexander F. Pugh Diary (Alexander F. Pugh Papers, LSU), January 18, 1865.

8. New Orleans *Tribune*, September 24, 1864. There were some that felt Banks should have been held accountable for his "failure." A Treasury Department official suggested to Benjamin Wade that "the com[mittee] on the conduct of the war would find profitable employment here." John Hutchins to Benjamin F. Wade, May 23, 1864, in Benjamin F. Wade Papers, LC. Despite varying definitions, the term Creole is used throughout this study to refer to prewar free blacks such as those associated with the *Tribune*. For more on who the Creoles were, see David Rankin, "The Origins of Black Leadership in New Orleans During Reconstruction," *Journal of Southern History*, XL, 417–40.

and partitioned among the tillers of the soil." At the same time the men should have been armed and drilled, educated, and "taught to act as free men." Implicit was the demand that "the horrible abuses [of] the present system" should end and the "relations between the government and the men of color should [be] based on justice and equality."[9]

From the fall of 1864 through the end of the war the *Tribune* reiterated these themes, made Federal officials aware of transgressions against the less fortunate of their race, and made suggestions on how best to improve the conditions of laborers. When Special Treasury Agent Flanders met with planters to work out the stillborn treasury regulations for 1865, the *Tribune* made a number of suggestions and observations. The paper wondered why representatives of the labor force were not present at the meetings: "It would be just and fair to hear the other party too." The idea that wages were being set for blacks without consulting them was ridiculed as a "new principle of . . . political economy." Under it "a man who rented a carriage . . . would fix the rate" and "a man who bought a loaf of bread would fix the price"; the new economics would cut down trade relations, since one would only have to pay what one thought a product was worth. As an alternative, the *Tribune* urged workers to send representatives from each plantation to New Orleans "to give expression of the wishes and wants of the laborers." The worker representatives and the employers would constitute a permanent system of councils which would have authority to judge whether contracts were fulfilled, to settle disputes, and to work for better employer/employee relations. The *Tribune* proclaimed that the time was long past when "the planter . . . [should] be a party and a judge in his own case."[10]

By 1865 the radical black newspaper was unremitting in its attacks on the labor system. Black "free labor" in Louisiana, insisted the *Tribune,* was not truly free. Early in the year a thoughtful editorial suggested that an uninformed observer would never

9. New Orleans *Tribune*, September 24, 1864; see also *L'Union*, January 6, February 28, 1863.
10. New Orleans *Tribune*, November 24, 26, 1864, June 3, 1865.

realize that slavery was abolished even with close observation. "Who are our 'free laborers?' " the writer asked. "They are the men who are not free to go where they choose; not free to contract for any length of time than the term prescribed by regulations; not free to lodge complaints . . . before ordinary courts for breach of contract by their employer." The editorial concluded that the workers involved were not free men, but serfs.[11]

"Slavery is dead, but 'free labor' lives, and 'free labor' is still to be killed," proclaimed the *Tribune* just days prior to the end of the war. What sort of free-labor system required passes to leave the plantation, had wages set by military order, and compelled men to work for those low wages? "Let the laborers alone," except to protect their rights and liberties as free men, urged the newspaper. The same sentiments were repeated in June under the caption of "General Banks' Record." The occasion was Banks's final departure from Louisiana. The *Tribune* lamented, "Louisiana, which was the best prepared state, which was ripe for the most thorough reform, reaped the worst system of 'negro labor' devised in the conquered states, and after two years she still retains it. The old organs of the slavery system remain in position."[12]

Black leaders in New Orleans offered innovative suggestions as well as criticism. They believed that, as long as freedmen were controlled by planters and overseers who worked them as slaves, there was no way for the laborers to receive "the benefits of a true and practical liberty." First preference was for a division of land among the freedmen. Failing that, what was needed was a model plantation program, which would restructure Banks's labor policy while introducing laborers to a new way of life. The requisites were capital, intelligence, and labor combined "harmoniously to equally protect the rights of the moneyed men, managers, and laborers, on the basis of individual freedom." The "associated managers" would

11. *Ibid.,* February 18, 1865.
12. *Ibid.,* April 9, June 10, 1865; see also Louis S. Gerteis, *From Contraband to Freedmen: Federal Policy toward Southern Blacks, 1861–1865* (Westport, Conn., 1973), 68–98, for an impressive study which substantiates the *Tribune's* contemporary conclusion that the Louisiana system was the "worst" of those devised by the military.

be men of intelligence, industry, experience—and opposed to slavery. Such men were available, and not all were white, said the *Tribune*; and men of that caliber would have no problems hiring an adequate number of laborers if land was available to them. Laborers would receive weekly or monthly wages and a share of the crop, with the wages providing the necessities of life and shares providing an inducement for steady work. Laborers would feed and clothe themselves as they wished and travel as they pleased "in order that they may get accustomed to self-reliance." (From the start the *Tribune* had objected to the paternalism of Banks's system.) The major obstacle was finding plantation owners willing to try the system. To circumvent that problem the *Tribune* suggested that the government, if it approved of the system, could make abandoned plantations available.[13]

The *Tribune*, in proposing a model labor system or supporting black land ownership, was not simply editorializing or offering idle suggestions; it was responding to the example set by many of the freedmen who managed to avoid the snare of Banks's labor program and who struggled to maintain themselves and their families on the land. Such struggle was, in part, a response to the free-labor plan and represents one of the more dramatic aspects of the wartime experiment in Louisiana. During the occupation period a large number of blacks established themselves as farmers independent of Federal control, and expectations of a developing black agricultural community were high. Black lessees, largely of abandoned land, showed that they had the necessary skills to survive and prosper if land and resources were available. They did much to discredit the myth that only by revitalizing white-owned and -operated plantations could the South's economy be revived.

A common black approach was individual sharecropping; instead of working for shares of the crop in gangs, which was common under Banks's system, sharecroppers leased plots of land and worked them independently. Normally, a fee of three-tenths was paid to the landowner with seven-tenths of the crop retained by the lessee. (The resources provided by these lessors varied, but

13. New Orleans *Tribune*, January 28, 1865.

seldom did they supply tools or seed.) The largest civilian example of this system was found in Terrebonne Parish, where twenty-seven freedmen families leased plots from 7 to 40 acres each. A black lessee, Gransion Hunter, divided 230 acres into tracts which were worked by twenty black families for shares.[14]

A majority of the new black farmers and planters leased land from the government, usually in return for a one-eighth share. Government assistance also varied from land only to land and all other necessary items, but more often than not it was the former. In Lafourche Parish eleven families worked 813 acres; some worked small family plots with no aid or with one hired hand, while others were able to undertake more ambitious ventures, working in excess of 100 acres with ten to twenty laborers hired under Banks's contract system. Activities of this type flourished throughout the state.[15]

While many of these black agricultural efforts were family subsistence affairs, clearly a large number were not, and some of the larger were quite successful. In 1863, for example, four freedmen leased 100 acres for $500 per annum. By the end of the first year they employed twelve hands, had 40 acres of corn, and had 60 acres of good cotton, which was projected to yield 300 pounds per acre, or $1,800 at the current market price.[16]

Freedmen frequently pooled their limited resources and established agricultural collectives. The success of these efforts varied, but a large number prospered. A report from one agricultural commune worked by seventy-five freedmen does much to discredit the insistence of Banks, Conway, and planters that white supervision and tight controls were necessary if blacks were to work. The inhabitants set their own rules and regulations, neither "allowing nor committing . . . misdemeaners [*sic*] among themselves." "They have worked hard," continued the report; but limited means

14. Report of Agreement with Freedmen on Woodlawn Plantation, September 7, 1865, Reese to Bagley [?], August 25, 1865, both XC, Louisiana, BRFAL. See Table 1.

15. R. K. Diossy Report, September 1, 1865, R. K. Diossy to Stickney, August 31, 1865, both *ibid.*; see also Proctor Moses Report of Lessees and Plantation, June, 1864, Mississippi, BRFAL.

16. New Orleans *Tribune,* August 13, 1864.

hampered progress. On another place it was reported that "the freedmen . . . have a good crop, have worked well, and conduct themselves creditably."[17]

The number of successful agricultural communes is difficult to determine, for no systematic records survive. But no less than nineteen of considerable size were functioning satisfactorily in the early fall of 1865 in Plaquemines, St. Charles, and Lafourche parishes alone—which only suggests how widespread they may have been. The largest had 750 acres in cultivation: 400 acres in corn, 100 in cane, and 250 in cotton. The cotton crop, hurt by worms, was expected to produce only one-half bale per acre; but even that low yield would be adequate to sustain the seventy freedmen for another season.[18]

Other communes were created as a natural result of wartime conditions. As planters fled before advancing Union armies, leaving blacks to fend for themselves, the freedmen often stayed on the plantation and continued working, choosing leaders and dividing the labor. Not infrequently troops arrived to find well-run places without whites.[19] But many groups of industrious blacks who found themselves in that position were subsequently incorporated into the Banks labor system. Former slaves in Terrebonne Parish were told by the provost marshal to remain on their deserted plantations and work until the government could help them. Sixty-one freedmen (only fourteen of them men) returned to their old plantation, organized themselves, and began working. When they had sixty acres furrowed and planted, the government leased the plantation, and the new manager claimed the results of the freedmen's labor.[20]

Black farmers had few resources and little power to make their economic gains secure. Even government plantations, which could have been showplaces for independent black capitalism, were not

17. John T. Harrison Report, September 15, 1865, XC, Louisiana, BRFAL.
18. See, for examples, E. L. Baxter to Stickney, September 30, 1865, J. S. Smith to Stickney, August 26, 1865, R. K. Diossy to Stickney, August 31, 1865, John T. Harrison Report, August 24, 31, 1865. all *ibid*. See Table 1.
19. Duganne, *Camps and Prisons*, 35–36, 62; Stevens, *50th Mass.*, 40.
20. C. C. Nott to Bowen, April 15, 1863, in Letters Received, Bureau of Civil Affairs, DGR(U).

trouble free. The government, no less than local whites, failed to provide mules, horses, seed, or implements; and animals and stock were usually missing from abandoned plantations. Newly emancipated blacks seldom left bondage with sufficient funds to sustain themselves for a season, much less outfit a farm. For example, a team of mules rented for twenty-five cents a day, roughly equivalent to the wages of a first-class hand, and they too required rations. Treasury agents, who considered abandoned plantations potential sources of revenue, rarely allowed undercapitalized blacks to lease land. The Freedmen's Bureau was more willing to lease to blacks, but it controlled the land for too short a period for most blacks to become secure on it.

The difficulties faced by the emerging black farmers were not ignored by all. Banks and the Bureau of Negro Labor paid little attention to them, but black and radical leaders in New Orleans did. From the pulpit of the New Orleans Third African Church came the call for a black farming association similar in mechanics to the communes. In response, a meeting was held that organized the Freedmen's Aid Association. In attendance were influential Creoles such as Joseph Montieu, Sidney Thazan, James Ingraham, Anthony Fernandez, V. L. Ceressolles, B. Cauloy, H. Stilles, Henry Train, Ernest Rillieux, C. J. Dallon, and Firanin C. Christophe. They assumed positions of leadership in the association as did two white radicals, Benjamin F. Flanders and Thomas J. Durant.[21]

The *Tribune*'s suggestions for model plantations and the examples and problems of the existing communes were points of initiative and discussion at the first meeting. The communes were cited as indications of how black field hands could organize themselves and work harmoniously. But certain variables were recognized in assessing possibilities, and the supply of capital, mules, seed, plows, tools, and general provisions (especially food to last until the first crop was in) certainly had to be taken into account. With that in mind the association stated its purpose as giving aid to freedmen farmers "by loans of money, means of education, and diffusion of

21. New Orleans *Tribune*, February 2, April 15, 1865.

Table 1

BLACK (FREEDMEN) FARMERS AND PLANTERS,
AUGUST THROUGH SEPTEMBER, 1865*

Individual

Name	Number of Acres Leased
Alfred Williams	15
Henry Speed	8
Stephen Clater	6
Campbell	5
Louis Fargo	30
Henry Warton	30
James Scolly	12
Joseph Robinson	4
Griffin Darling	12
Gowler	15
Watson	15
Anderson	25
Louis Hagen	25
Anderson	22
Smith Thomas	20
6 unidentified families	6–18 acres each
27 unidentified families	7–40 acres each

Individual with Laborers

Name	Number of Acres	Number of Hands
Jonas Brown	120	27
John Heinau	102	20
Madison Rhodes	175	12
Elijah Sears	110	8
Moses Thompson	125	11
Henry Morrison	58	8
Alex Pollard	30	2
Griffen Moore	18	2
John Neusten	10	3

Communal

Number of Freedmen (Including Women and Children)	Number of Acres
69	288
70	700
—	100
75	190
5	10
135	250
150	122
99	199
125	60

*See XC, BRFAL. These tables are in no sense complete. They represent compilations from one source for two months from five parishes. They should be considered only as indicators of what was happening with black land and capitalism.

useful information." Funds were to be raised by a twenty-dollar annual subscription per member. It was estimated that twenty thousand dollars would be required to meet the needs of the first year's work. The organizers were aware of the uniqueness of the situation: as upper-class Creole capitalists they were entering an association with field hands and were accepting on faith that the freedmen would honor the unsecured loans. Nevertheless, the *Tribune* was enthusiastic about the idea "of capital furnished by small shares of freedmen who possess nothing more than their industry, good faith, and courage."[22]

The association began work almost immediately. During the last week in February a committee was sent to visit plantations worked by groups of freedmen "to ascertain their condition and wants." The committee was enthusiastically received by the freedmen, who were eager to work and required only small amounts of aid in most instances. Laborers also came to New Orleans to meet and confer

22. *Ibid.,* February 23, 24, 1865, March 14, 1865.

with members of the association, and to make known their problems and complaints, the most common of which was working
without necessary resources. Abandoned plantations were just that
—seldom were seed, tools, supplies, or animals available.[23]

The associatiton was formed on February 22, 1865, and within
four weeks it had funded and helped establish four plantations run
by and for freedmen and had dispensed loans to an unspecified
number of other black plantations to help them survive. By July
"several plantations" were being worked by "free labor" under the
auspices of the association. Mules, plows, seed, and rations were
provided until the first crop was in. The loans were interest free.[24]

The association assumed responsibility other than funding, particularly concerning the communal efforts. When the bureau of
labor received complaints against freedmen working on their own,
Conway notified the association. Oscar J. Dunn, later a prominent
black politician, was sent to investigate. After visiting the two
groups in question, Dunn filed a report with Conway and the association. The freedmen, he concluded, were doing well, but white
planters in the area were distressed at the example they were setting
by their success. In reporting the incident, the *Tribune* suggested
that "the planters cannot be reconciled to the idea of the laborers
'enjoying freedom.' "[25]

To stimulate interest and competitive spirit, the associatiton
sponsored agricultural contests. Cash prizes were offered to the
freedman or group of freedmen who brought in the best samples
of cotton, brown sugar, and tobacco. The largest crop and the best
work animals were also rewarded with prizes ranging from $25 to
$250.[26]

The *Tribune*, involved from the start, soon brought to public
attention the significance of the Freedmen's Aid Association. The
success of the communal efforts demonstrated that former slaves

23. B. F. Flanders to Hurlbut, February 28, 1865, in Letters Received,
Bureau of Civil Affairs, DGR(U); New Orleans *Tribune*, March 7, April 15,
1865.
24. New Orleans *Tribune*, March 31, April 18, July 11, 1865.
25. *Ibid.*, May 16, 1865.
26. *Ibid.*, June 15, 1865.

could manage cotton and cane plantations, that blacks as well as whites responded industriously to fair profits, and that blacks working without white supervision were "perfectly orderly and of remarkable good conduct." If blacks working under the free-labor system responded differently, suggested the *Tribune*, then the fault lay somewhere other than with the workers. The association proved that free men making fair profits worked well. If less free, ill-paid, and over-worked men did not do as well, the planters and military had only themselves to blame.[27]

The continuation and success of individual and communal farming by freedmen was tied irrevocably to the fate of Louisiana's abandoned and confiscated lands. Some Federal officials encouraged independent black initiative and recognized black aspirations for land ownership. Pennsylvania congressman John Covode, sent to Louisiana in May, 1865, by Secretary of War Stanton, reported on a number of items, black farming among them. In his report Covode mentioned the contract-labor system but dwelled on black lessees. He concluded that "the best way is for the Freedman to have a small piece of land and work it himself." Such a system would increase management skills, self-reliance, and family stability, as well as stimulate the South's economic recovery.[28]

Similar reasons motivated many sympathetic members of Congress when the Freedmen's Bureau bill was debated. During the last year of the war there was some discussion of the Treasury Department's retaining abandoned lands, but Charles Sumner, among others, felt it was of primary importance to "get the abandoned plantations and colored peoples under one . . . supervision."[29] Congress was reluctant to create the bureau without that stipulation. The "one supervision" would be the bureau, and division of the land among the freedmen was a consideration from the start. By the end of the war the bureau was created and provisions were made for dividing the abandoned lands among the freedmen. In

27. *Ibid.,* July 11, 1865.
28. Covode to Stanton [June, 1865], in John Covode Papers, LC. Covode's report is an accurate statement of military failures in the Department of the Gulf.
29. James McKaye to Banks, April 29, 1864, in Banks Papers, LC.

Louisiana, before bureau agents were organized in most southern states, Conway issued Circular 10, a public announcement inviting freedmen who wanted "to procure land for their own use" to make application prior to January 1, 1866.[30]

The *Tribune* was ecstatic. For some time the black newspaper had labeled the government's policy on abandoned lands as "hasty, imperfect, and unwise." Anything less than a division of those lands was considered a reward to the planters, who were responsible for the war. Only by allocating it to freedmen could exploitation end and a "truly democratic system of labor" be created. Without land the former slaves would remain the "tools of capital"; with land they would have their own capital. Hence the radical press greeted Circular 10 as "the key to independence and a self-sustaining existence." But it was a guarded enthusiasm which prophetically asked what kind of title the freedmen would receive and whether they would live and work under the threat of eviction when rebels took "mock oaths."[31]

From the start many former slaves, in rejecting the free-labor system, had hoped and believed that the land would be theirs. Some had talked of seizing it. When the announcement was made on August 10, 1865, both freedmen and bureau agents responded quickly. By September 30, there had been 73 applications filed. Most were communal ventures—584 men, 458 women, and 644 children requested 16,482 acres. By October 10 the number of applications had jumped to 250. Horses, mules, carts, hogs, chickens, tools, and bales of cotton were listed as resources. Bureau Agent Conway created a Land Department to handle the requests. The prospects of black farmers' working as much as 40,000 acres in 1866 seemed a possibility.[32]

By 1865 Conway favored the division of land. He had skirted the issue in his *Final Report* of 1865. Under the caption "Wither-

30. *House Executive Document*, 39th Cong., 1st Sess., No. 70, p. 19.

31. New Orleans *Tribune*, September 10, 1864, March 8, August 31, 1865.

32. Stevens, *50th Mass.*, 101; James C. Patterson to Fenno, September 30, 1865, C. W. Hawes to Conway, October 10, 1865, W. B. Stickney to Conway, July 21, 1865, all in Letters Received, Assistant Commissioner, Louisiana, BRFAL.

ing Conditions of the Old Aristocracy" he proposed that the war and poor crops in 1864 had hurt the large planters, concluding that "another year will hardly leave any of the old planters on their feet." Even a "fair crop" in 1865 would not offset the unfavorable agricultural conditions and heavy mortgages facing many planters, claimed Conway. "It will be impossible to prevent a very early change in the ownership of the plantations. The thing is inevitable," he concluded.[33]

However inevitable it may have seemed to Conway in early 1865, Banks apparently remained unconvinced. Nor did he consider uniting two of the more significant but divergent forces at work in Louisiana—the independent black farming movement and the land division issue; and it was not until 1865 that Conway made an effort to make the two issues one. What Banks did do, along with his followers and subordinates in the Department of the Gulf, was to respond defensively to the growing criticism of the free-labor system emanating from the *Tribune*.

To offset the effectiveness of his bête noire Banks encouraged and subsidized a second Negro newspaper, the New Orleans *Black Republican*. Throughout the period it supported the "free labor system," and hailed Banks as a benevolent redeemer. It sniped at blacks of the *Tribune*'s persuasion, claiming they were rich and did not need Banks's assistance (as "nine-tenths of the race" did) and therefore could not appreciate his efforts. The Bureau of Negro Labor was defended as an agency which "manages the planters more than it does the freedmen," and the system was declared free because the freedmen were, after all, allowed to choose their own employers. The *Black Republican* embraced Banks's system because "not one in a hundred laborers would receive fair pay if the planters are not watched closely."[34]

The most thorough and comprehensive rebuttals came from Conway and from Banks himself. Conway issued two lengthy reports which explained the free-labor system and heralded it as a success. The first, issued in September, 1864, gave considerable attention

33. Conway, *Final Report*, 8.
34. New Orleans *Black Republican*, May 13, 1863, April 15, 1865.

to problems created by the Federal army's presence and the decay of slavery. Conway described the situation created by thousands of blacks fleeing to Union lines with few if any possessions and how after months of work, with proper regulations, "these people have been greatly improved and kept from idleness and persecution as well as from being an enormous tax upon the government." Initially they were placed back on plantations, but without controls, which gave rise to "evils and wrongs done by planters and some government officials." But Conway was quick to point out that those evils were not comparable to the "injury [which] would have resulted from idleness." Problems during the first year prompted the more comprehensive system outlined in General Order 23. Its purpose was to employ and protect the freedmen, "govern the planter, protect property, promote industry, supply the markets, and lay the groundwork [for] prosperity under the new . . . state of things." Justice was provided by freedmen's courts, and schools were established. The laborers, concluded Conway, reaped "marvelous benefits" from the new system. He acknowledged that the order was "strict and severe," kept them in one place, and regulated their conduct; but he also pointed out that it bound the planter. The second report, issued in February, 1865, endorsed black land ownership but continued to defend Banks's system by reiterating many of the same ideas developed in the first report and by stressing that laborers were paid wages which were protected by the labor bureau.[35]

Conway, through most of his tenure in Louisiana, tended to judge the system almost exclusively on the assumption that blacks were wage earners, and that their wages were protected by the bureau. He wrote Banks concerning the final report, "I will show that your [system] has never been so well tested as at the close of this year." He believed, optimistically, that "no more than one per cent of all our laborers will be unpaid."[36]

As is suggested by his letter to Banks, Conway's reports were

35. Thomas W. Conway, *Report of the Condition of Freedmen in the Department of the Gulf in 1864* (New Orleans, 1865); Conway, *Final Report.*
36. Conway to Banks, January 30, 1865, in Banks Papers, LC.

intended, at least partially, for consumption outside the Department; for increasingly throughout 1864 and into 1865, Banks found it necessary to defend his free-labor system in the North. As James M. McPherson has demonstrated, Banks's work in Louisiana was debated in the northern press and became a decisive issue among abolitionists. The columns of William Lloyd Garrison's *Liberator* are sprinkled with letters concerning Louisiana, most of them written by Banks's subordinates and most supportive of the system.[37]

Banks himself was drawn into the public debate in early 1865. From the *Liberator* he responded to his critics by proposing that "in the condition of the negro, there is not one solitary element or incident of serfdom." He offered a checklist of freedmen advances to support his conclusion: blacks were safe in their liberty, protected by the government, exempted from corporal punishment, allowed to choose their employers, compensated for their labor, limited in their working hours, united with their families, allowed to enroll in the militia, allowed to cultivate land for their own benefit, and provided schools for their children.[38]

Impressive though the list was, many of Banks's critics remained unconvinced. No less concerned and perceptive an observer than Frederick Douglass said of Banks's labor system, "I hold that that policy is our chief concern at the present moment." But Banks and his subordinates found an ally in Garrison, who, through the *Liberator*, suggested that the best means to settle the debate was to reprint Conway's laudatory report of early 1865.[39] Neither Douglass nor Garrison stilled the debate, which continued as long as the system was in effect.

Banks, no doubt in part to enhance his public image in the North, continued to defend his work in Louisiana even after leav-

37. See James M. McPherson, *The Struggle for Equality: The Abolitionists and the Negro in the Civil War and Reconstruction* (Princeton, 1964) 289–93, 299, for the effect of Banks's system on the abolitionists; *Liberator,* February 8, 22, 1865.
38. *Liberator,* February 24, 1865.
39. *Equality of All Men Before the Law And Defended* (Boston, 1865), 32; *Liberator,* April 21, 1865.

ing the Department and after the free-labor system was absorbed by the Freedmen's Bureau. He wrote and delivered on several occasions a lengthy address which later was published in pamphlet form (at his expense). He rationalized the system in much the same manner Conway had, stressing the chaotic conditions from which it sprang and how superior it was to slavery. He compiled considerable research and went to great lengths to show that Louisiana's black laborers received compensation respectable not only in America but on the world market. His findings are discredited by his valuing a set of freedmen's clothing at twenty dollars and claiming laborers made four to five hundred dollars yearly off their individual land plots when, in 1865, they were prohibited from growing anything other than vegetables.[40]

Banks believed he had done a fine job in Louisiana, given the conditions there when he arrived. Indeed the checklist of advances he offered in the *Liberator* is impressive, although it does little to discredit many of the charges made by the *Tribune* and others. As a temporary measure to aid the transition from slavery to freedom Banks's plan was sound, but only as a temporary measure. In many ways, as the *Tribune* suggested, it thwarted the transition. Free men, under Banks's program, were still dependent upon employers for food, clothing, housing, medical attention, and fixed wages; they were shackled to their place of employment for a year and allowed to leave only with permission. The *Tribune* succinctly phrased a comparison of Bank's policy and slavery: "If we except the lash . . . one is unable to perceive any . . . difference between the two sets of regulations."[41]

The *Tribune* suggested that the freedmen would never be able to do for themselves until allowed to do for themselves. The paternalistic features of Banks's system were as stifling as the repressive ones. As long as military personnel controlled the overall structure of their lives and planters controlled the day-to-day factors, the

40. Nathaniel P. Banks, *Emancipated Labor in Louisiana* (New York, 1865). For a comparison of cost of maintaining laborers see Home Place Plantation Journal, I, in Alexis Ferry Papers, TU.
41. New Orleans *Tribune,* December 8, 1864.

freedmen could not complete the transition to free men. They would remain caught somewhere between bondage and liberty.[42]

42. A number of studies suggest the inefficiency of free labor and tend to discuss the issue from planter sources. Charles P. Roland, *Louisiana Sugar Plantations During the Civil War* (Leiden, Netherlands, 1957); Roland, "Difficulties of Civil War Sugar Planting in Louisiana," *Louisiana Historical Quarterly,* XXXVIII, 40–62; J. Carlyle Sitterson, *Sugar Country: The Cane Sugar Industry in the South, 1753–1950* (Lexington, 1953), 203–227; J. Carlyle Sitterson, "The Transition From Slave to Free Labor on the William J. Minor Plantations," *Agricultural History,* XVII, 216–24; Bell I. Wiley, "Vicissitudes of Early Reconstruction Farming in the Mississippi Valley," *Journal of Southern History,* III, 441–52; Dorothy Lois Ellis, "The Transition from Slave to Free Labor with Special Reference to Louisiana" (M. A. thesis, Louisana State University, 1932); Josephine Luke, "From Slavery to Freedom in Louisiana, 1862–1865" (M. A. thesis, Tulane University, 1939); Gladys Stella Bringer, "Transition from Slave to Free Labor in Louisiana after the Civil War" (M.A. thesis, Tulane University, 1927).

V

Controls, Courts, and Violence

One country—one law.
—New Orleans *Tribune*

Louisiana's black population confronted tight controls and sometimes violent force throughout the war years. Confederate wartime
supervision was replaced by Butler's dictum to leave slaves "subject
to the ordinary laws of the community." Banks relaxed that restric-
tion, placing blacks on plantations under a program which retained
some of the controls associated with slavery. Crucial to Federal
occupation policy was the provost marshal, who in many instances
more closely resembled an antebellum patrol captain than an agent
of the liberating army. Even abolition of slavery did not materially
change the life of many of the state's blacks, for it brought few
changes in Banks's system.

Under General Order 23 plantation workers were given a choice
of employers, were paid wages, were protected from corporal punishment, and were afforded greater family security than in slavery;
but, many argued, that was the extent of their liberation. The
quantity and quality of their clothing and rations were set for them
as were their wages, and they were bound to the plantation for a
year under threat of loss of those wages. Plantation laborers were

also prohibited from owning various items, including weapons, and from growing certain crops and raising certain animals. A simple visit to a neighboring plantation required a pass from employer, overseer, or provost marshal. As late as January, 1865, blacks needed written authorization before they were allowed to enter Federal lines.[1]

The idea that any black should be unemployed or vagrant was abhorrent to Union officials. Blacks either worked on plantations or they were arrested and labored on public works for rations. Throughout the period of Union occupation vagrancy orders were repeatedly circulated. Occasionally the orders were sent to parish provost marshals when there was a shortage of laborers.[2]

The arrest of "vagrant" blacks occasionally became a knotty problem for Federal officials. Prior to the war slaves were jailed as a disciplinary measure, a common practice in urban areas such as New Orleans. During occupation, the practice was continued by civil and military authorities, and although Butler cautioned that only slaves of loyal masters should be interned, his warning often went unheeded. New Orleans police indiscriminately arrested blacks. They also assisted local slaveholders who, because of the dissolution of the old system, increasingly turned to civil authorities for slave discipline. The prisoner situation was solved in part with Banks's labor system; because of a shortage of labor, blacks could secure their release by signing contracts to work on plantations. That, however, did not lessen the enthusiasm of local policemen for arresting blacks—it only meant the freedmen were more likely to secure a rapid release.[3]

1. W. A. Fisk Orders to the Officer of the Day, January 7, 1865, in Letters Received, Provost Marshal Ascension, DGR(U).

2. Bowen to Porter, March 23, 1863, Letters Received, Provost Marshal Ascension; Page to Bowen, April 24, 1863, Letters Received, Provost Marshal General; Hanks to Stearns, July 18, 1864, Letters Received, Provost Marshal St. Mary, all *ibid.*; "Circular to the Colored People" by George Hanks, March 26, 1864, Bowen to Banks, March 28, 1864, both in Banks Papers, LC; New Orleans *Tribune,* August 31, 1865.

3. Receipt, August 31, 1863, in Gay Papers, LSU; *Official Records,* Vol. XV, Pt. 588, p. 602; Prisoners in the Parish Prison [New Orleans] to Butler, May 6, 1862, S. H. Stafford to Butler, July 21, 1862, both in Benjamin F. Butler Papers, LC; W. H. Gray to Banks, January, 1863, E. F. Brasin to Irwin, February, 1863,

The Creoles were particularly offended by the vagrancy laws and the controls. Free blacks were outraged at being stopped in the streets "while pursuing business" and arrested for not carrying free papers. Although usually able to escape the discomfort of the parish jail after presenting their papers, they were nevertheless incensed by the situation. In Baton Rouge and New Orleans they met as groups and drafted protests which were sent to Military Governor Shepley. But not until 1864 and emancipation did the free blacks in Louisiana feel secure in their status—as late as one year after the Emancipation Proclamation an antebellum registration process was still in effect which had been required of all free blacks who wished to remain in the state.[4] The rough and indiscriminate treatment the prewar free blacks received from Federals eventually pushed them toward an uneasy alliance with the freedmen. Normally very conscious of their status, they nevertheless came to realize that Federal controls would be enforced by virtue of skin color, not prewar status, and that they could share the fate of the newly liberated slaves.

Although the restrictions made life difficult for the Creoles, plantation hands fell under the tightest scrutiny. They were controlled by whites on plantations, as well as by local provost marshals who represented military and civil authority and functioned as mediators in affairs touching blacks and whites. A number of the provost marshals were honest, sincere, and overworked men serving in a truly thankless position. They were charged with supervising and enforcing labor contracts, seeing that blacks stayed on plantations, serving as judges in disputes, issuing passes, and generally protecting as well as controlling the black population.[5]

G. Heresa to Banks, January 14, 1864, H. Johnes to Banks, February 3, 1863, Mrs. Graham to Banks, January 28, 1863, all in Letters Received, Bureau of Civil Affairs, DGR(U); List of Colored Vagrants Now at the City Work House Suitable for Plantation Work [February 12, 1864], in Shepley Papers, MHSL.

4. W. A. Brice to Banks, January 3, 1863, in Letters Received, Bureau of Civil Affairs, DGR(U); Petition of Free Persons of Color to Governor George F. Shepley [undated], in Shepley Papers, MHSL; A. A. Hocha to Banks, March 18, 1863, Banks Papers, LC; Register of Free Colored Persons Entitled to Remain in the State, 1840–1864, New Orleans Public Library.

5. See, for example, W. Edwards to Dear Sir, February 18, 1863, Gay Papers, LSU. "All local matters about negroes . . . General Shepley leaves to local authorities—commanding officers [and] Provost Marshals."

But many of the provost marshals were troubled with color prejudice, became agents of planters, and assumed the worst qualities
attributed to overseers. One, described as being "pro slavery" and
"illiterate," was prone to committing "outrages" against blacks.
Another, initially dubbed too abolitionist to be effective, was, within
two weeks, caught up in the social whirl of wartime plantation
society and became "votre tres humble serviteur to all [whites] who
. . . choose to smile on him." On a plantation near Brashear City
the provost marshal and members of the guard were quartered at
the "big house" while they hunted, fished and had "a jolly time."[6]
Union soldiers frequently noted that provost marshals seemed rapidly corrupted after brief association with planters.

Blacks looked upon the officials with skepticism. Laborers protested that they lacked means of redress because provost marshals
were linked too closely with planters. They complained that most
gave justice for a few weeks until they were courted by planters
and then "we no longer have any rights, or very little."[7] Nor do
the complaints seem to be exaggerated. Provost marshals forced
laborers to forfeit wages as penalty for leaving the plantation even
when they were on legitimate errands for which the employer had
not issued a pass. In St. Charles Parish the provost marshal was
called after a theft of sugar and molasses; when unable to locate
the guilty party, he seized and sold enough livestock belonging to
the freedmen to compensate for the stolen goods. Other provost
marshals were charged with stealing produce from blacks, with
prohibiting blacks the rights allowed them under the labor contracts, and with refusing to issue passes.[8]

Reports of corruption and abuse were common and occasionally
resulted in courts-martial, but that did little to stop the infractions.
A dual system of justice and punishment permeated the Department. At Milliken's Bend insubordinate plantation hands were

6. R. K. Diossy to Conway, September 8, 1865, in Letters Received, Bureau
of Civil Affairs, DGR(U); Duganne, *Camps and Prisons*, 39, 43–44; Marshall,
Army Life, 397.
7. New Orleans *Tribune*, October 22, 1864, April 11, 1865.
8. C. Dewey to Bowen, February 19, 1864, J. H. Duganne to Bowen, April
13, 1863, Hanks to Chickering, July 29, 1864, Page to Bowen, February 28,
1863, in Letters Received, Provost Marshal General, DGR(U).

bound and gagged or put in the guard house; but the drunken overseer on the same plantation who beat laborers was cautioned not to repeat the act—"he did no permanent damage," concluded the investigating provost marshal. The provost marshal for St. James and St. John the Baptist parishes was typical of his type. Two blacks, "belonging" to one planter, "insulted . . . several planters," and men were sent to arrest them for that infraction. Another black, who was armed and "belonged" to a third planter, tried to prevent the arrests. All three were arrested.[9]

Corporal punishment bordering on the sadistic became common in some districts, and less severe punishment for minor offenses was routine. An observer in Terrebonne Parish, after listing a series of thefts and violent acts committed by the provost marshal, reported that the military agent "resorts repeatedly to the stocks and whips [and] I might multiply these complaints by scores." In Lafourche Parish black men and women were, "for the mildest offense," tied with their hands behind their backs, the rope passed over a hook on the wall, and "left hanging to await the pleasure of the owner or overseer." In that instance the charges were verified and the provost marshal relieved of duty.[10]

Freedmen who attempted to leave plantations to join the Union army were particularly offensive to provost marshals and were singled out for excessive punishment. A "literate black" man, arrested in New Orleans and sent to St. Bernard Parish as a plantation worker, was refused a pass to a recruitment station by Provost Marshal S. W. Sawyer. Attempting to take the journey without a pass, the man was arrested and returned to Sawyer, who "knocked

9. O. J. Flagg to Baird, November 15, 1865, in Letters Received, Assistant Commissioner, Louisiana, BRFAL; Hepworth, *Whip, Hoe and Sword*, 232; "Poor men become Provost Marshals and quickly become rich men," Wilkinson to Bower, March 30, 1863, Statement of J. B. MacMillian, February 21, 1863, both in Letters Received, Provost Marshal General, DGR(U); T. D. to John E. Fallon, January 4, 1864, in Thomas Durant Papers, NYHSL; D. McCall to Thomas, July 11, 1864, Mississippi, BRFAL. A Provost Marshal General of the Department was also relieved of duty; see Henri Robinson Papers, LSU.

10. Nott to Bowen, March 12, 1863, Duganne to Bowen, April 13, 1863, Rennis to Hanks, September 7, 1863, all in Letters Received, Provost Marshal General, DGR(U).

him down, kicked and beat him in the most brutal manner." The volunteer was still bleeding from those wounds when he was returned to the plantation. There he was punished by the planter without objections from the provost marshal: eighteen hours in the stocks, six hours with hands tied together in front and elbows bound behind with the aid of a stick and shirt pulled up so mosquitoes could cover his back; six additional hours in the stocks and twenty-five lashes. He was then made to "beg the pardon of his master." Sawyer, perhaps typical of his type, concluded that "the height of a negroes ambition is to have nothing to do and pleanty [*sic*] to eat."[11]

For the same offense—attempting to enlist without a pass—another black was sentenced by a provost marshal to twenty-four lashes on the bare back, eighteen hours in the stocks, twenty-five more lashes, and three hours tied to a tree after nightfall without a shirt so "that misquetos [*sic*], which fly in swarms, [could] bite him." Both of these cases were reported to the provost marshal general of the Department, who removed the provost marshals from duty and submitted charges against them.[12]

Violence and intimidation in the Union parishes during the war was not the exclusive work of Federal troops. Southern whites frequently beat, abused, and killed blacks. But whites tended to exercise greater restraint during the months of occupation than during the days of slavery and the period directly following the end of the war.[13] Such reserve did not imply that whites trusted blacks or felt they should be left uncontrolled or even left to the watchful eye of the occupying army. On the contrary, there were telegraphic rumors of insurrections, with whites convinced that every new freedom granted blacks would be followed by blood and

11. Ephraim Patterson to Bowen, July 18, 1863, Letters Received, Provost Marshal General; S. W. Sawyer to T. W. Sherman, May 19, 1863, Letters Received, Provost Marshal Orleans, both *ibid.*
12. Hepworth, *Whip, Hoe and Sword*, 236.
13. See, for examples, Negroe's Statement Concerning Hanging on Mr. Le-Sepps' Plantation [undated], in Shepley Papers, MHSL; Statement of E. Key, August, 1863, Statement of William Ruben, November 21, 1863, A. B. Long to Dwight, May 2, 1863, all in Letters Received, Provost Marshal General, DGR(U).

carnage. Butler's arrival was greeted by fears of black "insurrection and destruction" inspired by Creoles. The fears increased after Butler disarmed the white population, and they spread with the advance of the Union army. The local press tended to ignore the rumors for fear of causing a general panic. As explained by a Natchitoches editor, "we have failed to notice several things which have occurred within the last few days because we did not wish to increase public excitement."[14]

Occasionally whites banded together and formed vigilance committees, but that was relatively rare during the war years. More frequently they shared their fears with Federal officials and requested protection by Union troops. From the town of Vermillionville in Lafayette Parish came the cry that "the slaves . . . are banding themselves together resolved upon taking the lives of their masters." The citizens advised Banks that an armed guard was needed to keep order. A similar request came from Grand Coteau where blacks (described as "the slave population" four months after the Emancipation Proclamation was effective) were reputedly "in a state of disorganization and without control committing depredations that menace the honor, the virtue and lives of our families."[15]

Most white fears of mass insurrections were groundless. There is little evidence to support a thesis of widespread plotting by the black population. There is, however, clear indication that some freedmen in Louisiana resorted to violence, particularly in instances where whites continued to treat them as slaves. Few former masters were able or willing to acknowledge blacks as freedmen. Those who did and understood the dynamics of what was happening sel-

14. F. A. Pradhomme to his father, October 11, 1862, in Pradhomme Papers, LSU; "Journal of the War," *De Bow's Review*, XXXV, 327–28; P. L. Carrie to Colonel Irwin, March 10, 1863, A. B. Long to Banks, April 24, 1863, both in Letters Received, DGR(U); Banks to Halleck, December 24, 1862, in Banks Papers, LC; Natchitoches *Union*, May 18, 1862.

15. Vigilance Committee Documents, 1862–1865, in E. Cousinard Papers, LSU; Citizens of West Baton Rouge to Banks [?], 1863, Citizens of Vermillion to Banks, April 23, 1863, Citizens of Grand Coteau to Commanding General the United States Forces at Opelousas, May, 1863, all in Letters Received, Bureau of Civil Affairs, DGR(U).

dom had serious problems,[16] but those who refused to accept the new status of blacks, and complained of the need for controls often found themselves in violent situations.

Nat Becker was sent to a Federal post for striking an overseer "several times with a hoe handle over the face and arms"—an incident provoked by Nat's "insolent" refusal to obey an order and his resistance when the overseer tried to force his compliance. A similar incident occurred in Lafourche Parish when a black man refused to do as ordered. On the Louisiana-Mississippi border four black men were arrested for shooting a white man. The freedmen had left their place of work and joined several friends in a wooded area. Pursued by the employer and a number of whites (as they would have runaway slaves), the blacks resisted with violence, killing one of the whites. "A negro belonging to a man in St. Bernard Parish" was similarly shot and killed for attempting to leave the plantation. After being told to stop by armed guards, he continued to advance with a club and broke one man's arm before he was fatally wounded. On a plantation a few miles above New Orleans the workers exhibited the "symptoms of revolt" by organizing themselves and selecting leaders who were trying to negotiate grievances with the overseer. Instead of accepting blacks as wage earners with complaints, the overseer reported the situation to the owner, who in turn called in a black leader, ridiculed him, and had him whipped. At that point the "symptoms of revolt" erupted into the real thing—the overseer was killed, Federal troops had to be summoned, and five blacks were arrested.[17]

These were not isolated incidents. Black refusals to work under the conditions of the old system and white attempts to keep blacks working on plantations provoked considerable violence. An armed white who interfered during an argument between a planter and

16. See, for example, J. I. Scott to Buhler, June 28, 1865, in Buhler Family Papers, LSU.
17. Daniel Meames Statement, April 11, 1863, C. L. Colomb to Provost Marshal Donaldsonville, April 5, 1863, both Letters Received, Provost Marshal Ascension; Statement of George Lee, August 22, 1863, Miscellaneous Records, Provost Marshal General, all in DGR(U). New Orleans *Tribune*, August 23, 1865; New Orleans *National Advocate*, August 14, November 13, 1862.

his laborers was later found dead in the road, his head crushed with an ax. On another plantation, workers armed with cane knives and clubs refused to go to the fields until the provost marshal arrived with troops and arrested the leaders. Refusing to work and stealing were common irritants which prompted planters and overseers to call on outside assistance, but when local police or Federal troops were summoned, their presence often exacerbated matters and frequently brought violence. In Plaquemines Parish blacks systematically shot at police and patrols when they intervened in plantation disputes. During one exchange of gunfire a policeman was wounded and another killed.[18]

Stealing, burning, and violence over specific grievances were common; but the widespread, organized acts of black terrorism which the white population expected never materialized. Apparently the only large, armed group of blacks operated in Saint Mary Parish in the spring of 1863, and their activities, centered around the town of St. Martinville, were short-lived. They robbed no less than a dozen homes and rode the countryside disrupting work on plantations by telling laborers that they were not required to work and were free to leave if they wished, but there were no reports of violence against whites. Details are confused, but some of the men may have been army stragglers. A Creole, Theodule Melan, reputedly led the integrated band, but he later claimed he was forced to ride with them, and affidavits by his neighbors and by some of the victims support that statement.[19]

In late April the parish provost marshal was dispatched to St. Martinville with thirty men from the 52nd Massachusetts to investigate. On the evening of their arrival word was sent that about forty armed blacks were approaching the town. The military men, accompanied by sixty civilians, met the advance on a bridge. In

18. O. U. Lull to Emory, May 9, 1863, Sawyer to Bowen, June 3, 1863, both Letters Received, Provost Marshal General; Brown to Dunham, February 24, 1863, Letters Received, Bureau of Civil Affairs; Dudley to Irwin, August 2, 1863, Letters Received, all in DGR(U). Bayside Plantation Journal II (UNC), May 4, 1863; J. D. Smith to Lou, September 22, 1865, in J. D. Smith Papers, LSU; Magnolia Plantation Journal, III (in Warmoth Papers, UNC), August 12, 16, 1862.
19. See statements dated April 24, 1863, in Jarrard Papers, LSU.

the ensuing battle three or four blacks were killed and five were captured, as was Melan. The citizens offered the prisoners to the provost marshal, but he refused. Later the same day travelers on the bridge observed at least four of the blacks hanging there. Punishment had been swift.[20]

After the initial fight, local whites, fearful of retaliation, requested continued Federal protection. Their fears were justified. At 5 P.M. on a Sunday afternoon the troops returned to find "the citizens very excited, the women very much so," for word had been sent that the blacks were two miles away and approaching the town. Again a party of soldiers and civilians went out to meet the advance, but the outnumbered blacks melted back into the bayou before contact was made. A military post was established in the town, and soldiers traveled to outlying plantations sending laborers back to the fields. Local whites formed a patrol "for the protection of [their] properties against negro robers [sic]."[21] The military's presence apparently ended the activities of the St. Martinville gang, activities which, in fact, never matched the fears or expectations of the white population. The blacks committed no murders or rapes—most of their actions were confined to stealing food, money, and accouterments, and to "demoralizing" laborers in the area, a persistent source of irritation to local whites.

During the period of Federal occupation not all justice was meted out as it was at the bridge at St. Martinville or by provost marshals like Sawyer. Blacks received fair and impartial treatment from some provost marshals: one at Donaldsonville shocked the town's residents when he allowed blacks to testify against whites.[22] But despite isolated instances of blacks' receiving justice, there was an obvious need to standardize the Union judicial system relating to freedmen. Civil courts were disrupted in many locales, and in

20. Moors, *History of 52nd Mass.*, 127; A. B. Long to Banks, April 23, 1863, in Banks Papers, LC.

21. Henry L. Wood to Colonel, April 28, 30, 1863, Petition to Colonel 22nd Maine, both in Jarrard Papers, LSU.

22. J. M. Adderman, *Reminiscences of Two Years* (Providence, 1866), 34–35; see also J. H. Bradley to Bowen, May 21, 1864 in Letters Received, Provost Marshal General, DGR(U).

parishes where they were operating they frequently refused to hear black testimony against whites or excluded blacks altogether by refusing to entertain their complaints. Responding to that situation, a system of provost marshal courts was established. Although the courts were subject to the flaws of the individual provost marshals who sat as judges, by 1864 many of the more offensive had been removed. Those who remained were tempered in their decisions and punishments by a provision which allowed decisions to be reviewed. Increasingly throughout the occupational period the provost marshal courts became the vehicle of legal recourse for Louisiana's freedmen.

While the new system was an improvement and certainly was preferable to unilateral decisions by planters, overseers, and patrol captains, it often provided little real justice in a clinical sense. At best it occasionally and imperfectly protected black workers from the grosser injustices. Only infrequently is there evidence of a black bringing charges against a white. A majority of the cases which came before those courts involved blacks who were in violation of the law. Vagrancy was the most common charge; the guilty were usually sent to the bureau of labor. Refusals "to due duty" or to obey orders were equally common complaints; most offenders were returned to plantations with a loss in wages or sent to labor on the public works without pay. A number of blacks were found guilty of selling whiskey to soldiers and plantation hands and occasionally a freedman was charged with carrying a weapon.

Violence and contract violations were the two most common problems which brought blacks and whites before the bench. Numerous whites were found guilty in provost marshal courts of beating and whipping blacks. In Brashear City the usual fine was ten dollars or ten days, while in St. Bernard Parish fines were higher for the same offense—thirty dollars. Cases involving contract and wage violations indicate how widespread the problem was and suggest that a dual system of justice existed in those courts. Blacks who violated labor contracts (usually by leaving the plantation or refusing to work) frequently forfeited all or part of the wages due them. But whites who violated contracts (usually by not paying wages) were only made to pay the amount due. The case of Henry Cauldwell (black) versus G. P. Ayers (white) is typical. Cauldwell brought Ayers before the provost marshal court to collect his wages. Deciding in favor of Cauldwell, the court instructed Ayers to pay the back wages. Although Ayers was also fined ten dollars for being insolent to the court, he received no punishment for attempting to cheat his employee. Whites apparently had nothing to fear from the courts in trying to defraud their workers.[23]

The black relationship with white authority was one of the most difficult aspects of the experiment in wartime Louisiana. Blacks believed themselves free and responded accordingly, but in the Department of the Gulf few whites (blue or gray) were ready to accept the freedmen as free men and women. Native white planters frequently continued to consider their laborers as slaves, intimidating, flogging, and defrauding them. Nor could blacks feel secure in asserting their rights when they received inconsistent treatment from provost marshals. More often than not, those military agents, charged with mediating rural race relations, were willing partners of conservative local whites.

Flawed though it was by recalcitrant whites, unequal treatment in courts, and a dual system of administering punishment, the basis of the Reconstruction judicial system emerged in Louisiana during the war years. Blacks were allowed to testify against whites in the provost marshal courts which, if not free from color prejudice, at least opened courtroom doors to blacks and heard their cases. By the end of the war and the takeover by the Freedmen's Bureau, many of the more offensive provost marshals were removed and the court system was functioning smoothly if not always impartially.

23. See, for examples, CXXXIV, Louisiana, BRFAL. T. W. Greene to H. Robinson, October 31, 1864, G. Breuning Monthly Report, November 1864, both Miscellaneous Records, Provost Marshal General; Albert Stearns Monthly Report, March 31, 1864, Letters Received, Provost Marshal General, all in DGR(U). See G. Breuning Report for the Cauldwell versus Ayers case. Blassingame, *Black New Orleans*, 173–210, superbly carries race relations in the city through Reconstruction.

VI

"Men of Color—To Arms! To Arms!"

cO

If we must die, let it not be like hogs
Hunted and penned in an inglorious spot,
While round us bark the mad and hungry dogs,
Making their mock at our accursed lot.
If we must die, O let us nobly die,
So that our precious blood may not be shed
In vain.

— Claude McKay

Louisiana blacks had a long tradition of military service even prior to the Civil War. From 1729, free blacks, and occasionally slaves, participated in martial activities, the most notable being the assistance given General Andrew Jackson in 1815 at the Battle of New Orleans. With the start of hostilities in 1861, the black drummer boy from the battle in 1815, Jordan Noble, issued a call which eventually resulted in the creation of the First Native Guard Louisiana Militia. Confederate Governor Thomas O. Moore recognized the 440-man regiment as part of the Home Guard, and by the time the city fell to Butler's occupying forces, the Native Guard numbered about 1,500 men.[1] In rural parishes free-black planters responded by forming home guards whose primary responsibility was to prevent slave insurrections. It was rumored that a black planter from Pointe Coupee Parish financed a white guard to help protect the parish.

1. Mary F. Berry, "Negro Troops in Blue and Gray: The Louisiana Native Guard, 1861–1863," *Louisiana History,* VIII, 165–67; Everett, "Native Guard," 202–217; Blassingame, *Black New Orleans,* 25–47.

Such actions by black planters have been recognized generally as the product of class and property considerations, for indeed many of them had more to protect than a vast majority of white Louisianians. The activities of free blacks in New Orleans and the creation of the Native Guard has been less easy to understand. No doubt the tradition of 130 years of free-black military service to the territory and the state played a role, but tradition alone seems an inadequate explanation. New Orleans Creole Charles Gibbons reported that he enlisted in the Native Guard in order to save his life after a city policeman threatened him with lynching if he did otherwise. There is good evidence to suggest that white intimidation played a significant role, for there seemed to be a lack of enthusiasm on the part of the Guard. A white resident of the city described "the doings" of "our young Creoles" as "shameful." He believed that they "should be the first to offer their life's blood for their country," but as far as he was able to discern, all the Native Guard did was leave the city occasionally to go camping. He was distressed at their apparent reluctance to actively defend the Confederacy.[2] His concern proved justified, for when New Orleans fell to Union forces the Native Guard did not evacuate the city with the rest of the Confederate troops.

Butler was hardly settled in his command before officers of the Guard visited him and volunteered their services to the Union. Impressed though he was with the black delegation, he was reluctant to accept them as Union soldiers. He frankly outlined his reasons to Secretary of War Stanton: the light-skinned, well-educated officers of the Native Guard were not representative of Louisiana's black population, but their acceptance would signal acceptance of all black troops, and, he confided, "I hope . . . that this war will be ended before any body of negroes could be organized, armed, and drilled so as to be effective." Butler seemed torn between a fear of armed blacks and a contradictory belief that most were horrified of fire arms; they were, he wrote, "ludicrous in the extreme" when handling weapons.[3]

2. *House Reports,* 39th Cong., 2nd Sess., No. 16, p. 126; C. Nevins to Lou, March 2, 1862, in E. C. Wharton Papers, LSU.
3. Butler to Stanton, May 25, 1862, in Benjamin F. Butler Papers, LC.

While Stanton and officials in Washington pondered the question of the Native Guard and black troops, Butler wrestled with the contraband question and General Phelps. Butler insisted that Phelps close his lines to contraband blacks and use those within his lines for fatigue labor. Refusing in both instances, Phelps instead requested "arms, accouterments, clothing, camp and garrison equipage . . . for three regiments of Africans." Butler retorted that no authority existed for arming blacks but that he would forward the entire matter to President Lincoln. Until a decision could be reached, he ordered Phelps to stop organizing and drilling, and to put the blacks to "work they are fitted to do"—such as cutting trees and building defenses. Before Butler had Lincoln's decision Phelps resigned, preferring resignation to being a "slave driver."[4]

Less than two weeks after rejecting Phelps's plan to arm fugitive blacks, Butler decided to muster the Native Guard into Federal service; the acceptance was conditional upon approval from the president. Nevertheless, Butler did exactly what Phelps was told could not be done—he enlisted black troops without specific authorization. Phelps was pleased that the initial step had been taken but was critical of Butler's motives. The Native Guard regiments, claimed Phelps, were accepted by Butler "as the result of a low quarrelsome spirit . . . [and] because it had been previously accepted by the rebels, not because it is right in itself." Butler's attitude and official actions and decisions concerning Louisiana blacks were summed up by Phelps: "He is still on the old political issue instead of being occupied with the magnitude of the present crisis."[5]

Butler was not alone in being restricted by "the old political issue," and if he was cautious, Lincoln was even more so. Two months after requesting authorization for recruiting black troops,

4. Phelps to R. S. Davis, July 31, 1862, *Official Records,* XV, 534–35; Phelps to R. S. David, in Letters Received, Bureau of Civil Affairs, DGR(U); R. S. Davis to Phelps, June 18, 1862, *Butler Correspondence,* I, 615; Butler to Phelps, August 2, 1862, in Benjamin F. Butler Papers, LC; Butler, *Butler's Book,* 488–89.

5. Butler to Halleck, August 27, 1862, *Official Records,* XV, 555; John W. Phelps Diary (NYPL), August 15, 23, 1862.

Butler had received no answer. As with the contraband question, he received no specific instructions even after requesting them and was left with only vague guidelines and unofficial statements on which to base his policies. He protested to Chief of Staff Henry Halleck that many communications had come from the War Department and from the president, but none answered his questions concerning black troops. In the absence of a rejection to the proposal, concluded Butler, "I must therefore take it to be approved, but would prefer distinct orders on this subject." There the matter rested and the organizing continued.[6] Thus black Louisianians were given arms and uniforms and an opportunity to strike legally the institution which had kept them in bondage. But this was done not from the righteousness of their cause but from the tenacity of the Native Guard and Phelps, the vanity of Butler, and the cautious passivity of the president. The Native Guard was tentatively accepted by Butler in the absence of a rejection by the Government —hardly a forthright start.

Butler's letter to Halleck was no doubt prompted by mild desperation, for he had been recruiting for sixty days. By November he had mustered not only the Native Guard and free Creoles but also slaves freed by owners or by military courts and blacks who came from enemy lines. A sense of urgency prevailed because recruits arrived faster than they could be processed and organized. Despite enthusiastic enlistments, apparently neither the troops nor Butler received official notification of their acceptance until the Second Regiment was mustered and informed it would receive advance pay and bounty. By mid-November, 1862, Butler reported to radical Republican Senator Henry Wilson that he had "two regiments of Native Guards (colored) in good condition and doing good service in the field, [and] another of the same sort has recently completed its organization."[7]

6. Butler to Henry Halleck, November 7, 1862, in Benjamin F. Butler Papers, LC.
7. George Denison to Salmon P. Chase, September 24, 1862, *Butler Correspondence*, II, 328–29; George Denison to Chase, October 8, 1862, in Chase Papers, LC; W. A. Nichols to G. R. Gidding, November 15, 1862, Butler to

It is unclear why Butler changed his attitude. Just weeks before making the decision he ridiculed the idea of blacks trying to handle fire arms. Even earlier he asserted that fugitive slaves who came to his lines were "vicious and unthrifty," but they too were recruited. The shortage of white troops in the Department was certainly a consideration; repeated requests for reinforcements were ignored in Washington. Butler was probably prompted by the military situation, and Lincoln's passive approval was no doubt similarly motivated. From the start the president claimed that what he did or did not do regarding slaves and slavery would be dictated by military necessity. Secretary of the Treasury Chase had urged Butler in July to arm the contrabands, assuring him that public opinion was moving in that direction. With that Butler could count on some support within the cabinet. In the same month Congress gave the president authorization to recruit blacks, and while no action was taken by the administration, it must have indicated to Butler that at least Congress would not reject his actions. A final consideration was, as Phelps stated, that Butler was galled by the fact that the Native Guard had served the Confederacy and was not welcomed by the Union. For whatever reasons, the man who had cast fifty-two ballots at the 1860 Democratic Convention for Jefferson Davis was responsible for mustering the first three southern black regiments into the Union army.

In early 1863, recruitment of black troops in Louisiana was affected by a number of events. Banks replaced Butler; the Emancipation Proclamation and heavy Union losses generated greater acceptance of black troops throughout the North; and the Lincoln administration systematically began recruiting black troops. Brigadier General Daniel Ullman, lawyer and unsuccessful Know-Nothing candidate for governor of New York, was sent to Louisiana with instructions to raise one brigade of four regiments of black Louisiana volunteers. Ullman was given thirty days to raise the brigade and to report to Banks. The War Department informed

---

Henry Wilson, November 12, 1862, both in Benjamin F. Butler Papers, LC; George Denison to Jimmy, November 14, 1862, in Denison Papers, LC.

Banks that it wanted "a large military force from the colored population of Louisiana . . . raised immediately" and that Ullman had authority to assist in that. The secretary of war made it clear that he was committed to black troops and that their recruitment would take priority over the plantation economy: "Volunteers are to be allowed to come in from the plantations."[8] Such blanket authority and control over the more able-bodied former slaves was at variance with Banks's plans for the Department and produced considerable friction as recruitment progressed.

Even prior to Ullman's arrival in Louisiana Banks continued the recruitment started by Butler. A fourth Native Guard regiment filled quickly and was, according to one observer, moved by a "religious enthusiasm" for the task at hand. Estimates of the number of black troops that could be raised in Louisiana reached an exaggerated fifty thousand. This was qualified with the provision that the right man lead the project. It was implied in many quarters that Banks was not the right man; later events indicated that neither was Ullman. But, despite misgivings over Banks, black Louisianians responded to the call to arms. Ten New Orleans free blacks, six of whom served in the Confederate Native Guard, offered their services, requesting only that they be commanded by an officer "who will appreciate us as men and soldiers—and we will be able to surmount all other difficulties."[9]

With Ullman's arrival in Louisiana, recruitment activity increased. But recruitment was, in many instances, a mild euphemism for harsher activities. Blacks were marched to recruitment depots at gun point and forced to enlist; squads of soldiers, sometimes black, went to private homes and places of business and left with any and all able-bodied blacks. In New Orleans it was reported that "many negroes are afraid to go from home on business . . .

---

8. Thomas Vincent to Daniel Ullman, January 13, 1863, Stanton to Ullman, March 25, 1863, Stanton to Banks, March 25, 1863, all *Official Records,* Ser. 3, Vol. III, pp. 14, 102, 10; Stanton to Shepley, March 25, 1863, in Shepley Papers, MHSL.

9. George Denison to Chase, February 1, 1863, in Chase Papers, LC; Adolph J. Gla, *et al.,* to Banks, April 7, 1863, in Letters Received, Bureau of Civil Affairs, DGR(U).

Table 2

ESTIMATE OF NUMBER OF BLACK TROOPS
FROM LOUISIANA*

3,000 Infantry. Louisiana Native Guard raised by B. F. Butler. Later they were designated the 73rd, 74th, 75th, and 76th United States Colored Infantry (U.S.C.I.).

4,000 Infantry. Raised by Daniel Ullman. Later designated the 78th, 79th, 80th, 81st, and 82nd U.S.C.I. The 79th was later broken up.

8,400 Infantry. Raised by N. P. Banks. Later designated 83rd, 84th, 85th, 86th, 87th, 88th, 89th, 90th, and 99th U.S.C.I.

1,500 Heavy artillery and cavalry.

1,850 Infantry. Sixty-day volunteers.

_____

18,750 Total

_____

*J. Schuyler Crosby to Warmouth, November 14, 1865, in Henry Clay War-mouth Papers, UNC. These figures may be exaggerated and excessive. The total was probably closer to 15,000.

lest they should be picked up in the streets." Apparently those recruiting techniques were generated by an Ullman order authorizing recruiters to take any black male off the streets unless he had a signed pass. Impressments took place on plantations as well as in towns, and affected free blacks as well as contrabands, although undoubtedly former slaves suffered worse. At Brashear City a group of male contrabands and their families arrived at a labor depot with the understanding that the able-bodied men would be enlisted once their wives and children were settled; it was further agreed that those remaining, less-able men would be sent to plantations with their families. But upon their arrival, before any arrangements were made, all the men were marched away "by actual force, leaving their wives and children weeping and complaining that some soldiers forced them off."[10] These activities did not meet

10. See, for examples, E. H. Cummings to H. Pierson, August 6, 1863, Jules Blanc to Banks, August 11, 1863, A. Louisson to Banks, August 10, 1863, W. A. Emory to Irwin, August 13, 1863, C. T. Budduke to Banks, August 5, 1863, all in Letters Received, Bureau of Civil Affairs, DGR(U); George W. Hanks to

with Banks's specific approval, but little was done to stop them. (A member of Banks's staff wrote of one such instance: "This seems to be a case of oppression.")

Another recruitment method, the forced enlistment of "vagrant" black males, was consistent with Banks's orders. In many cases a vagrant apparently was defined as any black on the streets during working hours. A white recruiter for the Corps d'Afrique reported that black regiments were being filled differently from white ones: "Every male negro who was found about the streets was taken up and put in the [work house]. If they were able-bodied, they were scared into enlistment." White civilians reported any concentrations of isolated blacks with the assurance that they would be broken up by squads of blue-clad recruiters. Banks was quick to caution that employed blacks should not be impressed, but was equally adamant that the unemployed be placed in the service. One of Banks's subordinates boasted: "This policy [brought] their speedy removal from the streets and town."[11]

Many Louisiana blacks, particularly former slaves functioning in an alien environment, were no doubt bewildered by such treatment and reluctantly accepted it. Others did not. Armed guards were assigned at recruitment depots to prevent escapes by "volunteers." Frequently blacks protested directly to Federal authorities, as in the case of P. Bourgeois, a free black, who reported that a squad of soldiers accompanied by New Orleans city police went to his house to solicit his enlistment. When he refused, "they beat him, knifed him three times and took him away." Although Bourgeois' release was obtained the next day, George Hanks of the bureau of labor informed Banks that his office was "constantly

---

R. B. Irwin, July 11, 1863, Saul L. Kingston to Banks, May 3, 1863, both in Banks Papers, LC.

11. C. C. Morgan to Banks, January 19, 1863, George Drake to T. W. Sherman, August 15, 1864, S. B. Bevanst Co. to George Hanks, August 2, 1864, C. S. Sargent to [?], August 9, 1864, T. W. Sherman to Commander, Carrollton District, August 10, 1864, all in Letters Received, Bureau of Civil Affairs, DGR(U); Whitney to Ella, September 20, 1863, in William H. Whitney Papers, LSU; George Drake to Henri Robinson, September 5, 1864, in Letters Received, Provost Marshal General, DGR(U); Colonel Walker to Banks, May 14, 1863, in Banks Papers, LC.

besieged" by blacks with similar complaints against recruiters. Thirty-five black men from Baton Rouge indignantly reported: "We are hunted upon the streets, in the market house, and other places whilst engaged in our daily avocations, and marched off to the Penitentiary, where we are . . . forced into the service." They did not object to serving in the army, but asserted that as free men they were entitled to "be placed on the same footing with others who [were] subject to [military service]."[12] In these cases, like most others, responsible military officers acknowledged the damages done and attempted to prevent further abuses, but still they continued.

Throughout the spring and summer of 1863 there was increasing friction within the Department over the recruitment of black troops. A majority of the abuses, excepting the forced enlistment of vagrants, were probably the result of Ullman's activities. The New Yorker showed a wholesale disregard for the sensitivities, liberties, and families of Louisiana blacks. B. Rush Plumly—an aging Pennsylvania Quaker and Garrisonian abolitionist soldier who had served as a Treasury agent with the staff of John C. Fremont in Missouri prior to becoming involved in freedmen affairs in Louisiana—predicted that Ullman could not raise a brigade in "a thousand years." Success, claimed Plumly, required a personal appeal to blacks, something Ullman would not do. Plumly, whose son held a commission with the Corps d'Afrique, also suggested that potential black soldiers would not respond to a white leader unless they were convinced that he was "fighting for the principle of freedom by which they are to benefit—they don't want him to fight for 'niggers.' " Ullman's recruiting techniques showed that he did not measure up.[13]

Banks's antagonism toward Ullman did not stem from a desire to protect Louisiana blacks. Rather, Banks was concerned lest roughshod enlistment practices, particularly on plantations, disrupt

12. Robert A. Tyson Diary (LSU), April 3, 1864; George Hanks to Banks, August 5, 1863, Free men of Color of Baton Rouge to Lt. Col. Pardee, November 11, 1863, both in Letters Received, Bureau of Civil Affairs, DGR(U).
13. B. Rush Plumly to Chase, July 4, 1863, in Chase Papers, LC.

the labor system and thereby hurt the economy. Even before Ullman arrived in Louisiana, his authorization to recruit from plantations troubled many whites. Treasury Agent Benjamin F. Flanders,
who controlled numerous abandoned plantations in the state, wrote
the secretary of the Treasury in private that Ullman's orders, if
allowed to stand, would be a mistake. He felt that the Union parishes were then quiet and prosperous and that the plantations
being worked by Banks's labor plan would fall victims to the policy. Flanders forwarded similar complaints to Banks. The commanding general shared Flanders' concern but reported that he
would, from necessity, follow the orders of the secretary of war
concerning recruiting. But he also wrote Flanders and numerous
other Union officials in Louisiana suggesting that if they found the
policy "not in accordance with public interests . . . [then they]
should make it known at Washington."[14] Banks served notice that
he, as a soldier, would follow the instructions of the secretary of
war, but he, no less than they, was apprehensive about the contract-
labor system and advised them on a possible means of circumvent-
ing the recruitment order.

The protests were to no avail. Ullman arrived, set up rural recruiting stations, and disrupted the labor system as predicted—
hundreds of blacks left plantations and enlisted. Masters complained
of violated labor contracts and protested that blacks joined the
army illegally, for enlistment was a contract and under Louisiana
law no black could so bind himself. Irate and indignant planters
wrote military officials about recruiters "taking" laborers wherever
they could find them and "stopping all work on plantations where
they have been." Local provost marshals were besieged with complaints, but regardless of sympathy for planters or ill-treated freedmen, they ultimately were informed by Gulf headquarters that
Ullman's authorization came from Washington.[15]

14. Benjamin F. Flanders to Chase, April 30, 1863, in Chase Papers, HSP;
Banks to Benjamin F. Flanders, May 2, 1863, Banks to Michael Hahn, May 2,
1863, Banks to Cuthbert Bullett, May 2, 1863, all in Banks Papers, LC.
15. Plantation Journal (in Palfrey Papers, LSU), March 16, 1864; Magnolia
Plantation Journal (in Warmoth Papers, UNC), September 3, 1862; Mother to
Andrew, March 26, 1863, in McCollam Papers, UNC; Deer Range Plantation

Banks was disturbed over the effects of recruiting on labor, but he lacked the leverage or authority to change the situation. Apparently he raised the issue with Ullman, who claimed that he had not intended to interfere with the plantations. But Ullman had criticisms of his own and protested that he had received "little or no cooperation from officials here," that he had found "opposition to the policy of the government"; and he vowed to "represent this matter at Washington." Ullman was quick to refer to his instructions and invoke the name of the secretary of war to anyone he felt was hindering his efforts.[16] And he was correct in his accusations that military officials in the Department were uncooperative and that many openly opposed him. This was particularly true of the Quartermaster Department and engineers who were responsible for building roads and fortifications, repairing levees, and generally maintaining public works. On numerous occasions groups of blacks working under their control were enlisted en masse by Ullman's recruiters, and this did little to produce harmony.[17]

Banks's major concern was not with intraservice harmony but with the effect recruitment had on the plantation labor system and the economy. He could not prevent Ullman from carrying out his orders without breaching his own, but he felt compelled to do something. Planters protested that their best laborers were taken by the army, leaving them with only the old and infirm and thus unable to gather their crops. Banks ultimately found makeshift

---

Journal, III (in White Papers, UNC), November 18, 1863; J. S. Bands to Capt. Roberts, September 29, 1863, Letters Received, Provost Marshal St. James and St. John the Baptist; Petition of William Palfrey to C. P. Stearn, November 13, 1863, Andrew Robinson to Banks, March 23, 1863, both Letters Received, Bureau of Civil Affairs; S. W. Sawyer to S. H. Kallenstroth, August 21, 1863, H. M. Porter to Bowen, August 8, 1863, both Letters Received, Provost Marshal General, all in DGR(U).

16. Pierra Nougu to Banks, January 21, 1863, Eli Kinsley to Banks, April 11, 1863, C. C. Auger to Colonel Irwin, April 8, 1863, Fred Knapp to Banks, April 11, 1863, all in Letters Received, DGR(U). Daniel Ullman to Banks, May 15, 1863, in Banks Papers, LC; Daniel Ullman to Colonel Walker, May 13, 1863, in General Papers, AGO.

17. Colonel Walker to Banks, May 14, 1863, Frank Peek to Banks, August 18, 1863, both in Banks Papers, LC; Holabird to Irwin, August 4, 1863, Letters Received; Colonel Gooding to General Stone, October 2, 1863, Letters Sent, both in DGR(U).

solutions to the cases he considered most pressing. He first contacted the bureau of labor with instructions to supply workers for the beleaguered planters. If that proved unsuccessful, which it often did during the harvest season, then Banks released laborers from the army. As a common practice he furloughed a portion of the conscripts from a specific plantation, but occasionally he went further. Protests by a planter in Plaquemines Parish produced the return of all his laborers who had been inducted into the service.[18] Nowhere did Banks show skill as a political general more vividly than in dealing with loyal planters and black recruits. He was primarily a friend of the planters, who were necessary for reviving the state economically and politically. On the other side, blacks who considered themselves free and were willing to fight to sustain that freedom were shown that they had little more control over their own destiny under the military than they had had in slavery.

Eventually Banks smoothed out the situation by helping to fill the Ullman Brigade. Ullman's orders specified that he was to raise one brigade of black troops and then report to Banks, under whose command he would serve. The difficulties occurred in part because, as Plumly predicted, Ullman could not raise the troops. Black Louisianians lacked confidence in him. Banks placed two regiments of troops in Ullman's brigade in order to fill it. In that manner he curtailed Ullman's independent recruiting activities, and, with the brigade filled, Ullman, by previous orders, became subordinate to Banks.

By the fall of 1863, with Ullman's disruptive influence calmed, Banks created a more cohesive policy and organization to deal with Louisiana's black population. He established the Enrollment Commission, made up of three military men, which was empowered to deal with matters concerning the freedmen—specifically

18. P. F. Langville to Major Hambler, September 1, 1864, Philip Bacon to George Hanks, August 12, 1864, Mrs. Lavine Edwards to Major N. C. Mitchell, November 3, 1864, C. A. Weed to Conway, October 24, 1864, R. A. Minor to General Thomas, October 18, 1863, all Letters Received, Bureau of Civil Affairs; General George Cook to John C. Clark, October 19, 1863, Letters Sent; George Drake to Henri Robinson, October 3, 1864, Letters Received, Provost Marshal General, all in DGR(U). Samuel Hubler to George Drake, August 30, 1864, in Banks Papers, LC.

with education, employment, and recruitment of troops. With control of the Corps d'Afrique firmly under his auspices, Banks was assured that recruitment would not interfere with his labor policy. One of the first acts of the commission was to issue an order protecting planters: plantations where hands were conscripted were given certificates exempting them from further losses of their labor supply.

Banks was more concerned with the external relations of black troops as they affected the labor force than he was with internal affairs. A major problem throughout the period was the Corps d'Afrique's officers. Initially Banks announced that he wanted "capable and ambitious" men looking for a "great opportunity to serve with distinction," and while he did find men of that caliber, the methods of selection allowed a great number of undesirables to obtain commissions. Commissions were often obtained through political influence. Ullman, for example, received letters from members of the Senate, judges, governors, and from Lincoln's secretary, supporting various officers' candidacies. Others received commissions because they were effective as recruiters: "Any soldier who will recruit about a dozen or fifteen blacks can get a commission," claimed an officer of the Corps d'Afrique. Similar positions were offered to New England soldiers as inducements to reenlist, and Massachusetts privates became officers of black troops by extending their tour of service for two years. By late 1863 it was reported that "the fever for shoulder straps [is] quite prevalent, and many an ambitious young man . . . [has] secured a commission in the Corps d'Afrique."[19]

Commissions sought and accepted through political influence, enlistment incentive, and ambition produced predictable results. Sadistic misfits or incompetents often led the black regiments. Out-

19. Banks to Captain Dwight, August 1, 1863, in Banks Papers, LC; Ira Harris to Ullman, February 19, 1863, H. Hamlin to Ullman, January 23, 1863, Governor Andrew to Ullman, February 2, 1863, John Nicolay to Ullman, March 26, 1863, all in Ullman Papers, NYHSL; William Whitney to Ella, September 30, 1863, in Whitney Papers, LSU; William C. Harpell to Banks, January 22, 1863, in Letters Received, Bureau of Civil Affairs, DGR(U); Silas Fales to Mary, May 20, 1863, Silas Everett Fales Papers, UNC; Johnson, *Muskets and Medicine*, 152.

rages against black troopers became common. An irate chaplain reported seeing "abuses practiced by officers upon the men such as cursing and vilifying [and] striking and kicking with a manner that indicates it was practiced habitually." A black soldier who failed to travel with his company from one station to another was sentenced to 100 lashes by the regiment's colonel. A second soldier was ordered to administer the punishment with a tree root four and one-half feet long and three-quarters of an inch thick. After a half dozen lashes, the colonel called for them to be laid on harder. When told that was impossible, the colonel shot the second soldier. The original offender was given 101 lashes and left tied to a tree for two and one-half hours in the hot sun. Another trooper, whose offense was "shirking," was punished by being hanged by his hands. "His cries were heard one-half a mile."[20]

Whippings, beatings, and assaults were common in the corps, but not all black soldiers tolerated illegal punishment. At Fort Jackson, Louisiana, a lieutenant colonel proposed to whip two members of the Fourth Regiment Corps d'Afrique. One had disobeyed an order, and the other had been bothersome for several days but had committed no specific offense. When the regiment was assembled to watch the proceedings, a general revolt broke out to protest the excessive punishment. Although the disruption lasted for about an hour, there were no casualties; but the incident was serious enough to warrant an investigation which resulted in public disclosure of abuses. A number of higher-ranking officers were adamant that the lieutenant colonel be punished. Brigadier General William Dwight, commander of the corps, wrote that he "regarded it important that he should be convicted on a charge which could leave the court no discretion as to the degree of punishment." He believed it important that other officers understand the penalties if they "kick [and] strike soldiers." Even Banks was indignant. He felt that the officer "indulged in punishments . . . which are not only barbarous, but indecent and are interdicteds

20. S. L. Gardner to General Ullman, December 19, 1864, in General Papers, AGO. John Joyce to Banks, May 26, 1863, in Banks Papers, LC; Robert A. Tyson Diary (LSU), May 6, 1864.

[*sic*] alike by the considerations of humanity, the articles of war, the orders of the Department and the honor of a gentleman." All agreed that the previous actions of the regiment and the appearances of the fort reflected the success of the black soldiers, and that the officer's actions "could produce only the results they did —revolt."[21]

Many of the problems of the Corps d'Afrique could have been averted, or at least ameliorated, by the use of black officers who could have worked more harmoniously with the enlisted men. The experience of the first three Native Guard regiments bears this out. Staffed in part by blacks, those units suffered fewer difficulties than later regiments. The effectiveness of black officers, at least in the lower ranks, was acknowledged by the Enrollment Commission, which initially allowed the men to elect their own company officers. But these men and the officers of the Native Guard became a source of concern.[22]

General Lorenzo Thomas, the War Department officer in charge of recruiting black troops in the Mississippi Valley, opposed using Negro officers. He no doubt was influenced by Banks, who objected to black officers from the start. Banks initially inherited them from Butler as part of the first three regiments, but he was uncomfortable with the situation. He considered black officers "detrimental to the service . . . and a source of constant embarrassment and annoyance," apparently because of the reluctance of New England soldiers to give black officers proper respect and military courtesies. Instead of insisting upon proper protocol from white troops (for the uniform and rank), Banks began ridding his command of blacks with epaulets on their shoulders. He started by quietly trying to replace the blacks with whites as vacancies occurred. But, given the commitment of many blacks to the war of liberation, there were few vacancies. Determined to have the mat-

21. Banks to General Halleck, December 11, 17, 1863, Banks to Charles C. Dwight, December 16, 1863, W. Dwight to Stone, December 28, 1863, all in Banks Papers, LC.
22. John S. Clark and George Hanks to A. B. Botsford, September 12, 1863, in Ullman Papers, NYHSL; A. B. Botsford to J. J. Appleton, September 12, 1863, in General Papers, AGO.

ter done with, Banks finally called in the officers, explained the situation to them, and asked for their resignations. The officers suggested that many of the problems could be solved by making their regiments into a separate brigade and corps and thus minimizing contact with whites. Banks rejected the plan, eventually received the resignations, and the Department was rid of a source of "embarrassment and annoyance." The following year many of the black officers were drafted as privates into the service they had been asked to leave when officers.[23]

The loss of black officers was demoralizing to the troops. So, too, was the so-called "consolidation" movement, an attempt to systematize the black military units in the state. From the start, an overall organization of the black regiments in Louisiana was lacking: the three regiments enlisted by Butler and another by Banks made up a brigade called the Louisiana Native Guard; the five-regiment brigade raised by Ullman was called the Ullman Brigade; the remaining regiments recruited by Banks were called the Corps d'Afrique. Moreover, once a black regiment reached one-half normal strength (five hundred men) it was considered full; this may have been an attempt by Banks to show a large number of regiments without depleting the labor force.

By the summer of 1864 blacks were being recruited throughout the nation, and it was decided that the Louisiana regiments should become part of the United States Colored Infantry. But because of the numerical inferiority of the Louisiana regiments, they could not be mustered in their original form. Banks, claiming that there was not a sufficient number of able blacks left in Louisiana to fill the vacancies, decided to disband some regiments and fill the others with those men. The decision was disastrous for morale. By mid-1864 some of the men had fought as units at Port Hudson, Milliken's Bend, and other engagements, had developed pride in their

23. John S. Clark and George Hanks to A. B. Botsford, September 12, 1863, in Ullman Papers, NYHSL; L. Thomas to Banks, September 11, 1863, in Letters Received, DGR(U); Banks to L. Thomas, February 12, 1863, *Official Records,* III, 46; George Denison to Chase, in Chase Papers, LC; *House Reports,* 39th Cong., 2nd Sess., No. 16, pp. 125–26; Moors, *History of 52nd Mass.,* 62; New Orleans *Tribune,* May 14, 1865.

regiments, and did not want them disbanded. The resulting confusion and negative effects prompted Banks to telegraph the secretary of war and request that the orders be rescinded. He protested that "the movements here relative to colored troops were ruining the Corps." The order was rescinded, and the regiments were mustered in their original form and later filled. Unfortunately, the order suspending consolidation also stopped an examination program for white officers which had been part of the movement. But, although inferior officers remained, some were weeded out and many more resigned when advised of the examination.[24]

Soldiers in the ranks suffered from the loss of their black officers, from individual abuse by white officers, and also from demoralizing duties. Those who volunteered to fight against the system and class which enslaved them must have been disappointed, for once in the army they often performed many of the same duties they had during slavery. Black soldiers built dams, repaired levees and roads, constructed fortifications, and generally spent considerable time on fatigue duty.

"All colored force on . . . fatigue duty," reported an officer of the Corps d'Afrique on June 2, 1864. He reported the same for June 6, 8, 10, and 11. On June 15, he concluded, "The regiment is on fatigue at the Fort every day." It remained on fatigue until leaving for Port Hudson on June 24. At the new location the men continued the old work through August. Not until September did they drill and acquaint themselves with weapons, and then it was only for a half day—the remainder was spent on fatigue. Another officer complained that "the men have been kept so constantly at work on the place they have not had . . . much time to drill." An inspection of several black regiments by an aide from the Office of the Inspector General confirmed the observations of individual officers. After visiting a number of regiments, he made similar remarks on each: "Owing to the great amount of labour which the

24. W. B. Pearsall to Banks, August 31, 1864, in Banks Papers, LC; Tyson Diary (LSU), July 15, August 7, 12, 1864. Technically what happened was that the First Louisiana Native Guard became the 73rd United States Colored Infantry; the 2nd Louisiana Native Guard became the 74th United States Colored Infantry, etc.

troops had been required to bestow . . . they had not received much instruction in drill." Banks, although he never said so, probably considered black troops laborers, not line soldiers, and it is likely that fatigue duty was the role he felt they should play in the war. Despite poor duty and inadequate leadership, the men matured as soldiers. The inspector reported that the Second Corps was fair at battalion drill, good at handling heavy guns, and had weapons in excellent order.[25] Other regiments made similar gains proportionate to time in service and time on fatigue duty.

Only in the area of health did the black troops seem to have an advantage. Throughout the Department black soldiers suffered less than one-tenth as much as whites from malaria. But even with that comparative advantage there was considerable illness. During the month of August 245 members of the Fourth United States Colored Cavalry suffered from some form of fever. Black recruits often presented major health problems, for many were escaped slaves who had spent days in swamps without adequate clothing or food. Once in the service, they were the last to receive medical attention, clothing, blankets, and tents. Separate hospitals were authorized for the Corps d'Afrique, but it is doubtful that any were established. Despite this, the black mortality rate from illness was lower than that of whites, according to medical reports. No doubt that was due in part to the proportions of blacks from Louisiana and whites from New England serving in the Department.[26]

One of the more positive aspects of the black military experience was the attention given to education—it was a part of wearing the uniform. One of the Enrollment Commission's earliest orders provided education for the soldiers. The commission assigned teachers

25. Tyson Diary (LSU), June 2, 6, 8, 10, 11, 15, 24, September, 1864; T. E. Gammons to Captain Burt, March 14, 1864, T. E. Gammons Papers, TU; March Report, 152, 153, 163, Letters Received, IGO; Francis Lubor, *Memoir on the Military Use of Colored Persons that Come to Our Armies for Support or Protection* (N.p., n.d.).

26. W. A. Hammond to Stanton, June 30, 1864, *Official Records,* Ser. 3, Vol. III, pp. 454–55; Report of Sick and Wounded, 4th U.S.C. Cavalry, August, 1864, Daniel D. Slauson Papers, LSU; A. B. Botsford to Daniel Ullman, May 28, 1863, in General Papers, AGO; Banks to Commissioner of Enrollment for Corps d'Afrique, September 2, 1863, in Banks Papers, LC.

to each regiment and the Quartermaster Department distributed books paid for by the Corps d'Afrique fund.[27]

In the commission's first educational program officers doubled as teachers; a captain served as corps instructor, and a lieutenant from each regiment was tapped as a teacher. But these men also had military duties to perform and were thus limited in their effectiveness. Moreover, men qualified and willing to assume the role of educators were scarce—few soldiers volunteered for duty with black troops to serve in pedagogical positions.[28]

Difficulties arising from using officers as teachers were among the reasons the American Missionary Association (AMA) became involved in black military education. Early in 1864 the northern abolitionist and philanthropic association asked Ullman to assign civilian teachers to each regiment. Ullman was enthusiastic about the idea and suggested that the War Department provide transportation. He also contacted other benevolent societies soliciting their aid. Stanton and Banks shared his feelings, and Banks, true to form, promised "every assistance," writing appropriate commanders and sharing his views with them.[29] Under the new system the military corps instructors remained, but civilians served as regimental teachers. The AMA and other benevolent societies provided books and supplies, and while the association paid the teachers' salaries, there was discussion about having the men assume that responsibility. The teachers were kept busy instructing the rudiments of mathematics, reading, and writing. When not in the classroom they spent considerable time writing letters to families of illiterate soldiers.[30]

27. Banks to the Commissioner of Enrollment for the Corps d'Afrique, September 2, 1863, Endorsement by Banks, December 12, 1863, both in Banks Papers, LC.

28. S. W. Magill to Secretaries AMA, January 21, 1864, in AMA Papers, DU.

29. Ullman to Stanton, January 1, 1864, George Andrews to Banks, January 22, 1864, both in AMA Papers, DU; Dudley T. Cornish, "The Union Army as Training School for Negroes," *Journal of Negro History,* XXXVII (October, 1952), 373–74; Banks to George Andrews, January 22, 1864, in Banks Papers, LC.

30. T. A. McMasters to George Whipple, March 24, 1864, Charles Strong to Whipple, May 9, 1864, Conway to My Dear Brother [Whipple], April 5, 1864, all in AMA Papers, DU; Conway to Ullman, March 16, 1864, in General Papers, AGO.

Whereas black soldiers, like their civilian counterparts, were anxious for education, the very nature of the military posed problems. The fatigue duty required of black troopers left little time for instruction or energy for studying. When the soldiers were not attending to manual labor, military training took precedence over education. Activities in the field and temporary duty away from camp also proved troublesome. Frequently regiments were transferred before a suitable building was secured and outfitted or before books and supplies were obtained. An occasional officer encouraged and supported black education, but others hampered progress by their passivity and some were openly hostile.[31]

The overall effectiveness of the military education policy was lessened by internal problems and by the short life of the program. It was not functioning properly until the spring of 1864, and the consolidation and eventual mustering of the Corps d'Afrique into the regular service all but eliminated it during the summer of that year. The confusion and uncertainty caused by the changes disrupted the educational activities. When the matter was finally settled, the civilian teachers were confronted by regular army rules and regulations which did not provide for civilian teachers or civilians in any capacity. The typical black soldier found it increasingly difficult to obtain an education. As John Blassingame has suggested, that made army life less appealing to blacks. Because clerical work was done by sergeants and noncommissioned officers, men filling those positions had to be literate. Thus, the lack of education left many blacks unqualified for even minor advancements within the enlisted ranks.[32]

Despite its failings, the army education program had positive aspects. Many men received the rudiments of education, and others were exposed to it for the first time and returned to school once

31. Thomas McMasters to George Whipple, June 4, 1864, Huston Reedy to M. E. Streeby, April 1, 1865, W. B. Whitcomb to Whipple, June 2, 1864, Fannie Campbell to Whipple, March 16, 1865, F. A. McMasters to Whipple, May 20, 1864, James H. Schneider to Mr. Jocelyn, January 8, 1864, all in AMA Papers, DU.

32. C. B. Whitcomb to George Whipple, June 27, 1864, *ibid.;* John W. Blassingame, "The Union Army as an Educational Institution for Negroes, 1862–1865," *Journal of Negro Education,* XXXIV (Spring, 1965), 155.

out of the service. The thirty schools in the corps produced good results while they lasted, given the circumstances. Black students with blue uniforms must have been an inspiration by their example. One observer reported the scene of a black soldier at Port Hudson walking "with his gun upon his shoulder, and hanging from his bayonet by a bit of cord was a Webster's spelling-book." The observer was moved to remark that "this newly acquired liberty is secure. The negroes fight, and the negroes read. The bayonet wins victories, the spelling-book makes them secure."[33]

While there is some question whether education made black troops secure, there was no question about their willingness to fight. Prior to the battle at Port Hudson, Banks was besieged by requests from the three black regiments to allow them to lead the assault. The story of their performance is legendary, as is the number of losses they suffered. Banks was impressed. He wrote his wife that they "fought splendidly! Splendidly!" The three charges upon the rebel works "exhibited the greatest bravery." But his praise was probably as much a product of surprise as a change in attitude toward blacks. He noted that the regiments "mostly composed of slaves exhibited equal courage and capacity with those who had been free." Banks concluded that "they require only good officers to make the best troops the government will have."[34] By his previous actions Banks indicated that "good officers" were by definition white.

Black troops at Milliken's Bend showed the same tenacity and courage as those at Port Hudson. Many had received only a few hours of drill and had little or no experience with their weapons, described as faulty and "very inferior." They engaged rebels who poured over the works in hand-to-hand combat until forced back by superior numbers and heavy volleys from the flank. The courage

33. Hattie E. Whiting to Mr. Hunt, April 29, May 31, 1866, in AMA Papers, DU; New Orleans *Tribune*, September 20, 1864; *American Missionary Magazine*, VIII (October, 1864), 247.
34. Denison to Chase, January 8, 26, July 15, 1863, in Chase Papers, LC; Gould to Ned, June 6, 1863, in Gould Papers, UNC; Banks to his wife, May 30, 1863, in Banks Papers, LC.

of the black troops at Milliken's Bend was acknowledged by some southern whites. One reported that "the negroes fought desperately and would not give up until our men clubbed muskets upon them."[35]

Black soldiers fought desperately for good reason. They were not recognized as soldiers by the Confederacy—black prisoners were often shot, sold into slavery, or released to planters as laborers. Captured officers of black troops suffered the same fate. A captain and a lieutenant of the Corps d'Afrique were reportedly hanged at Monroe, Louisiana; and at Shreveport, corps officers were separated from the other prisoners and singled out for special abuse. Confederate attempts to intimidate whites and blacks in uniform were futile. Murders and reenslavement did not keep black Louisianians out of the Union service but did make them more determined fighters. Faced with probable death if captured, most preferred to take their chances on the battlefield. On occasion they stayed and fought after white troops retired; they were also more apt to attempt battlefield rescues of the wounded.[36]

The southern-white attitude toward black soldiers was ambivalent. They despised, ridiculed, and murdered blacks in uniform, but rebel soldiers came to respect and fear them as fighters. Initially the recruitment of former slaves caused "much excitement" among native whites, even though predictions were rampant that blacks would not fight for the Union. The New Orleans *Picayune* suggested that blacks would be reluctant, not from "natural dullness and cowardice," but from a lack of sympathy with the Union cause; "the vast majority of negroes are contented with their situation in life." A Shreveport editor implied that there was little to fear from black soldiers on the battlefield. With a note of irony and exaggerated accuracy, he explained that the "descendants of

35. Ellis Dennis to John A. Rawlings, June 12, 1863, *Official Records*, Vol. XXIV, Pt. 2, p. 447; Wadley Diary (UNC), June 9, 1863.
36. Tyson Diary (LSU), June 5, 1864; Power Diary (UNC), August 4, 1863; Statement of E. J. Corwen, November 19, 1863, in Letters Received, Provost Marshal General, DGR(U); Henry Johnson to Reynor, January 28, 1863, in Henry Johnson Papers, LSU; M. M. Kinney to Banks, September 20, 1863, in Banks Papers, LC; Bacon, *Among the Cotton Thieves*, 185.

Ham are placed into the fatigue corps, furnished with 'bosses,' a pick, and a spade, and a place to dig."[37]

Attitudes changed quickly when black troops moved into an area as occupational forces. It was a surprise that placid blacks fit only for manual labor suddenly "demoralized entire communities" with their arrival; satisfied field hands "content with their situation in life" awaited but "a signal to commence bloody work" once in uniform. Wherever they went, black troops intimidated and outraged the white population. A resident of Clinton recalled, "I never had such feelings as I did to think we must be ruled by a set of black negroes." A man of the cloth in Franklin exclaimed, "Oh! I had indeed hoped that we would be spared the degradation of having our towns garrisoned by negro troops." A Shreveport editor, when considering a rumor that black troops would soon occupy the town, serenely claimed that the "total absence [of Federal troops] would not endanger the peace of the community."[38] The fact that black troops spent a disproportionate amount of time guarding rails, depots, prisoners, and on garrison duty made their presence more noticeable and galling to southern whites.

Southern whites were not alone in finding black troops offensive. New England soldiers wrote critically about serving with "niggers" and about fighting "a damn 'nigger' war." Their reluctance to show proper respect for black officers was a major reason for Banks's insistence on all white officers. Nor was such criticism confined to enlisted men. The provost marshal of St. James and St. John the Baptist parishes proposed he would leave the service before leading black troops, and Brigadier General George Weitzel, under whose command the first three black regiments served, similarly claimed: "I cannot command these negro regiments." He did not believe they would fight. Racial antagonism between whites and blacks in blue uniforms frequently resulted in violence. On one

37. James E. Bradley Diary (LSU), August 16, 1864; New Orleans *Picayune*, July 30, 1862; Shreveport *News*, November 29, 1864.
38. Monroe *Weekly Telegraph*, October 5, 1865; Tyson Diary (LSU), June 12, 1864; Adderman, *Reminiscences of Two Years*, 15–16; Power Diary (UNC), August 2, 1863; Hilton Diary (TU), May 31, 1865; Shreveport *Semi-Weekly News*, June 20, 1865.

occasion about forty white soldiers attacked a group of black troopers, wounding several. Slurs, segregation, intimidation, and racial insults in the form of habitually poor duty assignments were also common. Butler, for example, was quick to agree that the three Native Guard regiments should do little more than guard the railroad.[39]

The more positive features of black involvement with the military concerned things yet to come, things not fully realized in April, 1865. As soldiers, the former slaves were exposed to education for the first time and were made aware of its benefits; many Reconstruction classrooms were filled with returning black soldiers. Most of the veterans correctly believed that they had contributed to the Union war effort and victory in the field. They expected changed attitudes after the war and pointed to their military service as the basis for demands for equality before the law, social and economic justice, and, eventually, the franchise.

39. Eben Roberts to Cousion [*sic*], April 16, 1863, E. S. Calderwood to his wife, April 16, 1863, both in Eben S. Calderwood Papers, MHSL; Edward Page to John S. Clark, January 18, 1863, in Letters Received, Provost Marshal General, DGR(U); George Weitzel to George Strong, November 5, 1862, *Official Records*, XV, 171–72; George Strong to George Weitzel, November 6, 1862, *Official Records*, XV, 164–65; Henry to Dear Ma, Andrew and Edmond, December 11, 1864, in McCollam Papers, UNC.

VII

Education

What the emancipated man wants now is knowledge.
—Frederick Douglass

Black education did not come to Louisiana with Federal troops. Starting in the 1830s New Orleans free blacks attended private schools such as St. Baete Academy, Pension des Demoiselles des Coleur, and the Institution des Orphelens. Opelousas blacks boasted of the Grimble Bell School, which had 125 pupils, each paying fifteen dollars monthly for board and tuition. Nearly every center of free-black population provided a privately maintained educational facility. Slave children occasionally received the rudiments of education on plantations, but that was unusual and outside the law. The majority of Louisiana's blacks were uneducated and illiterate at the outbreak of the Civil War.[1]

1. [Nathan Willey], "Education of the Colored Population of Louisiana," *Harper's News Weekly Magazine*, XXXIII, 1866, 248; Betty Potter, "The History of Negro Education in Louisiana," *Louisiana Historical Quarterly*, XXV (July, 1942), 728–31; James E. Winston, "The Free Negro in New Orleans, 1803–1860," *Louisiana Historical Quarterly*, XXI (September, 1938), 1082; Annie Lee Stahl, "The Free Negro in Ante-Bellum Louisiana," *Louisiana Historical Quarterly*, XXV (January, 1942), 360–61; Maria S. Hawes Reminiscences, in Maria S. Hawes Papers, UNC. One observer claimed that free blacks in New Orleans paid taxes in excess of $11,000 yearly to support white schools which their children

The decision to educate Louisiana's black population came slowly, even after the Union occupation of New Orleans. Federal officials were preoccupied with more pressing matters: winning the war, recruiting black troops, reviving the economy, and controlling black laborers. Moreover, until the legal status of contrabands who came to Union lines was determined, black education was not a serious consideration. The term *contraband* as applied to escaped slaves suggests the dilemma—were they property that would be dealt with as spoils of war, or humans needing assistance in adjusting to a new life? During Butler's administration white schools in New Orleans were reorganized and reopened, but no attention was given to establishing black schools.[2]

The first efforts to educate contraband slaves were individual ones. Prior to the war Mrs. W. A. Brice, a graduate of Antioch College and later an employee of the American Missionary Association, operated a free-black school which was branded abolitionist and closed in 1861. Back at her profession in November, 1862, she wrote that blacks coming into the lines "are already being taught to spell and read." Overwhelmed by the work that needed to be done and the short supply of teachers, Mrs. Brice wrote Banks in early 1863, suggesting that day and night schools be established for blacks, free and slave.[3]

Throughout the winter and summer of 1863 blacks in Louisiana made their educational aspirations known, and as various military personnel who worked with contrabands became aware of the needs, they forwarded the information to Banks. George Hanks, George Hepworth, and Thomas W. Conway were the most active. In early summer Conway shared with Banks his concern over the future of the contraband in United States lines. He particularly stressed the need for schools and, though not sure how best to establish them, he proposed that black education would be in the

could not attend. See I. G. Hubbs to Jocelyn and Whipple, January 8, 1864, in AMA Papers, DU.

2. *Daily Picayune*, September 6, 1862.

3. W. A. Brice to Editor, *American Missionary Magazine*, November 13, 1862, in AMA Papers, DU; W. A. Brice to Banks, January 3, 1863, in Letters Received, Bureau of Civil Affairs, DGR(U).

best interest of the government. George Hepworth, who had daily contact with the freedmen, wrote Banks that the possibility of education "has been pressed on me daily." He suggested a board of education made up of military officers and a system of schools in cities, villages, and on plantations. Teachers and books could be provided by northern aid societies. Hepworth was confident that all blacks in the Department could be reached at a minimal cost to the government.[4]

Black education received endorsements from outside the Department also. The Freedmen Inquiry Commission concluded that it could not overestimate the importance of the "enlightened institution." The commission was impressed by the outpouring of freedmen "eager to obtain for themselves, but especially for their children, those privileges of education which have . . . been . . . withheld from them." No doubt a stronger stimulus for Banks was the sentiment of President Lincoln, who also stressed the need for educating young blacks in the Department of the Gulf.[5]

Banks, never a friend of Louisiana blacks, moved slowly despite encouragement from blacks, whites, and the president. Not until August, 1863, did he create the Enrollment Commission, whose responsibilities included education. Nevertheless, the nucleus of an education administration was established. Army officer W. B. Stickney was appointed Superintendent of Public Schools for Colored People in New Orleans. He administered scattered schools such as the Union Public School which had been opened by Hanks in June but was desperate for books and supplies by August. During the early stages Hanks, more than the other members of the commission, took an active interest in black education. Within a short period he collected numerous applications from teachers and secured buildings suitable for schools. Both he and Conway were anxious for a northern tour to collect educational resources—

4. George Hanks to Chief of Staff Stone, January 12, 1863, in Letters Received, Bureau of Civil Affairs, DGR(U); Conway to Banks, June 1, 1863, George Hepworth to Banks, June 15, July 2, 1863, both in Banks Papers, LC.
5. Freedmen Inquiry Commission to Edwin M. Stanton, June 30, 1863, *Official Records*, Ser. 3, Vol. III, p. 447; Lincoln to Banks, August 5, 1863, *Collected Works Of Abraham Lincoln*, VI, 365.

funds, supplies, and philanthropic assistance. Hanks was allowed to go. By mid-October, 1863, the fledgling school system had seven schools, twenty-three teachers, and 1,500 students, all in New Orleans; no attention had yet been given to plantations or towns in the rest of the Department.[6]

A major influence in advancing black education was the American Missionary Association, which sent teachers to Louisiana shortly after the occupation. Banks's feeble attempts apparently encouraged the association to redouble its efforts in early 1864. Isaac G. Hubbs was sent to New Orleans as its official representative. Shortly after his arrival, his reports were filled with optimism. From the Enrollment Commission he received a promise of "aid and facilities" and an endorsement of two American Missionary Association proposals: one for creating normal schools for training teachers and another for establishing schools on plantations, a feature which later was much disputed. Hubbs was equally pleased to report that Banks "grants us cheerfully all we ask." Rations and housing were promised for association teachers in New Orleans, Baton Rouge, and Donaldsonville, and for those on plantations. Also important was an order for free transportation for fifteen new teachers, ten of whom were slated for plantations.[7]

During January Hubbs had reason for optimism. Black educational facilities moved out of New Orleans and into the countryside with some semblance of order. Responsive military authorities seemed eager to assist, buildings were being sought for additional day schools, and one evening school was set for opening with sixty adult students. The future looked bright. Hubbs was poised with additional plans. Because of the taxes paid by New Orleans' free

6. J. A. Norager to Banks, July 29, 1863, in Letters Received, Bureau of Civil Affairs, DGR(U); George Hanks to Banks, September 26, 30, 1863, Conway to Banks, August 13, 1863, W. P. Stickney to Banks, October 19, 1863, all in Banks Papers, LC; Banks to Stanton, October 14, 1863, in Banks Papers, LSU; E. M. Wheellock to John Clark, March 19, 1864, in Letters Received, Bureau of Civil Affairs, DGR(U).

7. Isaac G. Hubbs to Jocelyn and Whipple, January 8, 14, 1864, in AMA Papers, DU; *American Missionary Magazine*, VII (March, 1864), 68. See also Richard Bryant Drake, "The American Missionary Association and Southern Negroes, 1861–1888" (Ph.D. dissertation, Emory University, 1957), for the best available study on the AMA.

blacks to support white education, he hoped to procure one each of the city's white grammar and high schools for black use. He also envisioned a school on every plantation that could service two hundred or more blacks in the vicinity. To circumvent planter hostility to plantation schools, Hubbs, "with others," lobbied for an education clause in all labor contracts. He believed the labor shortage would ensure the plan's success.[8]

On the surface it appeared that Louisiana blacks were well on the way to having their educational needs and aspirations met. Yet problems remained, as Hubbs reluctantly acknowledged. He skirted the issue by suggesting that it might be best to wait before sending additional teachers to Louisiana and by complaining that school furniture and supplies were scarce. AMA teacher the Reverend Charles Strong, a more perceptive observer who did not share Hubbs's optimism, reported that the Louisiana situation was not what Hubbs claimed it to be. While Banks gave "all that was requested," part was given in orders and part in promises. "We find it one thing to obtain a promise," wrote Strong, "but quite another to realize its fulfilment [sic]." Orders, once issued, brought no guarantee of success, he continued, for those who "savour either . . . advantages of money or political influence" easily evaded the orders. He cited the issue of living facilities for teachers as an example. Banks promised housing, and the missionaries were sent to the Quartermaster Department to secure it. There they were informed that the Treasury Department controlled all confiscated property. The Treasury Department eventually released one house (for which Strong had to "bow and scrape"), but the Treasury agent's gubernatorial candidacy prompted its repossession. Strong described the military education program as "nondescript in its character" and inefficient.[9]

In an atmosphere of increasing distrust and friction between the military and the AMA, the administrative system for black education in Louisiana was reorganized. The new system called

8. Hubbs to Jocelyn and Whipple, January 8, 14, 1864, in AMA Papers, DU.
9. Hubbs to Jocelyn and Whipple, January 8, 1864, Charles Strong to S. S. Jocelyn, February 19, 1864, both *ibid.*

for a separate Board of Education for Freedmen to be appointed by Banks. Financing would be shared by blacks and whites, but, for reasons which were never made clear, the board was given the power to levy taxes. Buildings would be obtained through local provost marshals from among the confiscated properties. The board would employ and compensate all teachers.[10]

The new board was comprised of three members. Forty-eight-year-old B. Rush Plumly, the experienced member with service on the Enrollment Commission was appointed chairman. Secretary of the board was Edwin M. Wheelock, a Unitarian minister from Dover, New Hampshire, who, prior to the war, had been a frequent guest in the pulpit of radical abolitionist Theodore Parker. The "John Brown abolitionist" came to Louisiana as the chaplain of a New Hampshire regiment and served as a lieutenant with the Corps d'Afrique before going to the board. Isaac Hubbs, representing the AMA, was the third board member and its only civilian.[11]

Hubbs was not perhaps the best man available for the job, but undoubtedly was appointed because of his association with the AMA. Jealous of his position, he complained to Banks's aide that the new system had been his idea, not George Hanks's, who had taken it to Banks and received the credit. Hubbs made departmental officials aware that he represented not only the AMA but the "Presbiterian [sic], Congregational and Dutch Reform Churches of the North," and that his appointment to the board was part of "the very plan they would desire me to fill." He concluded his pontifical note by asserting that "without vanity I may say of myself . . . no man can bring to this work a better experience than I." There were those working with the freedmen who disagreed. Foremost was Thomas W. Conway, who contacted Hubbs's AMA superiors and suggested "in confidence" that they replace Hubbs with a more able man devoted to missionary work, not business. That

10. George Hanks to Banks, February 24, 1864, in Letters Received, Bureau of Civil Affairs, DGR(U).
11. Charles Kessel, "Educating the Slaves—A Forgotten Chapter of Civil War History," *Open Court*, XXXXI (April, 1927), 241; Charles Kessel, "Edwin Miller Wheelock," *Open Court*, XXXIV (September, 1920), 562, 567.

was the first hint of corruption surrounding Hubbs, an issue which loomed larger in coming months.[12]

Within a matter of weeks after the board began operation it was split over personalities and policies. Several AMA teachers and many of the military personnel working with the freedmen lacked confidence in Hubbs, who controlled the AMA schools as well as served on the board. One teacher accused Hubbs of "double dealing," but was not more specific. Nor were the military members of the board exempt from criticism; they were accused of hiring disloyal and "irreligious" teachers, and of being jealous of the AMA.[13]

While matters of personalities and power were causing problems, matters of policy widened the split. Due to planter pressure, Banks rescinded the order establishing plantation schools in favor of one creating a district school system. Hubbs was incensed that his plan was changed after initial approval by Banks. He agreed a district system was a consideration for the future but termed it impractical for the present. Hubbs properly resented the influence of the planters, who under the old system would have had to pay for teachers and school buildings. He was also aware that a more permanent system would eventually cost him control of the AMA teachers already in Louisiana, plus the fifty to one hundred additional teachers he had recently requested for plantation schools.[14]

It is difficult to judge whether the new plan was designed to remove Hubbs, the AMA, or both from black education in Louisiana. Certainly the military members of the board would have been pleased to see Hubbs eliminated. A second policy change and later events suggest that both objectives were desired. In early May, 1864, while Hubbs was in New York, Plumly and Wheelock initiated a drive to bring the AMA schools under control of the Board of Education. Their initial proposal included controlling

---

12. Hubbs to James Bowen, March 4, 1864, in Letters Received, Provost Marshal General, DGR(U); Conway to Brother Jocelyn, April 22, 1864, in AMA Papers, DU.

13. C. F. Tambling to Jocelyn and Whipple, May 11, 1864, Charles Strong to S. S. Jocelyn, February 19, 1864, both in AMA Papers, DU.

14. Hubbs to S. S. Jocelyn, February 6, March 4, 1864, *ibid.*

and supplying the schools but not retaining the teachers. This was later amended, allowing the missionary teachers to remain but at the expense of the AMA, which would be responsible for salaries. In essence, the board wanted to ease out the AMA; failing that, it was content to claim the schools as its success without increasing its responsibilities. A compromise was eventually worked out whereby the board assumed complete responsibility for the schools, providing the teachers with salaries as well as housing and rations. Although many of the missionaries were reluctant to sever ties with the AMA, they agreed to the change to conserve association resources. Understandably they were leery of the board.[15]

Hubbs and Strong both claimed the military members of the board were intent upon destroying AMA influence. Prior to leaving for New York, Hubbs had agreed to the transfer of schools, provided the missionary teachers be retained and funded by the board. Strong claimed that in Hubbs's absence the board attempted the transfer but "refused to employ our teachers." He objected to the idea of retaining the teachers on the association payroll while losing the schools, asserting that "the foot-hold which we by persistent efforts have gained" would be lost. Strong was correct. By mid-summer the transfer of the schools and teachers was complete, and for the most part the work of the AMA was finished in Louisiana for several years.[16]

Of the AMA influences only Hubbs remained, and his time was short. He resigned from the board in September, 1864, amid protests to his superiors of "a vigorous persecution of us and all our interests," and of a "formidable plot to *destroy* me." There were charges and countercharges against Hubbs of immoral conduct, corruption, fraud, and theft. Special Order 280 ended the entangled matter by expelling Hubbs from the Department. He was officially

15. Charles Strong to Whipple, May 7, June 23, June [?], August 5, 1864, Hubbs to Whipple, June 17, 1864, E. H. Allen to Whipple, June 1, 15, 1864, E. M. Wheelock to Whipple, July 1, 1864, F. A. McMasters to Whipple, July 29, 1864, Josiah Beardsley to Whipple, June 27, 1864, F. H. Bartlett to Whipple, July 30, 1864, all *ibid.*

16. Hubbs to Whipple, June 17, 1864, Charles Strong to Whipple, May 7, 1864, both *ibid.* The AMA returned to Louisiana in 1869 when the Freedmen's Bureau relinquished control of black education in the state.

charged with "gross failure of duty," with violating instructions of the board, with profiteering from the purchase of freedmen's libraries, with collecting portions of teachers' salaries, and with "conduct and language wholly unbecoming his position as a clergyman and his dignity as a man." It is impossible to judge fairly all the charges, for Hubbs never adequately responded to them. Instead he attacked Plumly and Wheelock over petty matters and generalities. At one point he requested the AMA to send him copies of invoices for all books and supplies that the association had sent, including seven thousand Bibles. Along with the invoices he requested the *"market value of each."* If Hubbs was not guilty of all or part of the charges, then indeed there was a plot to destroy him. Hubbs's parting shot was a demand that the board return the seven thousand Bibles which the AMA had sent for distribution among the freedmen.[17]

The controversy between personnel of the AMA and the military ran deeper than personalities and jealousies. There was outright competition between the two groups, competition concerning the philosophy and the direction that black education in Louisiana would take. Despite his faults, Hubbs was correct on the issue of plantation schools. A district system would take longer to establish, would probably reach fewer plantation children, and would be costly—something to work for in the future. No doubt misled by Banks's early promises (many of which were never fulfilled), Hubbs failed to recognize the general's basic tendencies. To the end the AMA official believed Banks supported the military members of the board over him because of the greater influence of Plumly. However true that may have been, Banks was not one to align himself with the cause of black education on plantations when confronted by a committee of "loyal" white planters who opposed it. He was a politician, and from the start many consider-

17. Hubbs to Jocelyn and Whipple, September 23, 24, 1864, Special Order 280, Headquarters, Department of the Gulf, October 16, 1864, Hubbs to Whipple, September 16, October 13, October 15, 1864, Conway to S. H. Tyng, October 1, 1864, Conway to Whipple, October 4, 20, 1864, Hubbs to Banks, September 17, 1864 (copy), all *ibid.*; *Special Report of Board of Education for Freedmen*, September 20, 1864, in Letters Received, Bureau of Civil Affairs, DGR(U).

ations in the Department of the Gulf required political skills, not military, and certainly not philanthropic.

If the attempt to rid the Department of AMA teachers was not endorsed by Banks, it was at least in keeping with his philosophy. He believed that the wartime reconstruction program was best served by employing southern teachers. The AMA teachers were used early on because of the initial shortage of southerners willing to assume the task. But by the fall of 1864 the situation was reversed. Secretary Wheelock of the board wrote the AMA that the supply of local teachers had increased to a point where there was no longer a need to send northerners to Louisiana. He frankly acknowledged the reason: "Banks has informed us that sound policy demands that we should employ mainly southern teachers." Public opinion was cited as the main consideration for the policy. After the war the Freedmen's Bureau was confronted by the same opinions and continued the policy. By the fall of 1866 one source claimed that two hundred northern teachers had been fired from black schools.[18]

Despite the AMA's premature departure from the Department, it made significant, positive contributions to black education. It provided teachers when few were to be had; it provided schools where none existed. Figures on the number of teachers and schools controlled by the association are vague because of the tendency of the military agencies to claim AMA schools as their own. Yet the much-praised showcase of black education in New Orleans, the School of Liberty, originally was an association school. The missionaries (and that they were) were eager to take black education out of New Orleans and into towns and plantations. While timorous military commanders tested the winds in hesitation, the AMA provided an impetus for white involvement by action, hard work, and results.

The controversy surrounding Hubbs was unfortunate. Egos, petty jealousies, personality conflicts, fraud, corruption, and power struggles affected all involved. But black Louisianians seeking

18. E. M. Wheelock to Whipple, September 12, 1864, Frank Chase to Whipple, September 18, 1866, both in AMA Papers, DU.

education ultimately suffered most; for time, energy, and probably funds which should have been spent on education were wasted. The dedication and the resources which the AMA brought to other southern states during Reconstruction were lost to Louisiana blacks for a number of years.

The Board of Education for Freedmen was beset by external as well as internal difficulties. Structures suitable for use as schools were in short supply until Banks authorized the use of deserted or confiscated properties. If none were available, property could be seized for educational purposes. The authorization was not a panacea, particularly in the interior parishes where provost marshals, who were responsible for securing buildings, tended to identify more with planters than with black education. Those who were eager to assist met resistance from hostile whites, particularly those individuals whose property was being seized. Fortunately the provost marshal general of the Department was an advocate of black education and supported the seizures. Occasionally he instructed owners not only to turn over buildings but to make necessary repairs on them. Throughout the Department, churches, homes, sheds, stores, warehouses, and white schoolhouses were transformed into centers of black learning. The board assumed responsibility for furnishing them.[19]

Many of the same problems were confronted by teachers trying to obtain living quarters. Here, too, greater resistance was found in the rural parishes. Although earlier Banks had not adequately housed AMA teachers in New Orleans, he was insistent that teachers be boarded at local expense in the interior. Referring specifically to housing teachers on plantations, he reiterated a favorite theme: "It is indispensable to the cultivation of the soil, that

19. H. H. to E. M. Wheelock, July 1, 1864, Letters Received, Provost Marshal General; E. Offner and V. Sawman to Captain Dunham, September 7, 1864, in Letters Received, Provost Marshal Orleans; J. H. Bradley to Henri Robinson, August 27, 1864, Letters Received, Provost Marshal General; L. P. Newman to Banks, May 29, 1865, Letters Received, Bureau of Civil Affairs; E. M. Wheelock to George Dawling, April 11, 1864, Letters Received, Provost Marshal St. John the Baptist and St. James, all in DGR(U). Whitlaw Reid Diary (LC), June 8, 1865; B. Rush Plumly to Banks, September 19, 1864, William White to George Hanks, April 18, 1864, both in Letters Received, Superintendent of Education, Louisiana, BRFAL.

schools for colored children shall be maintained." In essence Banks told plantation owners that if they wanted to make money, they would have to tolerate the schools and house the teachers. The commanding general was aware of the freedmen's commitments to education and of their reluctance to work where schools were not available. In attempting to aid economic recovery, Banks tried to wed black education to Yankee capitalism.[20]

As suggested previously, recruiting an adequate number of teachers also proved difficult. The AMA, the National Freedmen's Relief Association, and the American Freedmen and Union Commission all eventually sent instructors to Louisiana. But until 1864 teachers were in short supply, and even the AMA schools were forced to rely on southern teachers initially. Banks eventually made their use a matter of policy. He believed native teachers would make black education more palatable to southern whites. He could not have been more incorrect. Southern whites, rather than embracing black education, ostracized their own people who took up the cause. A white teacher in New Orleans was thrown out of her family home by her brothers. Another in Baton Rouge was retired into a "solitary" life, and a local minister requested that "God be merciful to her and guide her to His throne" despite her transgression. Generally, the southern teachers "quietly bore the load of calemny [*sic*], sneers, and social proscription that fell to their lot."[21]

For different reasons, Louisiana's black leaders found themselves on common ground with local whites on the issue of employing southern white teachers. The New Orleans *Tribune* published

20. Charles Strong and E. H. Allen to Banks, June 23, 1864, Letters Received, Bureau of Civil Affairs; William J. Fiske to Captain Bigelow, December 24, 1864, Letters Received, Provost Marshal Lafourche; Banks to Provost Marshal, June 27, 1864, Letters Received, Provost Marshal St. James and St. John the Baptist; Banks to T. E. Chickering, August 13, 1864, Letters Received, Provost Marshal General, all in DGR(U). Wheelock to Holabird, April 19, 1864, in Letters Received, Superintendent of Education, Louisiana, BRFAL.

21. W. B. Stickney to Banks, October 13, 1863, in Banks Papers, LC; *American Missionary Magazine*, VIII (January, 1864), 6–7; Hubbs to Jocelyn and Whipple, March 24, 1864; Mary O. Quaiffe to S. S. Jocelyn, July 26, 1864, both in AMA Papers, DU; The Reverend Charles Whitehorn Hilton Diary (TU), December 26, 1865; E. M. Wheelock to John S. Clark, March 19, 1864, in Letters Received, Bureau of Civil Affairs, DGR(U).

a letter from "Liberty," protesting the use of teachers of questionable loyalty (i.e., southern). "Liberty" proclaimed that the black race had "men of ability among us born and raised upon the soil of Louisiana identified with us by blood and by birth, by thoughts and feelings." Indeed there were native Louisianians who were eager to teach and who were associated with the freedmen by "blood and by birth." Thomy Lafon ran a prewar school for free blacks which was bilingual and taught grammar, history, geography, bookkeeping, mathematics, and moral and natural philosophy. Joseph Craig requested permission to open a similar school shortly after the Federal occupation of New Orleans.

In many cases white teachers sent to the interior arrived only to find that local blacks had already established schools and had educational matters well in hand. At Tigerville, Louisiana, a former slave organized a plantation school using books another worker procured from children's libraries of local plantations. In New Orleans, Baton Rouge, Goodrich Landing, Port Hudson, and Brashear City, as well as on scattered plantations, blacks pooled their resources and initiated educational efforts. Black teachers were active throughout the period. They taught in numerous schools and served as assistants in still others. The Reverend Huston Reedy was a black representative of the AMA and a strong advocate of normal schools to train black teachers. Another black educator, referred to only as Mather, was described as "the pioneer colored teacher of Baton Rouge." Mather eventually left the capital to carry his work to plantations in the area. At one point it was estimated that eighty-five black teachers worked in government schools in Louisiana.[22] Other blacks aided in ways they were best able. Land suitable for building sites was a common donation, as

22. New Orleans *Tribune*, March 4, 1865; *L'Union*, January 12, 1864; Joseph Craig to George F. Shepley, October 28, 1862, in Shepley Papers, MHSL; L. M. Birge to Secretary, AMA, March 27, June 27, 1864, John C. Tucker to Jocelyn and Whipple, March 30, 1864, Huston Reedy to AMA, March 28, 1865, Mary O. Quaiffe to Jocelyn, July 26, 1864, all in AMA Papers, DU; *American Missionary Magazine*, VIII (January, 1864), 5–6; A. M. Roberts Report, September 26, 1865, Superintendent of Education, Louisiana, BRFAL; Duganne, *Camps and Prisons*, 86–87; Howard A. White, *The Freedmen's Bureau in Louisiana* (Baton Rouge, 1963), 171.

were labor and material for constructing schools. Blacks sought out an educational representative and expressed their willingness to finance a school by contributions.[23]

Teachers (black and white), students, school buildings, and black education in general attracted white hostility and abuse. Northern teachers coming to Louisiana were warned that they would face ostracism, isolation, and "the curse of the planters." Often short of funds and unable to obtain credit or housing, many teachers were befriended by blacks who provided food and lodging. Military insistence that planters house teachers of plantation schools did not always bring positive results. One planter sent his family away and converted his residence into a "sort of bawdyhouse" that drove the teacher away. Educators were often pelted with mud and stones, verbal abuse, and threats to life and limb.[24]

In Thibodaux a woman teacher received almost daily abuse, but remained at her job until the school was broken into and "excrement voided" upon her desk. The following morning the offender watched through the window as she discovered it. He "laughed, used obscene language and threatened to repeat the outrage, which he did that evening." The teacher went to the local provost marshal but, receiving no redress, moved on to New Orleans; and the school, described as "large and useful," was closed. Numerous schools were broken up and various teachers left as a result of intimidation. In many areas the creation or continuation of black schools depended upon the attitude of local provost marshals or the presence of troops. The withdrawal of Union forces was frequently the signal for dismantling black schools.[25]

23. G. F. Ruby to A. G. Studer, April 12, 1866, William Guest to W. M. Wheelock, March 30, 1865, Conway to Board of Education, March 28, 1864, all in Letters Received, Superintendent of Education, BRFAL.

24. Hubbs to Jocelyn and Whipple, January 8, 1864, in AMA Papers, DU; R. B. Fulks to E. M. Wheelock, January 4, 1865, in Letters Received, Superintendent of Education, Louisiana, BRFAL; New Orleans *Tribune*, September 13, 1864; W. E. Thrall to Henri Robinson, August 20, 1864, in Letters Received, Provost Marshal General, DGR(U); E. M. Wheelock to Dear General, August 9, 1864, in Banks Papers, LC.

25. E. M. Wheelock to T. E. Chickering, August 9, 1864, in Banks Papers, LC; J. Horace McGuire to Edward Hemmingway, November 18, 1865, General Canby to General Baird, November 7, 1865, both in Letters Received, Assistant Commissioner, Louisiana, BRFAL.

White reaction to black education was not uniform throughout the state, but generally it was hostile. There seemed to be fewer objections in New Orleans than in the rural parishes. That no doubt was the product of a number of forces. Foremost among them was the presence of Union troops and officials in the city. In addition, New Orleans was the cosmopolitan, urban center of the south and had more sophisticated citizens. There also was the example of the prewar free-black schools, which were usually tolerated in a passive and silent way. Equally important was the example of the Creole leadership in New Orleans, whose chief organ, the *Tribune*, quickly brought transgressions to the attention of appropriate officials.

Black education faced greater resistance in the rural parishes, and often that resistance was proportionate to the proximity of Union troops. The representative of the Board of Education in Franklin, Louisiana, reported "unanimous" opposition to black schools. The local citizens, he claimed, "are determined to break them down." Their objections were based on the premise that educated blacks were blacks striving for equality, a goal which would not be tolerated. But not until Federal soldiers left the town was opposition active. The day they departed, a meeting was held in the town marketplace and open acts of aggression began. Under similar circumstances the process was repeated in other parts of the state: teachers and students were abused, schools were destroyed—and often nothing was done to stop the outrages. In the Red River area agents of the Board of Education were forced back into their boats and warned that if they tried to establish schools the buildings would be burned and the teachers killed. The only schools established there were on military posts.[26]

26. H. M. Roberts Report, November 22, 1865, Superintendent of Education, Louisiana, BRFAL. E. M. Wheelock to Bigelow, January 8, 1865, Letters Received, Provost Marshal Lafourche; Nathan Willey to George Darling, March 17, 1863, Letters Received, Provost Marshal St. James and St. John the Baptist, both in DGR(U). U.S. Congress, *Report of the Joint Committee on Reconstruction* (1866), 63, 79–80. In contrast, see R. R. Brown Report, April 30, 1866, in Letters Received, Assistant Commissioner, Louisiana, BRFAL, for an example of planters supporting black education at their own expense.

Despite difficulties within the board and problems with obdurate whites, black education in Louisiana made gains during the war years. Edwin Wheelock, in summarizing the early educational work of the Enrollment Commission, pointed to a number of them. As we have seen, in New Orleans during a six-month period (October, 1863–March, 1864) seven schools with twenty-three teachers served an average of fifteen hundred students. The pupils, described as perceptive and orderly, learned to spell, read, write, and do written and mental mathematics. The advanced students were using the third and fourth readers at the end of six months. Wheelock closed his report with sentiments appropriate to his calling: "Behind the advancing lines of our armed forces follows the small pacific army of teachers and civilians, and the school house takes the place forever of the whipping post and scourge."[27]

Wheelock was correct that schools and teachers followed military advances, even if he overzealously described the permanent effects of education. As areas outside New Orleans became secure, schools were established. The advances coincided with the creation of the Board of Education for Freedmen and the decision to establish a district school system. The board sent representatives into the parishes instructed to work with local provost marshals in obtaining buildings and housing for teachers. Through the spring and summer of 1864 parish schools made reasonable headway given the circumstances, and by June the board reported 51 schools, 93 teachers, and 5,747 students in fifteen parishes. However, approximately 30 percent of the schools, 40 percent of the teachers, and 50 percent of the students were in Orleans Parish. A shortage of teachers prevented 14 additional schools from being opened in four parishes. In St. James Parish it was reported that 9 schools were ready, but "in no case in that parish can [the agent] obtain board for a teacher in consequence of the existing hostility to establishment of these schools." Such problems in the interior ac-

27. E. M. Wheelock to John Clark, March 19, 1864, in Letters Received, Bureau of Civil Affairs, DGR(U).

count in part for the predominance of educational facilities in the city.[28]

In the next six months education was made available to an even greater number of former slaves. By November, 1864, the board boasted of 84 schools, 142 teachers, and 8,761 students. This put the board approximately half way toward its two main objectives: a school in all the 168 districts of the fifteen parishes under Union control, and school attendance of all black children between the ages of five and twelve in those parishes. These advances were made during the period when board members were actively assailing each other and struggling for control.[29]

By the end of the war the board claimed 121 schools, 216 teachers, and 13,462 students within the fifteen parishes. It also planned for an additional 57 district schools which were needed to reach the 4,728 young blacks not in attendance. Approximately 3 of every 4 black children between the ages of five and twelve in the Department were enrolled in military schools when the Board of Education for Freedmen relinquished the system to the Freedmen's Bureau in June, 1865.[30]

Clearly the Board of Education, with all its failings, did positive work in Louisiana despite difficulties. Troubles with transportation, food and houses for teachers, school buildings, and educational materials, as well as petty jealousies, political intrigues, and white hostility and violence, all hampered progress. Banks's chameleon-like nature and his obvious white bias were troublesome at times, but credit is due him for insisting that local whites support the

28. Report of the Number of Schools Established and Teachers Employed by the Board of Education, June 1, 1864, in Letters Received, Bureau of Civil Affairs, DGR(U); E. M. Wheelock and Hubbs to Banks, June 20, 1864, in Letters Received, Superintendent of Education, Louisiana, BRFAL. See Table 3.

29. B. Rush Plumly to General Hurlburt, November 5, 1864, in Letters Received, Bureau of Civil Affairs, DGR(U). See Table 4.

30. Report of the Number of Schools Established and Teachers Employed by the Board of Education, May, 1865, in Letters Received, Superintendent of Education, Louisiana, BRFAL. See Table 5. See also Blassingame, *Black New Orleans*, 107–137, for urban education in Reconstruction; and see Robert Stanley Bahney, "Generals and Negroes: Education of Negroes by the Union Army, 1861–1865" (Ph.D. dissertation, University of Michigan, 1965), for a comparison of education in other occupied areas.

Table 3

NUMBER OF SCHOOLS, TEACHERS, AND STUDENTS
UNDER BOARD OF EDUCATION FOR FREEDMEN
JUNE 1, 1864*

Parish	Schools	Teachers	Students
Ascension	3	3	185
Assumption	5	5	310
Baton Rouge	3	11	715
Iberville	1	2	135
Jefferson	3	7	437
Lafourche	3	4	220
Orleans	15	38	2,453
Plaquemines	1	1	35
St. Bernard	4	5	240
St. Charles	2	2	74
St. James	—	—	—
St. John the Baptist	4	4	315
St. Mary	3	5	315
Terrebonne	4	6	310
Totals	51	93	5,744

*Report of the number of schools established and teachers employed by the Board of Education for Freedmen, June 1, 1864, in Letters Received, Bureau of Civil Affairs, DGR(U).

school system, and for, failing that, funding the schools from military sources. It was indeed ironic that one of America's traditionally conservative institutions, the military, was responsible for one of the earliest and most successful black educational efforts in the nation's history.

The truly positive aspect of black education in Civil War Louisiana was the response of the black population. Freedmen and Creoles participated in and contributed to every phase of the experiment. They collected funds, donated land, labor, buildings, and books, and often supplied the staff. Many times they did so without the aid of the military or northern aid societies.

Table 4

NUMBER OF SCHOOLS, TEACHERS, AND STUDENTS
UNDER BOARD OF EDUCATION FOR FREEDMEN
NOVEMBER 1, 1864*

Parish	Schools	Teachers	Students	Districts Without Schools	Children Not in School
Ascension	2	3	177	8	631
Assumption	7	8	493	12	685
Baton Rouge	3	9	698	—	309
E. Baton Rouge	2	3	173	7	250
Iberville	1	3	232	11	268
Jefferson	8	16	823	4	27
Lafourche	3	4	348	7	38
Orleans	19	51	3,291	—	1,184
Plaquemines	5	5	345	2	61
St. Bernard	6	6	317	3	652
St. Charles	6	8	421	3	317
St. James	2	2	120	14	1,053
St. John the Baptist	9	9	431	1	316
St. Mary	4	5	274	—	176
Terrebonne	7	10	618	13	1,112
Totals	84	142	8,761	85	7,079

*B. R. Plumly to General Hurlbut, November 5, 1864, in Letters Received, Bureau of Civil Affairs, DGR(U).

The response of students was no less significant. Blacks made their desire for education known to officials and flocked to the schools as they opened. From May, 1864, to the end of the war the student-teacher ratio in the Department never fell below an average of sixty to one. While this reflects, in part, the difficulty in obtaining teachers (particularly early in the program), it also reflects the desire of the freedmen for education—being forbidden in slavery, it took on magical qualities with freedom. Four generations often studied from one text, and many black students achieved

Table 5

NUMBER OF SCHOOLS, TEACHERS, AND STUDENTS
UNDER BOARD OF EDUCATION FOR FREEDMEN
MAY, 1865*

Parish	Schools	Teachers	Students	Districts Without Schools	Children Not in School
Ascension	5	5	316	5	491
Assumption	13	16	997	5	181
Baton Rouge	4	12	902	8	528
Iberville	1	5	466	11	34
Jefferson	11	19	1,130	1	120
Lafourche	9	12	817	1	169
Orleans	28	84	4,756	—	844
Plaquemines	7	9	449	—	57
St. Bernard	7	7	515	2	485
St. Charles	6	8	607	3	193
St. James	12	14	836	4	337
St. John the Baptist	8	9	637	2	163
St. Mary	4	6	372	—	78
Terrebonne	6	10	662	14	1,068
Totals	121	216	13,462	57	4,728

*Report of Schools Under Board of Education for Freedmen, May, 1865, Superintendent of Education, Louisiana, BRFAL.

third- and fourth-year reading proficiency at the end of six months; one source claimed that fifty thousand freedmen had learned to read by the end of 1865. Without question the education system of 121 schools and over thirteen thousand students was the greatest accomplishment during the wartime experiment in Louisiana, excepting only emancipation.

VIII

The Family

c∕∕∽

The family, more than any other aspect of Afro-American life during the Civil War era, typified the troubled relationship between Louisiana's slaves and freedmen and the state's slave holders, Confederate military officials, Federal occupying forces and postwar planters. A sense of family was part of the meager baggage which the bondsmen brought with them out of slavery.[1] But, ironically, throughout the war and into the early days of emancipation the struggle to maintain the family seemed to intensify, seemed to be confronted by new and unexplained difficulties. As slaves became wartime laborers, runaways, contrabands, and finally freedmen, their families were assaulted and strained by forces unknown in the antebellum period: Confederate impressment of slave labor, refugee masters, Federal recruitment of black troops, the free-labor system, and the exigencies of the war itself. Available evidence

1. See Blassingame, *The Slave Community*, 77–103, for the best study of the slave family. See also Genovese, *Roll, Jordan, Roll*, 70–75, 450–58; and see Robert William Fogel and Stanley L. Engerman, *Time on the Cross: The Economics of American Negro Slavery* (2 vols.; Boston, 1974), I, 126–44, for an overstatement about the slave family.

suggest that whites (blue and gray) frequently ignored black concepts of reality and insisted (as paternalistic owners or self-righteous liberators) that blacks conform to white norms; it further suggests that slaves nevertheless had a sense of what their lives should be about and that blacks could look only within their own community to protect the handholds and footholds gained by emancipation.

In antebellum Louisiana some planters acknowledged slave marriages (and thus the family) and encouraged both within the limits of the institution of slavery. For some masters, conjugal relationships meant something more than pairing off slaves by sex to produce offspring for the plantation and greater tranquility in the quarters. On the plantations of William Minor marriages and divorces were serious matters. Minor instructed his overseers that "marriages must not take place until after a months notice . . . [and] divorces can only take place after similar notice." He discouraged changing mates by insisting that "parties once divorced can not remarre [*sic*] without agreeing to receive 25 lashes well laid on unless they have agreed to take that for the privilege of parting."[2] A month's waiting period before either marriage or divorce and twenty-five lashes for a second marriage indicates that Minor took the marriage of his slaves seriously, and there is no reason to believe that his slaves viewed those unions any less seriously. Minor was perhaps exceptional for the controls he exercised over slave relations, but he was not unique in his paternalism and the importance he placed on marriage.

Occasionally, planters took their obligations to the black family seriously even beyond the economic convenience of the plantation and the social confines of the slave community. When an estate in Iberville Parish was being divided, an exchange was worked out with a second plantation to prevent the separation of husbands and wives.[3] A second incident indicates the commitment of a slave to

2. Southdown Plantation Journal, 1861 (in Minor Family Papers, LSU), Instructions to the overseer.
3. Statement of P. K. Owen and C. D. Craighead, September 20, 1862, in Gay Papers, LSU. This transaction took place under the threat of advancing Federal troops.

his wife, and how, by aggressive action and an appeal to planter paternalism, a bondsman exercised control over his family's destiny. Prince's master was considering his sale to a speculator. After informing his master that he did not wish to leave, Prince went to his wife's master and proposed that his family not be separated. As a result, Prince was purchased by his wife's master.[4]

Although there were many instances wherein families were indeed broken up by sales, there was an interaction between planter and slave which benefited both and strengthened the family. The mechanics of good plantation management reflect this interaction in that the arrangement was often family oriented. Marriages were a recognized means to greater slave contentment; slave quarters were equally family houses; garden plots were likewise family plots; food, although rationed individually, was prepared for the family; and women were occasionally allotted time for cleaning the family cabin and mending the family clothes.[5] Thus the desire for efficiency and greater profit often aided the black family.

When masters—through plantation organization and paternalism—encouraged the black family, they contributed to a stronger sense of family than could reasonably be expected within the perimeters of institutional slavery. And the fact that the lives of the slaves were centered around the family unit had a reciprocal effect on masters. Not uncommon were planters who regarded their slaves as family units rather than number of male hands, number of female hands, and number of children. For Louisiana planters such as George Marshal and Andrew McCollam, who each had over one hundred slaves, to consider them as man, wife, and children bears strong testimony to the strength of slave families, at least on those plantations.[6]

Yet maintenance of the slave family was not a primary concern of the planter class; those families that survived did so, no doubt,

4. Wadley Diary (UNC), August 27, 1863.
5. See, for example, Robert Collins, "Essay on the Management of Slaves," *DeBow's Review*, XXXII (1862), 154–57.
6. See, for example, Cresant Plantation Journal, 1853 (in George Marshal and Family Papers, LSU); and Ellendale Plantation Journal, 1863 (in McCollam Papers, LSU).

in spite of the planters. Data from certificates of marriages performed in Union-occupied Concordia Parish, in late 1864 and
early 1865, give strong testimony to the stability and importance
of slave marriages. The records also give some indication of social
norms in slave society. Of a large number of former slaves married
at that time, 454 acknowledged a "previous connection" while in
slavery and gave a discernible reason for the dissolution of that
slave connection."[7]

Table 6

REASONS FOR DISSOLUTION OF MARRIAGES
AMONG BLACKS IN CONCORDIA PARISH

Years Married	Reasons for Separation					Totals
	Death	Force	Mutual Agreement	Desertion	Moral Reasons	
0–5	108	92	21	16	4	241
6–10	62	47	9	2	3	123
11–15	29	12		1		42
16–20	18	6		1		25
21–25	8	3				11
26–40	9	2	1			12
Totals	234	162	31	20	7	

Couples separated by force amounted to 35.7 percent, which
indicates that planter paternalism vis a vis slave marriages was not
universal, and that slave marriages of many years were obliterated
at the whims and needs of masters. But the majority of the dissolved marriages (64.3 percent) were terminated for reasons beyond the planters' immediate control. From this it may be inferred
that some planters acknowledged the slave family, or at least did
not tamper with it.

More revealing about the black community are the 87.2 percent
who remained with one mate until events or conditions not of their
making (death or force) ended the partnership. This would cer-

7. Marriage certificates, Louisiana, BRFAL.

tainly indicate that stability and faithfulness characterized these marriages; conversely, the low percentage (.044) of desertions would indicate the same. Perhaps equally revealing about slave society are the separations resulting from what are designated moral reasons by traditional Judeo-Christian standards. The figure is a miniscule .015 percent and does not support the concept of promiscuous slave quarters. To the contrary, the fact that any slave marriage was ended by one partner because of an adulterous relationship by the other partner suggests that a moral code existed in slave society and that at least some members lived by it.

Black religion during the slave period probably strengthened the moral code. Black churches thrived throughout the state, in towns and on plantations. Over forty black churches flourishing at the end of the Civil War were still operating well into the twentieth century.[8] Other churches with mixed congregations—usually made up of masters and their slaves—also served to reinforce morality in slave society. For example, one black member of the Hepzibah Baptist Church was recommended for expulsion because of "immoral conduct," *to wit*, "dancing."[9] The predominance of strict Baptist and Methodist doctrine in Louisiana and the widespread inclination to give slaves religious training in both black and mixed churches reinforced the moral code and thus the family structure in slave society.

The stability and commitment evident in the marriage certificates is reflected in the register of contrabands received at one of Louisiana's Federal home colonies. In January, 1863, over 50 percent of the adult arrivals considered themselves married, and 73 percent of the males arrived with their wives.[10] This latter figure suggests that running away during the war years was frequently a family operation.

8. See, for example, Church Archives, LSU, which are Historical Records Survey materials of the Works Project Administration.
9. Hepzibah Baptist Church Record Book, April 12 [1859], in Hepzibah Baptist Church Records, LSU.
10. Register of Contraband, Greenville Colony, January 1863, CLXIX, Louisiana, BRFAL.

Slave marriages were nurtured by strong, long-lasting commitments and a supportive moral code. Stable social patterns and values emerged in the slave subculture to a point far beyond that warranted by the institution of slavery. Later events indicate that those values were carried over to the days of contrabands, freedmen, and citizens. During the war, actions by planters, the Confederate States government, and Federal authorities weakened the black family through separation and dislocation.

With the outbreak of fighting, slave controls became tighter, and marriages outside the plantation, always frowned upon, were further discouraged. This limited the selection of potential partners, which must have been burdensome, particularly for bondsmen of smaller slaveholders. Marriages that did exist between servants of two masters were subject to greater restrictions, as in Lafayette Parish where owners of slaves with wives off their plantations were allowed to grant only "monthly passes which [were] good only for Wednesdays [and] Saturdays."[11]

The Confederate government's policy of hiring and impressing slave labor for the military effort also had a negative effect. One-fifth to one-half of the male slaves were subject to duty, a prerogative which was widely exercised in Louisiana. When the male was impressed, he went alone—no provisions were made for his family. Separation by this method was common from the start of the war and increased after the Federal occupation of southern Louisiana.

With the arrival of blue-clad liberators the process of dislocation and separation was accelerated, particularly as Union troops made excursions into the interior of the state. With each new piece of Federally controlled territory, more planters fled deeper into the state, to Texas, or to Mississippi. A British traveler near the Louisiana-Texas border in the spring of 1863 reported, "The road today is alive with negroes who are being 'run' to Texas out of Banks' way. We must have met hundreds of them." The same was true to a lesser extent of the Mississippi-Louisiana border.[12]

11. Joseph Embree to Henry Marston, August 10, 1861, in Henry Marston Papers, LSU; Lafayette Parish PJM, June 3, 1861.
12. Fremantle, *Three Months in the Southern States*, 85, May 10, 1863; your bro[ther] to Albert, April 28, 1863, in Cummings-Black Papers, TU.

"Running" slaves devastated families. Males, more valuable and more mobile, went with the planter, while planter paternalism and slave families were often discarded along the route. Women and children were frequently left to survive as best they could, which often meant avoiding Confederate raiders (who ironically would probably have taken them to Texas) and finding their way to Union lines. There they posed a problem for Federal officials who complained of having to issue rations to women and children because most of the men had been taken to Texas and could not provide for them.[13] The extent to which such situations were common is reflected in the records of contraband camps established by Federal authorities to care for the migrants: at one camp over 70 percent of the adult arrivals in one month were females.[14]

Increased contact between Union authorities and slaves had varying effects on black families. Where there was close and constant contact, much the same type of interaction that existed between slaves and planters also developed between Federals and Louisiana blacks. But regulations protecting the black family were slow to emerge, and early policies governing contrabands, labor, and military recruitment did considerable damage before they were arrested.

As Union troops and bondsmen made initial contact, many were impressed by the slaves' concern for their families. A constant question posed by blacks was whether they were free to join wives or husbands.[15] Some military commanders shared the slaves' concern and made a conscious effort not to further separate families; when the commander of the District of Western Louisiana ordered a cavalry sweep of a hostile area for horses and mules, he included in the instructions male "negroes without families" but cautioned

13. Robert Gaskill to Henri Robinson, October 19, 1864, in Letters Received, Bureau of Civil Affairs, DGR(U); Thomas Calahan to Conway, October 2, 1865, in Letters Received, Assistant Commissioner, BRFAL; Winslow Roberts to E. G. Beckwith, September 23, 1863, in Letters Received, Provost Marshal General, DGR(U).

14. Register of Contraband, Greenville Colony, January, 1863, CLXIX, Louisiana, BRFAL.

15. Marshall, *Army Life*, 398; Hepworth, *The Whip, Hoe and Sword*, 141–42.

that "no negroes who have families dependent upon them for support [should] be taken."[16]

As blacks evaded rebel raiders and made their way to Union lines or followed troops back from excursions into the interior, Federal authorities were forced to deal with them. The routine that developed was to gather freedmen at the contraband colonies established by the Bureau of Negro Labor. From there able-bodied males were either enlisted into the army or sent to work on fortifications, public works, or plantations. Only a portion of the men sent to labor on plantations were able to remain with their families. Most women and children either stayed at the home colonies or went to plantations without husbands and fathers.[17] Except for those few who went to plantations, families were separated indiscriminately, and, despite any rhetorical concern on the part of authorities in the Department of the Gulf, the need for black laborers and black troops took precedence over the desirability of keeping black families together.

As the Union commitment to black troops increased, the situation for families worsened. In Louisiana the squads of soldiers (often black) who made up recruiting parties had a wholesale disregard for the families of men they were enticing to join the army of liberation. Frequently blacks were taken off the streets and out of the fields and "enlisted" into the army at bayonet point. Many were not given time to notify their families before being marched to recruitment depots.[18] But not all of the Federal officials were as callous as some of the recruiters, and not all the former slaves tolerated such treatment. Thomas W. Conway of the Bureau of Negro Labor wrote an organizer of two black brigades that the troops had requested him "to keep a record of their wives [and] children [in order] to prevent such a separation as will result in

16. W. B. Franklin to A. L. Lee, October 25, 1863, *Official Records*, Vol. XXVI, Pt. 1, p. 755.

17. S. B. Holabird to J. W. McClure, May 17, 1863, General Papers, AGO; John Clark to Norman Leiber, October 23, 1863, in Letters Received, DGR(U).

18. Plantation Journal (in Palfrey Papers, LSU), October 9, 11, 1863; William J. Minor Diary (LSU), September 29, 1863; Conway to Ullman, May 15, 1863, Generals Papers, AGO.

their not knowing where their families are." Conway, more sensitive than most to some of the blacks' needs, began a tour of plantations making a registry of families of black soldiers, a program which continued throughout the war.[19] In the fall of 1864 the bureau announced that it had a registry of all laborers on plantations and asked commanders of black troops to advise their men of its existence. Its purpose was twofold: to establish mail communication between soldiers separated from their families, and to obtain certificates for the families so they might receive the Federal rights and protection due them as military dependents. The service was necessary, acknowledged the bureau, because of the early recruitment methods. The postal service was widely used, and teachers assigned to black regiments spent considerable time writing letters to families of illiterate soldiers. But it is difficult to evaluate its success, for when the war ended, the bureau had failed to locate the recipients of some four hundred letters, and no doubt a portion of that number represents families that were not reunited.[20]

Some new recruits, reacting to crude enlistment methods and abrupt separation from their wives and children, did not wait for the bureau to reestablish contact with their families—they took their own leave of the army and rejoined them in person. This practice was common enough to force the military to place guards over recruits to prevent their escape.[21] Federal authorities, in attempting to meet military needs, showed little concern for black families until black soldiers by their own actions made many of the whites around them aware of their concerns.

Much the same was true for black laborers on plantations. Abandoned plantations run by the Treasury Department for the profit

19. Conway to Daniel Ullman, May 15, May 27, 1863, Generals Papers, AGO.

20. New Orleans *Tribune*, November 16, 1864; Thomas D. Howard Diary (in Charles Howard and Family Papers, UNC); New Orleans *Black Republican*, April 15, 1865.

21. Van Alstyne, *Diary of an Enlisted Man*, 16, October 16, 1863; Marshall, *Army Life*, 398; Wadley Diary (UNC), November 11, 186[3]; Tyson Diary (LSU), April 13, 1864; Untitled, undated Manuscript, in Edmund Kirby-Smith Papers, UNC.

of the government received the best laborers not taken by the army. But even agents of those plantations were reluctant to accept the added responsibility of providing for laborers' families until forced to. Finally, Treasury officials in Louisiana were informed through the bureau of labor that unless provisions were made immediately "to support the families of said laborers on the plantations . . . they [the laborers] must be returned."[22] Not surprisingly, much the same methods had to be used to force planters to care for their laborers' families. While this threat was in part a means of shifting and designating responsibility for the care of women and children, it also reunited families, and as the practice became policy, it prevented additional separations.

Throughout the war years probably the greatest strain on the black family resulted from the conscription of married males. Problems arose because of their absence, and because families of black soldiers were targets of white abuse merely because they were families of black soldiers. Even with efforts to reestablish contact with separated military families, there still remained the question of who would care for them. Many planters simply forced wives and children off plantations once husbands and fathers were in the army. The military frequently returned them, informing planters that as slaves they had served him and now he should care for them.[23] But this policy had limited success, for enforcement was difficult, and many planters refused to assume the responsibility; women and children were turned out of plantation cabins and abandoned homes which by law they were entitled to occupy, leaving garden plots, animals, and what possessions they had accumulated in a lifetime of labor. Others were allowed to stay but were issued no rations, or were charged for them. Although by the fall of 1864 provisions were made for families of soldiers to draw rations from the Army Quartermaster Department, the program was

22. J. S. Clark to B. Rush Plumly, October 27, 1863, in Letters Received, CWSATD.
23. Winslow Roberts to E. G. Beckwith, September 23, 1863, in Letters Received, Provost Marshal General, DGR(U).

not a cure-all.[24] A wife had to present a certificate proving she was married to a Union soldier before she was eligible for rations. The widespread separation of families made that difficult and often impossible despite the coordinating activities of the Bureau of Negro Labor relating to the certificates. Nor was this service widely available except in the New Orleans area or near military posts of some size.

The freedmen, particularly those in uniform, were quick to respond to the opportunity to sanctify their marriages by white man's standards. The 478 ceremonies in Concordia Parish can be supplemented by 56 marriages on two occasions in Iberville Parish in June, 1864, 12 in St. John the Baptist Parish the previous month, and 28 in St. Mary Parish in January, 1865. The ceremonies were performed by authorized military personnel, justices of the peace, priests, and white ministers.[25] But no group was more adamant about having their slave marriages recognized by white society than black soldiers. The chaplain of a New York regiment wrote Banks that black soldiers frequently asked him to legalize the unions they had made in slavery, and he wanted assurance that it was within his power to do so before proceeding.

Former slaves they may have been, but they recognized the importance white men suddenly placed on formally validating the obvious, and they were reluctant to be separated from their wives unless this was done for fear their women and children would have no legal claims in the event they were killed. Subsequent events proved their fears correct; wives needed proof of marriage to draw rations once they were available to soldiers' families. Banks assured

24. George Hanks to J. T. Tucker, July 21, August 14, 1863, Letters Received, Bureau of Civil Affairs; W. Marston to Captain Stearns, August 23, 1864, J. M. White to Captain Stearns, August 24, 1864, both Letters Received, Provost Marshal St. Mary Parish, all in DGR(U). F. M. Frisbie to Conway, September 18, October 2, 1865, in Miscellaneous Records, Assistant Commissioner, BRFAL. E. G. Beckwith to Lt. Col. Crosby, May 16, 1865, Letters Received, Bureau of Civil Affairs; Conway to Henri Robinson, September 17, 1864, Letters Received, Provost Marshal General, both in DGR(U).
25. Marriage certificates, in Gay Papers, LSU; George Daley to George Bowen, May 13, 1864, in Miscellaneous Records, Provost Marshal General, DGR(U); J. S. Clark to Conway, August 13, 1865 in Letters Received, Assistant Commissioner, Louisiana, BRFAL; Hilton Diary (TU), October 12, 1865.

the chaplain that the marriages would be legal and authorized a special order allowing any minister to marry blacks free of charge.[26]

Despite legal marriages and letters of protest by black soldiers and their commanders, and despite protective actions by the Bureau of Negro Labor, abuses continued throughout the war years. What should have been a simple matter of black soldiers and civilians visiting their wives and children on plantations was often an ordeal. Overseers and planters particularly resented visits by black troopers because of their reputedly bad effect on laborers. Many soldiers were turned away at gun point, and blacks not in uniform fared even worse. At least one man was hanged as a result of a visit to his wife; beatings, arrests, and imprisonments were more common.[27] Eventually black troops were forbidden to visit their families on plantations without specific written authority from their commanders; during visits they were prohibited from carrying weapons.

Those black families not separated by planters, by Confederate labor policies, by Federal recruiters, or by dislocations of wartime society struggled to stay together as best they could. Ghettos sprang up near urban areas. A settlement near Gretna and Algiers, Louisiana, reportedly housed "700 black families," with grocery stores, boardinghouses, whorehouses, and other services mirroring white society.[28] While some came as families, blacks drawn to towns and military posts came as much in search of lost families as for a desire to leave the plantation and to test new freedoms. Once reunited, many stayed. A majority of the freedmen, however, remained on the land. They stayed on plantations abandoned by their masters, living in their quarters and working their garden

26. Job G. Bass to Banks, June 17, 1864, in Letters Received, DGR(U); marriage certificates, General Records, BRFAL, in which 31 percent of the males married in Concordia Parish were in the military service.
27. George Converse to George Cozzens, June 15, 1864, CWSATD. Waterloo Plantation Journal (in Minor Papers, LSU), April 10, 1865; Statement concerning the hanging on Mr. LeSepps' Plantation [June, 1862], George F. Shepley Papers, MHSL; George Hanks to Banks, April 18, 1863, in Letters Received, Bureau of Civil Affairs, DGR(U).
28. William Dougherty to Captain Hayden, January 31, 1866, Assistant Commissioner, Louisiana, BRFAL.

plots in order to keep their families together. Or they were able to lease small plots of land from black and white lessors.[29] Most laborers and their families found themselves working on large plantations again. A reading of plantation journals and labor contracts indicates that a great many of them were hired as family units, but in some instances contracted families were kept together at the expense of women and children working for lower wages than they otherwise could have received.[30]

From slavery to freedom the black family, more than any other facet of the Louisiana experiment, exemplifies a sense of black community, a sense that black Americans brought with them out of bondage, a feeling of what their lives should be about. That feeling of family, rooted in the antebellum era, sprang from slave marriages with strong commitments, buttressed from the outside by planter paternalism and plantation organization and from the inside by a pragmatic cultural code. The abuses properly ascribed to slavery and inherent in the institution give an extra dimension to the significance of the durability of the black family.

Equally revealing, no facet of race relations quite as vividly details the ambivalent relationship between whites (blue and gray) and blacks in wartime Louisiana. Paternalistic planters, when confronted by a hostile advancing army, abandoned homes, crops, and more often than not the families of their male slaves and became refugees: economics dictated that when time and circumstances permitted, all movable property accompanied them; when survival dictated, slave families were separated, wives and children were abandoned, husbands and fathers went on to Texas. Confederate military impressment of slave labor had a similar effect.

Escape to Federal lines or liberation by an advancing army did not guarantee family security. Federal officials considered black

29. M. Hawke to Bagley, August 22, 1865, R. K. Diossy to C. R. Strickney, September 1, 1865, XL, Louisiana, BRFAL.
30. See, for example, Greenwood Plantation Contract, March, 1866, in D. Weeks Family Papers, LSU, for contracts made with families; and see, for example, Fairchild and Smith Contract, February, 1865, in Miscellaneous Records, Provost Marshal General, DGR(U), for contracts made with families and wage discrimination against wives.

men soldiers and workers first, husbands and fathers second. A shortage of labor meant a constant demand for laborers on public works, fortifications, and plantations. Recruitment of black troops produced wholesale separations, and the conscripts protested with pen and paper, voices, and feet. Individuals and agencies eventually modified abusive Federal policies and attempted to compensate for past abuses but with varying degrees of success. And that suggests the confusion of the Yankee relationship to the black family. Federal officials, including Banks, repeatedly and publicly stressed the need to encourage family stability among the freedmen. But the freedmen frequently brought with them to Union lines not only a sense of family, a commitment to family, but their families themselves. And more often than not those families were challenged, pushed, pulled, strained, and separated by the Federal officials who proposed to inculcate family stability among the former slaves.

Despite these influences it is obvious that slaves and freedmen had strong family commitments. They proved it by running away or by remaining on plantations, whichever might preserve the family unit; they proved it by the length of their slave marriages and their eagerness to legalize those marriages when free; they proved it by protest and action and concern for their families when separated by military duty; and they proved it many times in spite of planters and liberators alike. And that points to perhaps the ultimate irony of the Louisiana experiment. In matters of the family —as with emancipation, labor, land, and education—blacks had an immediate and real awareness of their best interests; but those interests were frequently frustrated by both blues and grays.

IX

"Give Us a Free State Reorganization"

The deep-rooted prejudice against this people
still remains in all its pristine vigor, in
the North as much as the South, and will so
continue till public opinion shall be brought
up to a higher standard and recognizes the
true principle of politics that, *before the
law all men are equal.*

—New Orleans *Tribune*

Black political aspirations were clearly defined and articulated during wartime Reconstruction in Louisiana. Convinced that economic security and freedom itself were closely tied to political clout, the Creole leadership, in particular, struggled for black voting rights. But the political opportunity for Louisiana's blacks was dependent upon the success of the local white radical politicians who favored black suffrage. The black movement could not succeed alone. It needed allies from the established political system. If the radical white movement could control the state politically, that would pave the way for black advancement and gains. But if the whites failed, it would ultimately mean the defeat of the black cause as well. Both movements were dependent, to a great extent, upon the Lincoln and Banks administrations. Lincoln, as commander and chief of the army and wartime architect of Reconstruction, had final authority over the state. And although he was passive about some matters there, he was attentive about politics. Banks, as military commander of a department under martial law, had authority where and when Lincoln did not exercise it. Military

Governor George F. Shepley, normally in charge of civil matters in Louisiana, deferred for the most part to Banks and Lincoln.

Wartime political activists in Louisiana focused on three larger events: the gubernatorial election of February, 1864, the state constitutional convention which met from April to July, 1864, following a March election, and the state and national elections of the same year. In each case black suffrage and the future of Louisiana freedmen were significant and volatile issues. After those crucial events ran their course, the major political issues of Presidential Reconstruction in Louisiana were resolved.

Political maneuvering began in earnest in Louisiana in the spring of 1863. After a year of intramural, background skirmishes, two leading parties emerged. The first, the Free State party, was the vehicle of the radical Union clubs of Orleans and Jefferson parishes. New Orleans lawyer Thomas J. Durant was its titular head. A prewar Democrat, Durant was primarily a constitutionalist, both as an attorney and as a politician. He had opposed the annexation of Texas without losing his political influence. He managed the statewide presidential campaign of James K. Polk, an effort which earned him appointment as United States District Attorney for Louisiana. In 1860, Durant, successful lawyer and wealthy slaveholder, supported Lincoln's election and opposed secession. A man of genuine principle and integrity, Durant consistently refused to run for political office. If the "sad-faced and thin featured New Orleans unionist" had a fault as a political manager, it was his tendency to allow theoretical arguments to obscure political realities and goals.

A case in point was the argument, put forth by Durant and adopted by the radicals, that secession had voided the Louisiana Constitution of 1852 and that a new constitution, without slavery statutes, had to be written before further political reconstruction could be considered. That assumption was the basis of the radicals' political activities throughout 1863. Working on that premise, a Free State General Committee, made up of five delegates from each of the Union clubs, planned to register loyal voters in the Union parishes as a necessary step leading to an election of delegates to a constitutional convention. Durant was president of the committee, and under his name the registration and constitutional convention plan was submitted to Shepley in May, 1863. After the military governor approved it (and appointed Durant state attorney-general and commissioner of voter registration), the radicals began registering loyal citizens.[1]

The so-called Planter party represented the opposition. Like the radicals, the Planters professed loyalty to the Federal government and repudiated secession. The major point of contention between the two groups was the state constitution. The Planters wanted the 1852 constitution reinstated in toto, including the provisions protecting slavery. Arguing that because only southern Louisiana was being considered at that time, and because slavery still existed there by virtue of the exemptions in the Emancipation Proclamation, they saw no reason why the old constitution was not valid. Thus a general election for state offices was planned for November, 1863, as outlined by the 1852 document. A Planter party committee went to Washington in late summer to discuss the matter with Lincoln. They hoped for his approval but, more importantly, needed him to instruct Shepley that the election should be held. Lincoln apparently gave neither and reputedly informed the delegation that he would not interfere in the state's internal politics. Undaunted, the Planter party went ahead with its election plans, which included an invitation to the radicals to participate. The offer proved unsuccessful; the radicals refused on the grounds that the 1852 constitution was void and that the election would be illegal. Without the cooperation of the radicals, or the support of Shepley and Lincoln, the election lacked legitimacy; the two congressmen "elected" were never seated. The resounding failure of

1. John Rose Ficklen, *History of Reconstruction in Louisiana (Through 1865)* (Gloucester, Mass., 1966), 40–47; I rely on Ficklen for material on the general shape of Louisiana politics; for a solid study of the political failures in wartime Louisiana see J. P. McCrary, "Moderation in a Revolutionary World: Lincoln and the Failure of Reconstruction in Louisiana" (Ph.D. dissertation, Princeton University, 1972); for the radical plan see Thomas Durant to Shepley, May 23, 1863, in Shepley Papers, MHSL, and Reports of the General Committee of Union Association in New Orleans and Jefferson, Louisiana, May 8, June 12, 1863, NYHSL.

the conservative Planter party did, however, boost the stock of the radicals.[2]

While the conservatives organized and executed their unauthorized election, Durant, B. F. Flanders, and the radicals continued their voter registration. They also planned an election for delegates to a constitutional convention under guidelines newly approved by the Lincoln administration. Lincoln's plan was essentially the one Durant had sent to Shepley in May. It acknowledged that the loyal citizens of the state desired a new constitution, provided for a registration of qualified voters who had taken the oath, and set the procedure for the election of delegates.[3] As of early fall, 1863, the radicals' plan was gaining favor; it had become Lincoln's as well as their own.

The president's involvement in Louisiana's political reconstruction increased steadily from the time of occupation. In November, 1862, he wrote Shepley that he did not need or want northerners filling Louisiana's congressional seats. That, he concluded, "would be . . . at the point of the bayonet [and] would be disgusting and outrageous," and he would not favor seating them. Repeatedly he stressed that he did not think it proper for Louisiana to be reconstructed from Washington; rather, he wanted the impetus and involvement to come from the state's loyal citizens. In August, 1863, while radicals were registering voters and the planters were organizing their abortive election, Lincoln wrote Banks outlining his feelings on executive involvement in Louisiana politics: he would like to see a new constitution acknowledging the Emancipation Proclamation throughout the state, including the exempted parishes; he favored "some practical system by which the two races could generally [work] out of their old relation" and one which would include education for young blacks; but he also stressed that

2. Ficklen, *Reconstruction in Louisiana*, 47–50; George Denison to Chase, July 15, November 5, 1863, Thomas Durant to Chase, November 6, 1863, all in Chase Papers, LC; Committee to Shepley, September 19, 1863, Durant to Shepley, October 23, 1863, both in Shepley Papers, MHSL; B. F. Flanders to Chase, November 27, 1863, CBSA.

3. Edwin M. Stanton to Shepley, August 24, 1863, in Shepley Papers, MHSL. The instructions were sent by Stanton, who made it clear that they were Lincoln's.

"while I very well know what I would be glad for Louisiana to do, it is quite a different thing for me to assume direction of the matter."[4] A few weeks later he deviated somewhat from that position by adopting Durant's plan—but Durant's was an indigenous proposal, not a dictate from Washington. Nonetheless, Lincoln clearly leaned toward the radicals by endorsing their plan while rejecting the planters'. Additionally, he informed Banks that the contents of his August letter could be shared if that would help matters. Banks took Lincoln at his word and circulated the letter; the effect was euphoric for the radicals.

While Lincoln tried to stay neutral and the radicals and the planters jockeyed for position, New Orleans' Creole leaders were busy organizing a black suffrage movement. In early November, 1863, they held a mass meeting of six or seven hundred to petition Governor Shepley for the vote in the upcoming elections. The principal speaker was P. B. S. Pinchback, the shrewd and capable mulatto politician who would later serve as interim governor of Louisiana. He frankly outlined the group's position: Louisiana blacks were fighting the nation's battles; they believed that they were citizens and as such had a right to vote. If they were refused the franchise, then they expected exemption from the draft as well.[5] While the meeting and the demands elicited no response from Shepley, they set the tone for black political demands and action.

The Free State radicals, no less than Shepley, publicly ignored black demands for suffrage, but they did include emancipation as a major platform plank. The committee was primarily concerned with registering voters, a cause which was going slowly. Durant had difficulties finding a sufficient number of qualified registrars in the rural parishes, and loyal citizens willing to take the oath and

4. Lincoln to Shepley, November 21, 1862, in Shepley Papers, MHSL; Lincoln to Banks, August 5, 1863, in Flanders Papers, LSU. See also Philip D. Uzee, "The Beginnings of the Louisiana Republican Party," *Louisiana History*, XII, 197–211, for a sound overview which is flawed only by a misunderstanding of the 1863 radical phase.
5. *National Anti-Slavery Standard*, November 28, 1863; *American Missionary Magazine*, VIII, February, 1864; Donald E. Everett, "Demands of the New Orleans Free Colored Population for Political Equality, 1862–1865," *Louisiana Historical Quarterly*, XXXVIII, 41–64.

register to vote seemed even scarcer. Radical enthusiasm and optimism of late summer tended to lessen as fall turned to winter. In October, Flanders went to Washington to meet with Lincoln and explain the party's difficulties. Lincoln, anxious to recognize a government in Louisiana, agreed to recognize any they might organize. After Lincoln's urging, the Free State committee asked Shepley to set a date for the election of delegates even though the number of registered voters was not as high as they wished (Durant claimed four thousand). Shepley agreed and the election was slated for February 25, 1864. No doubt Lincoln's urging prompted the decision to hold the election at that time, and despite the problems, Flanders reported that "our great cause is prospering well here . . . and [I] have little doubt of a favorable result" in the upcoming election.[6] Flanders had reason to be optimistic—Lincoln had all but assured him that *any* legitimate government would be recognized.

December was pivotal for the radical and black movement in Louisiana. During the first week Lincoln announced his 10 percent plan for Reconstruction. He offered amnesty to all Confederates except high-ranking civilian and military officials, individuals who had joined the Confederates after taking an oath of allegiance to the Constitution, and those declared outlaws for abusing black troops. All others could take an oath of allegiance to the Constitution and the Union. When 10 percent of the number of voters in 1860 had taken the oath, a new state government could be formed.[7] On the surface the 10 percent plan was consistent with the advice and counsel Lincoln gave Flanders. The governing 10 percent in Louisiana could be radical as well as moderate or conservative.

By the end of the month matters had changed. Lincoln again met with the delegation of the Planter party, and this time the conservatives found a more sympathetic president than they had

6. Ficklen, *Reconstruction in Louisiana*, 57; Thomas Durant to W. O. Fiske, December 18, 1863, in Durant Papers, NYHSL; George Denison to Chase, October 10, 1863, in Chase Papers, LC; B. F. Flanders to Chase, December 4, 1863, in Chase Papers, HSP.
7. William B. Hesseltine, *Lincoln's Plan for Reconstruction* (Chicago, 1967), 70–71.

in late summer. They cautioned the president that the citizens of Louisiana would accept the Emancipation Proclamation "provided they could come back to civil government under their constitution and laws," that is, the Constitution of 1852. Under it blacks, military personnel, and residents of the state for less than one year could not vote. And that question was central to the constitutional struggle between the radicals and the conservatives—who would vote. The conservatives told Lincoln that the plan of Durant and Shepley allowed illegal votes and was unacceptable to the residents of the state.[8]

It is not clear how directly the Planters' meeting influenced Lincoln, but the president began moving away from the radicals as 1863 drew to a close. Lincoln increasingly looked to Banks for political advice, which was a departure. Although Banks had final authority in the Department, his was a military bailiwick; Shepley, as military governor, was charged with overseeing political matters. But in late December, 1863, Lincoln turned away from the radicals and Shepley, as well as his previous posture, by writing Banks: "You are master of all, and . . . I wish you to . . . give us a free state re-organization of Louisiana in the shortest possible time." Banks immediately abandoned the radicals and their plan for a constitutional convention election on February 25; instead he issued a proclamation calling for a general election of state officers on February 22. Although the decision was a conservative victory, which frustrated the radicals, Banks also alarmed the Planter party by scheduling an April election for delegates to a constitutional convention, designed to eliminate the proslavery features of the 1852 constitution.[9]

8. J. L. Riddell to Banks, December 23, 1861, in Banks Papers, LC. Riddell was chairman of the executive committee of the Planter party. His reporting to Banks on the Lincoln meeting is not insignificant.

9. Banks to T. P. Sullivan, January 16, 1864; Boutwell to Banks, December 21, 1863, both in Banks Papers, LC; Banks to Stanton, January 11, 1864, *Official Records*, Ser. 3, Vol. IV, pp. 22–32; Lincoln's instructions are quoted by Banks in the letter to Sullivan; Ficklen, *Reconstruction in Louisiana*, 56. Everett, "Demands," 52–53, has a view of Banks's involvement which suggests that Banks supported black suffrage.

The radicals were stunned and exasperated. After months of organizing under a plan approved by Lincoln, their efforts were undermined by the administration. Flanders wrote his mentor Chase, "I will not attempt to describe the feelings of those who have labored incessantly for months in developing and organizing the Union sentiment for a free state government, at this turn of affairs." Members of the Free State General Committee were described as "unanimously against General Banks' plan and proclamation." Their main fears were that Banks's action would destroy the radical movement by making a more moderate position acceptable to Union people and that the votes of soldiers recruited in the state would be controlled by Banks. Both fears were to be realized. In protest, Durant resigned his position as attorney general.[10]

What prompted Lincoln to desert the radical and black movements is unclear, although a number of historians have offered explanations. William B. Hesseltine believed that the president "had grown weary of searching for competent Unionists to organize the rebellious states." The Free State committee had registered only four thousand voters at the end of the year, a rather unconvincing number to present to congressional skeptics and conservatives. But the problem was not simply to find "competent Unionists" but Unionists of the correct political persuasion, for Louisiana Republicans were divided into two rival groups—Banks's military people, allied with Lincoln, against Flanders' treasury clique, which looked to Secretary Chase for leadership. Indeed the struggle between Banks and Flanders over control of abandoned and confiscated property, black labor, and the Bureau of Negro Labor were symptoms of that rivalry. Ludwell Johnson argues that "the real issue among Louisiana Republicans [was] . . . whether the government of the state would be loyal to Lincoln or Chase." Johnson suggests that personal political loyalties and patronage were the spoils at stake in Louisiana; he rejects the idea that the question of Negro rights played a significant role. Louis Gerteis,

10. Flanders to Chase, [?], January 14, 1864, in Chase Papers, HSP; Durant to Shepley, January 13, 1864, in Durant Papers, NYHSL.

in a perceptive article treating Chase's wartime career, proposes that the treasury secretary's presidential challenge in the fall of 1863 was the last best hope of the radicals. The challenge was easily sidestepped by Lincoln and shortly thereafter Chase resigned from the cabinet. With that, concludes Gerteis, the single radical spokesman for southern blacks within the administration was gone.[11] Chase's presidential aspirations best explain why Lincoln abandoned the Louisiana radicals. A number of the leading advocates of the Durant plan were Chase supporters; Durant was very much his own man but Flanders and others in the radical group were Chase's. Politically, Lincoln could not allow Louisiana, which was testing his reconstruction program, to fall to a radical Republican challenger.

But the struggle between Chase and Lincoln and the abandonment of the radicals has implications beyond partisan rivalries. What was at stake was the future status of the freedmen. Chase, the highest-ranking radical friend of the freedmen in Washington, had objected to exempting the southern Louisiana parishes in the Emancipation Proclamation, and had pushed Butler toward arming contraband blacks. He was openly hostile to Banks's contract-labor system, and, more important, he actively proposed a program for dividing plantation lands among the freedmen. He consistently urged his subordinates in Louisiana, who were involved in politics, to support black suffrage. Chase clearly viewed black Reconstruction differently from Lincoln. Because of that, the abandonment of Louisiana radicals and the failure of Chase's presidential challenge affected the course black Reconstruction would take.

Lincoln's actions reshaped the political landscape in Louisiana. By January, 1864, some elements of the Planter party aligned with the moderate Banks-Lincoln faction, which now stood in a commanding position over the dispirited Flanders-Chase faction. The

---

11. Hesseltine, *Lincoln's Plan*, 70; Carl Sandburg, *Abraham Lincoln: The War Years* (4 vols.; New York, 1939), II, 570–71; Ludwell H. Johnson, "Lincoln and Equal Rights: A Reply," *Civil War History*, XIII, 71 n.; Louis S. Gerteis, "Salmon P. Chase, Radicalism and the Politics of Emancipation, 1861–1864," *Journal of American History*, LX, 42–62.

two rival Republican groups looked to the February 22 governor's election as a test of strength.

Michael Hahn was Banks's candidate. Born in Bavaria but a resident of Louisiana since childhood, Hahn attended the local school system before reading law with Christian Roselius' firm. A Douglas Democrat, Hahn had canvassed the state opposing secession and refused to take an oath to the Confederacy. A scholarly man of some ability and principle, Hahn remained active in Louisiana politics throughout the Reconstruction era even though he was shot and crippled in the New Orleans riot of 1866. But in early 1864 it was predicted that he would run for governor without party or nomination if necessary.

On February 1, three weeks prior to the election, the Free State party met at the Lyceum Hall in New Orleans to select a candidate. But the unity of the radical movement had been broken by Banks's plan, and the convention split. Flanders and Durant found themselves leading a faction, not a party, which had been co-opted by moderate Unionists. The more radical element nominated Flanders for governor and J. Madison Wells for lieutenant governor. The moderates also endorsed Wells for second place on the ticket; but they nominated Michael Hahn for governor.

Excepting one issue—the future status of Louisiana blacks—there was little separating the two gubernatorial candidates. Both candidates opposed slavery, but Flanders, tagged as the black candidate, was accused of favoring black suffrage and equality. He clearly was the more problack of the two but did not advocate black voting rights during the election. He privately wrote Chase that he "was not ready for that question."[12] Although the conservatives also ran a candidate, neither he nor Hahn nor Flanders was the central figure of the election. Banks controlled the situation by virtue of the authority given him by Lincoln.

12. Ficklen, *Reconstruction in Louisiana*, 58; George Denison to Chase, February 5, 1864, in Chase Papers, HSP; see also Amos E. Simpson and Vaughn B. Baker, "Michael Hahn: Steady Patriot," *Louisiana History*, XIII, 229–53, for more information on Hahn. The authors suggest that Hahn's friendship with Lincoln was significant in wartime politics in Louisiana.

Whether or not by design, Banks successfully co-opted both left and right in Louisiana. By moving to abolish slavery in the exempted parishes and by requiring voters to take the oath prescribed in the 10 percent plan, he hurt the conservative effort. By recognizing the Constitution of 1852 he destroyed the base on which the Free State party was building. He further eroded the radicals' position by offering Union people a less difficult route to reunion. In so doing he split the party, rallied the moderates around Hahn, and destroyed the possibilities of radical success. Banks also aggravated both sides by allowing white resident soldiers recruited in Louisiana to vote in the governor's race and by using military personnel to register them.

On the eve of the election Flanders accurately reported that "the whole power of the Government is used against us, and of course we shall be defeated." The Hahn and Wells ticket swept the field. Flanders later claimed that the election "was a foregone conclusion of the Commanding General" because "every employee of the city, [the] government, . . . the state, and all the quartermasters men and the Louisiana soldiers were made to vote for the General's candidate."[18] Although usually intemperate when discussing Banks, Flanders was correct that the commanding general did all he could to ensure Hahn's success. Lincoln had what he requested—a new government in Louisiana in the shortest possible time.

In addition to creating the new government, Banks reduced the possibility of white radicals and blacks coalescing into a viable political force in wartime Louisiana. Moreover, Hahn's victory ensured that few friends of black suffrage would sit at the constitutional convention. Under Durant's plan the radicals controlled the registration process and thus stood a good chance of directing the creation of the new document. But once the moderates controlled the state offices they, as incumbents, were all but assured of dominating the election of convention delegates and the writing of the new constitution.

13. Flanders to Chase, February 16, 23, 29, 1864, all in Chase Papers, HSP.

The radicals were both disappointed and outraged at the election results (Flanders finished third in a field of three). Durant wrote numerous letters to influential Washington politicians, including radical Congressman Thaddeus Stevens and Congressman Henry L. Dawes, Chairman of the House Committee on Elections. He tenaciously argued that the election held under the 1852 constitution was illegal, that Banks's actions were inappropriate, and that the new state government should not be recognized. He also wrote Lincoln, pointing out irregularities and violations of the state constitution that surrounded the election. In bold terms Durant described Banks's actions as those of a military despot: "What sort of a state is this . . . where one man, not a citizen of the state, and having none but military power, is entirely master of its civil destiny, calling a convention at his will to nullify or abolish its government?" Durant asked Lincoln not to recognize the new state government. The upcoming constitutional convention, he hoped, would be free from military manipulation.[14]

Lincoln gave Durant no encouragement, and the radical and black political activists in Louisiana turned their attention to the delegates' election for the constitutional convention which was set for March 28. But neither group had realistic hopes of dominating the convention, with the state's political machinery so firmly controlled by Hahn and Banks. The election went as predicted—a majority for Banks's people, with the conservatives filling a lesser number of seats. A Treasury agent reported that the radicals claimed only four delegates.[15]

With few exceptions the convention was a homogeneous group; points of conflict arose largely over the future status of blacks. Slavery was abolished (after five days of discussion), but the question of compensation was long debated. The more conservative forces won out with passage of a resolution endorsing Federal compensation for loyal and disloyal slaveholders. Black education

14. Thomas Durant to Thaddeus Stevens, March 2, 1864, in Thaddeus Stevens Papers, LC; Thomas Durant to Dawes, February 8, 1864, in Dawes Papers, LC; Thomas Durant to Lincoln, February 26, 28, 1864, in Durant Papers, NYHSL.
15. George Denison to Chase, April 1, 1864, in Chase Papers, LC.

was also an issue. Although the final document supported black schools, some convention members objected to the provision in Banks's General Order 38, which provided for white taxation to support black education. A resolution was offered declaring that the tax was unconstitutional, that the collection should be suspended, and that Banks should find an alternate means of financing black education. The resolution was tabled by a comfortable margin, no doubt partly because of a letter from Lincoln to Governor Hahn strongly endorsing black education; but its introduction gave credence to the popular myth that the tax was unconstitutional and made collection more difficult.[16]

Throughout the period of the convention (April–July, 1864) black suffrage was debated both in and out of the meeting halls. Just prior to the opening of the convention, Lincoln cautiously and privately wrote Governor Hahn suggesting that perhaps "some of the colored people may be let in [to the elective franchise]—as, for instance, the very intelligent, and especially those who have fought gallently [sic] in our ranks." Despite Lincoln's urging, Hahn apparently never used his position to advance black suffrage.[17]

Few observers were optimistic about black suffrage as the convention opened. The radical black newspaper *L'Union* hoped for "humane legislation" and stated unequivocally that it wanted "full equality before the law and full civil equality [for all] native and freeborn Americans" as well as full governmental rights for all freedmen. But *L'Union* expected little from a convention controlled by "a miserable prejudice against a certain class of native born Americans [and which] refuses to recognize . . . the generous principles of impartial justice, and universal equality before the law." Chase's Customhouse man in New Orleans reported little chance for even free-black suffrage; he assigned ultimate responsibility for the failure to Banks, whose people controlled the convention.

16. Ficklen, *Reconstruction in Louisiana,* 70–71; *Official Journal of the Proceedings of the Convention for the Revision and Amendment of the Constitution of the State of Louisiana* (New Orleans, 1864), 3–6.

17. Lincoln to Michael Hahn, March 13, 1864, *Collected Works of Lincoln,* VII, 243.

Durant, more in tune with black political actions and aspirations, accurately reported, "We have no hope now but in Congress."[18]

Black suffrage activity was constant despite increasingly pessimistic reports and attitudes. Blacks organized Union radical clubs, held meetings, and signed petitions. The major petition was circulated in the spring of 1864 and was endorsed by a thousand free blacks, including twenty-four veterans of the War of 1812. The culmination of those activities was the presentation of the petition in Washington by J. B. Roudenez and Arnold Bertonneau, editors of the New Orleans *Tribune*. The black leaders met with Lincoln and with members of Congress, but they expected their "rights and protection from the Congress of the nation," not from Lincoln and certainly not from the state convention.[19]

Their pessimism about the Louisiana convention was well founded. The convention debated black suffrage and, failing to reach a decisive agreement, compromised—voting was restricted to white males of twenty-one years of age, but the constitution permitted the legislature to extend suffrage to those "citizens of the United States, as by military, by taxation . . . or by intellectual fitness, may be deemed entitled thereto."[20] That vague and hollow promise for the future is as close as Louisiana's blacks came to the franchise under Presidential Reconstruction.

The two major provisions relating to blacks in the Louisiana Constitution of 1864 reflected Lincoln's influence. Lincoln wrote Hahn strongly endorsing black education—the constitution so provided. Lincoln later wrote Hahn privately suggesting that black enfranchisement be considered—that possibility was provided for in the future. Both constitutional provisions owed something to Lincoln's intercession with Louisiana's governor. The president was pleased with the new constitution; he wrote Banks complimenting him on his work and stressing, "I am anxious that it [the

18. New Orleans *L'Union*, April 9, 1864; Denison to Chase, April 1, 1864, Durant to Chase, March 5, 1864, both in Chase Papers, LC.
19. *National Anti-Slavery Standard*, April 16, 1864; William Viger, Corresponding Secretary, Union Radical Club (Black) to Charles Sumner, May 27, 1864, in Sumner Papers, HLHU.
20. *Official Journal of the Convention*, 175.

constitution] be ratified by the people." He also told Banks to let it be known to state officials "holding [office] under me . . . that this is my wish, and let me know at once who of them openly declare for the Constitution, and who of them, if any, decline to so declare." Clearly, by late summer, 1864, Lincoln was taking a firm hand in Louisiana's political reconstruction, and was content with its more moderate direction.[21]

A majority of the federally appointed officeholders in Louisiana followed Lincoln's lead, but the same cannot be said for the state's black leadership. By the time the constitutional convention adjourned, the Creole leaders were disillusioned and alienated from the state government and from the Lincoln administration. Aware of the need and the possibilities for real reform in Louisiana, the *Tribune* had hoped "to see an example of liberty . . . that other free states could emulate for the elevation of the black race"; instead they found "some of our best and wisest men" moving away from that idea. The radical organ applauded the constitutional provision abolishing slavery and supporting black education, but it was disappointed that blacks were denied the right to vote— "which would not be a favor, but an act of justice."[22] The *Tribune* recognized that "the deep-rooted prejudice against this people still remains in all its pristine vigor, in the North as much as the South, and will so continue till public opinion shall be brought up to a higher standard and recognizes the true principle of politics that, *before the law all men are equal.*"[23]

Black disillusionment and criticism was not confined to the new state constitution. In mid-August the *Tribune* complained of the lack of progress in Louisiana during two and one-half years of occupation. Its editors recounted the "means employed to carry out" the governor's election of February, 1864, the poor men selected as candidates (the *Tribune* had reluctantly endorsed Flanders), the "intimidation and other malpractices of the police offi-

21. Lincoln to Banks, August 5, 1863, *Collected Works of Lincoln,* VI, 364; Lincoln to Hahn, March 13, 1864, *ibid.,* VII, 243.
22. New Orleans *Tribune,* July 23, 28, 1863.
23. *Ibid.,* August 11, 1864.

cers," and the removal of problack military officials. The constitution was described as "conceived in the fraudulent design of getting up a sham electoral ticket in Louisiana [and] carried through by military violence against the will of the people." The *Tribune* concluded that the constitution "had no lawful authority, [was] based on Executive usurpation [*sic*]," and was framed "by men who had no higher principle of action than hatred of their fellows of African descent." The *Tribune* refused to support the constitution for adoption.[24]

Free-black alienation from the state and Federal governments ran deep. There was considerable discussion within the Creole community of a mass migration to Mexico, and J. B. Roudenez, influential editor of the *Tribune*, was one of the more vocal advocates. The month after the constitutional convention adjourned, it was reported that "a suitable person to institute the suit to test the rights of colored citizens to vote" could not be found. Why? Because there was a loss of confidence in the political machinery and because "a large majority of them are going to Mexico . . . because they have been deceived so often."[25]

The recent French installation of Maximilian as ruler of Mexico undoubtedly heightened Creole interest in migration. The Creoles had affection for French institutions and for France. Many had been educated there and the experience had converted them to unabashed Francophiles. Moreover, before Louisiana was sold to the United States by France, free blacks had enjoyed the rights and protection of free citizens, something being denied them in America. Apparently contact was made with Maximilian and the emperor was "guaranteeing to them that which *France* . . . concedes to all its citizens but which [the United States] prohibits: *tourt* 'Equality to all castes before the law.' " At least one white observer was concerned about the potential international complications resulting from the migration. There was talk in Washington about invoking the Monroe Doctrine and pushing Maximilian and Na-

24. *Ibid.*, August 13, 1864.
25. P. M. Tourne to John F. Collins, August 12, 1864, Conway to Dr. Roudenez, August 19, 1864, both in Banks Papers, LC.

poleon's army out of Mexico by force if necessary. There was fear that exiled Confederates and black veterans in Mexico would join Maximilian's army or would support his army as a fifth column in the United States if fighting occurred between the two nations.[26] Although there is no evidence that suggests Creoles in any numbers crossed the border from Texas, the episode is an indicator of alienation and frustration in the black community.

New Orleans' Creoles and radicals were not alone in their alienation from Lincoln and his reconstruction plan. Congressional opposition to the Lincoln-Banks government in Louisiana was a major consideration in passage of the Wade-Davis Bill, an attack on Lincoln's reconstruction program. Briefly, the bill provided for a registration of all white male citizens in the state. When a majority (as opposed to Lincoln's 10 percent) of those registered took an oath of allegiance to the Constitution then a new state government could be organized. No one who had held an office in the Confederacy or had voluntarily fought for the Confederacy could vote or hold office. The bill never became law and had little effect in Louisiana, yet it was an indication of congressional response to the political situation which had developed in the state since Lincoln's letter to Banks in December, 1863. It also served notice that senators and representatives sent to Congress by the existing state government might have difficulty being seated.[27]

Despite signs of congressional disaffection, the Hahn-Banks-Lincoln organization continued to reorganize the state government. September 5 was the date set for elections to the state legislature. Banks was anxious for a good voter turnout to indicate the loyalty and popularity of the Hahn government. He instructed the state auditor to find "respected men" to go into the parishes to urge people to register and to vote. He further ordered that residency

26. T. B. Thorpe to Banks, April 12, 1862, in Banks Papers, LC; Alfred Jervis to Thaddeus Stevens, April 8, 1864, in Stevens Papers, LC.
27. Randall and Donald, *Civil War and Reconstruction*, 552–53. Lincoln vetoed the bill. See also Herman Belz, *Reconstructing the Union: Theory and Policy during the Civil War* (Ithaca, N.Y., 1969), 190. Belz suggests than congressional opposition to Lincoln gained considerable ground when the president abandoned the Durant plan and changed his reconstruction program in Louisiana.

papers be issued without charge (the normal fee was five dollars) and for the courts to remain open extra hours to issue the papers. The "respected men" sent into the parishes and court clerks who worked extra time were guaranteed wages by the government.[28] Criticism by black and white radicals in Louisiana and by Congress put Banks on the defensive about his political creation, and he was, at Lincoln's urging, doing all he could to insure its success.

The fall and winter of 1864 was a political season in Louisiana. A majority of the winners in the legislative election were moderate and moderate-conservative. The new legislature filled the two United States Senate seats vacated by Confederate resignations by electing Michael Hahn and King Cutler. (Hahn resigned his governorship to accept the seat.) But opposition to Lincoln's reconstruction plan, particularly as it was unfolding in Louisiana, was growing in Congress and neither senator was seated. Their arrival in Washington was preceded by a petition from the Durant faction challenging the election. Cutler claimed that he and his colleague were not seated only because the congressional session was too short to complete the investigation. In an open address Cutler assured the citizens of Louisiana that a vast majority of the cabinet and both houses of Congress approved of their new state government. But Banks, Lincoln, and the moderate Unionists in Louisiana completely misread Congress—neither Cutler nor Hahn was ever seated and the same fate awaited three members of the House of Representatives who were sent to Congress the next fall.[29]

The final official order of political business for the fall was the national presidential election. Lincoln fought off the move within the Republican party to replace him, while General George McClellan represented the Democrats. Neither radical whites nor blacks gave the president enthusiastic support. Durant was an active speaker, and although he endorsed Lincoln over McClellan, his speeches were critical of the Lincoln administration and its

---

28. Banks to A. D. Dostie, August 23, 1864, Dostie to Banks, August 23, 25, 1864, Banks to John W. Thomas, August 26, 1864, all in Banks Papers, LC.

29. Ficklen, *Reconstruction in Louisiana*, 88–91; *Address of Hon. R. King Cutler, United States Senator of Louisiana to the Citizens of the State of Louisiana* [N.p., n.d.], 1–4; New Orleans *Tribune*, December 23, 1864.

Louisiana handiwork. The *Tribune* was not as guarded. The contest was, claimed the newspaper, between Lincoln and McClellan —a civilian and a military man; a Kentucky-Illinois man and an Ohio-New Jersey man; an old-line Whig and a war Democrat; one in office for four years who was slow and often failed to act, the other who led his army to defeat in the peninsula and to victory at Antietam—"both . . . third- or even fourth-rate men and utterly unworthy to be the head of a great nation like ours." With that as background the *Tribune* concluded, "We are not prepared to advocate the claims of either McClellan or Lincoln for the next presidency."[30]

After the election, which Lincoln won (although Louisiana's electoral votes did not count), Louisiana blacks persisted in their efforts to attain suffrage. Late 1864 through early 1865 was spent organizing and trying to construct a united front, particularly in the black community. The Creoles were split over two issues. The first was a matter of tactics—whether to work through the state legislature (which met from October, 1864, through early 1865) or to spend the fall organizing and then petition the United States Congress when it reconvened. The other issue was who should vote —would the movement support limited or universal male black suffrage?

The National Equal Rights League (NERL) represented the more radical black faction, which looked to Congress for black suffrage unencumbered by property or educational restrictions. The *Tribune* acknowledged the social and economic difference separating the older free-black community from the freedmen but stressed that both groups were "equally rejected and deprived of rights [and] cannot be . . . estranged from one another." Indeed, under the Banks administration upper-class, wealthy Creoles as well as unlettered, twelve-dollar-a-month field hands were arrested as vagrants and sent to plantations as laborers or were "enlisted" into the army at bayonet point. The *Tribune* did not idly editorialize

30. George Denison to Jimmy, September 16, 1864, in Denison Papers, LC; B. R. Plumly to Banks, October 20, 1864, in Banks Papers, LC; New Orleans *Tribune*, September 22, 1864.

about breaching class lines, for its editors realized that race, not class, would shape legislation affecting the postwar black community. No less an observer than New York newspaperman and Louisiana plantation lessee Whitelaw Reid noted that the Creoles, who "have not been in the habit of caring much for rights of any negroes except themselves, [are] making common cause with even plantation hands."[31]

A few weeks later the *Tribune* announced the results of the first state meeting of the Louisiana chapter of the NERL. Officers were selected with Captain J. H. Ingraham of the Corps d'Afrique serving as president. Of greater significance, the *Tribune* felt, were the convention delegates sent from the rural parishes: "Seated side by side [were] the rich and the poor, the literate and the educated and the country laborer." The meeting was a congregation of landowners, laborers, tradesmen, freedmen, Creoles, ministers, and soldiers. "All classes of society were represented and united in a common cause . . . the actual liberation from social and political bondage," reported the black newspaper.[32]

The NERL failed to achieve its goal of black harmony. The *Tribune* and the league believed that any overt political move should be preceded by a sound organization reflecting a united black front with clearly defined strategy and objectives. There were, however, blacks in New Orleans who felt differently. They, apparently in conjunction with some white radicals, began a petition campaign aimed at the state legislature. Its objective was *limited* suffrage, or, as described by the *Tribune*, "claiming for certain classes of colored citizens the right of suffrage." The radical newspaper was skeptical. It expected little from the state legislature and warned that blacks who petitioned that body were doing so as individuals. They did not represent the black people; the league did that. The *Tribune* questioned why the petitioners did not wait "in order to obtain the franchise for all without distinction of

31. New Orleans *Tribune*, December 29, 1864; Whitelaw Reid Diary (LC), June 6, 1865.
32. New Orleans *Tribune*, January 15, 1865. As a postscript to the article the *Tribune* noted with approval that "the country delegates were generally more radical than most of the city delegates."

classes." As critical of its own people as it was of unresponsive whites, the black organ wondered who "would be selfish enough to vote when thousands of his brethren cannot. Who is willing to abandon his race for a short and void gratification?" The most effective course, insisted the *Tribune*, was to maintain racial unity and petition Congress when it met to discuss the Reconstruction bills.[33]

By early 1865 white and black radicals in Louisiana were troubled from all sides. They had worked and organized under a plan approved by Lincoln only to have the president abandon them. Reluctantly, they adapted their efforts to meet the new situation, participated in the state elections, and saw the elections manipulated by military authority. Frustrated and angry, the black leadership talked of migrating to Mexico, but chose instead to remain and work for equality for all their race; they rejected attempts at division by both blacks and whites who tempted them with rights and privileges based on a caste system. Rebuffed by the Lincoln administration and the state legislature, the radicals looked to the United States Congress and postwar Reconstruction to protect those limited gains made since occupation.

33. *Ibid.*, February 19, 21, 24, 1865.

X

"Slavery Is Reestablished"

In June, 1865, when the Bureau of Free Negro Labor and the Board of Education for Freedmen were transferred to the Freedmen's Bureau, Louisiana blacks looked to some advances from slavery: emancipation, a substantial school system, access to military courts, the promise of land, and greater family security. Although many of the wartime gains were incomplete and insecure, the possibility existed in Louisiana in mid-1865 for an innovative Reconstruction. An effective Freedmen's Bureau and the full force of Washington could have smoothed the military programs and made Louisiana a showplace for black aspirations and achievements and a model for Reconstruction in the rest of the South.

But through the summer and fall of 1865 the fragile wartime advances were besieged with challenges in Louisiana and Washington. The military programs were confronted by a more active and hostile local white population and an increasingly conservative political atmosphere. By the end of the year the question was not whether Louisiana would serve as a model for Reconstruction but, rather, whether any of the advances from slavery would survive, save emancipation.

Politically, the Lincoln-Banks plan for creating a moderate Unionist government in Louisiana went afoul. By destroying the base of the radicals and blacks, the Lincoln administration ultimately opened the way for conservatives, not moderates. In June, 1865, Banks was cautioned that the "copperheads are gaining power," and indeed they were. The following month Congressman John Covode, in a letter to Benjamin F. Wade, warned that Union men in Louisiana had been betrayed and that matters there were in "bad shape, probably more so than at many other [southern] points." A local and experienced political observer vividly described the changing situation. The men gaining control, he reported, "dress like Union men, look like Union men, talk like Union men, and have ears like Union men, but they don't smell much like Union men."[1]

At the center of the controversy was Governor J. Madison Wells, who had been nominated on both the Hahn and Flanders tickets in 1864, and had come to power when Hahn resigned to accept a senate seat. Wells brought a strange and varied background to Louisiana politics. Born in Louisiana, he was orphaned at eight, attended a Jesuit school in Kentucky, a military school in Connecticut, and read law in Ohio. Having returned to Louisiana in 1829, he was one of the largest planters in Rapides Parish when the war started. Despite his large holdings in land and slaves, Wells actively opposed secession and spent the first year of the war hiding from Confederates and Confederate sympathizers who found his political posture offensive. He eventually made his way to Union lines and into Union politcs. One of the more overt political opportunists in a state full of the species, Wells was willing to flow with the source of power as long as it was blue not gray. By June, 1865, the power source was coming more and more from the right. Lincoln was dead; Johnson was president; the rebels had received a

---

1. Conway to Banks, June 10, 1865, in Banks Papers, LC; John Covode to Benjamin F. Wade, July 11, 1865, in Wade Papers, LC; J. Hawkins to Taliaferro, September 22, 1865, in James G. Taliaferro Papers, LSU.

nearly blanket amnesty. During May, Wells had gone to Washington, met with Johnson, and came away a strong supporter of the new chief executive. Anxious to stay in office, Wells began courting local conservatives. He removed the military mayor of New Orleans, rejected Banks's original voter registration, and ignored selective provisions in the 1864 constitution.[2]

Wells also initiated mischief regarding the freedmen. He replaced military personnel with antiblack officials who began harassing and arresting black "vagrants." He and the newly appointed mayor of New Orleans, Hugh Kennedy, began a concerted effort to discredit radical Unionists, to destroy the black educational system, and to systematically deprive the freedmen of their civil liberties. Wells accused the Chase people in Louisiana of trying to overthrow the government and he poisoned the president against the Freedmen's Bureau in general and Conway in particular. Wells was eroding some of the wartime work and was turning the state toward conservative planter control.[3]

Wells courted planters, President Johnson, and a conservative Reconstruction in a number of ways. His actions concerning black garrison troops, whom local whites found particularly offensive, suggest the changed situation. Planters protested the "unsafe condition of the country"—black soldiers were accused of robberies, outrages, and murders. The mere presence of black troops, charged former slaveholders, "demoralized" the labor force. The citizens of Monroe threatened to take "matters into [their] own hands" if no action was taken. Wells was attentive to white protests. He promised St. John R. Liddell—Catahoula Parish planter, former Confederate general, and postwar militia director—that the troops would be removed, and, whenever possible, they were. Political pressure from the Louisiana governor, coupled with the cooperative spirit of General Edward Canby, new commander of the De-

2. Ficklen, *Reconstruction in Louisiana,* 104–107.

3. A. F. Fenno to [?], April 30, 1865, Michael Hahn to William Seward, May 19, 1865, J. Madison Wells to Andrew Johnson, July 3, 1865, all in Andrew Johnson Papers, Microfilm copy in LC. See also Wells to Johnson, July 29, 1865, and Hugh Kennedy to Johnson, July 21, 1865, both *ibid.,* for statements on Wells's ideas and work.

partment of the Gulf, brought the recall of many black garrison troops throughout the fall of 1865.[4]

More significant was Wells's attempt to abolish the provost marshal-bureau courts and return judicial control of the freedmen to the newly reestablished civilian courts. Wells insisted on the transfer, but bureau Assistant Commissioner Conway was hesitant. Conway feared that blacks would not be allowed to testify and would not receive proper treatment, even though Wells assured Conway that he had instructed all judges to deal fairly with freedmen. Not satisfied, Conway required the judges to sign a circular stating that they would be impartial in their decisions. Gradually he relinquished judicial control over freedmen affairs, but he reserved the right to establish a tribunal to hear cases when he felt whites were not treating blacks fairly.[5]

Conway had ample reason for concern. Although he received assurances of impartiality from Wells and judges, he continued to receive reports from his agents that indicated the courts were not without prejudice. Civilian governments tended to treat blacks unfairly and unevenly and resented efforts by the bureau to intercede on behalf of the freedmen. In St. Landry Parish the provost marshal fined two whites for the brutal beating of a black man, "which [seemed] to stir up the civil authorities of [that] bastard machine." Blacks were waiting lengthy periods for trials and then receiving outrageous sentences for petty offenses. One freedman was given six months in prison for stealing a peck of corn. Agents apprised Conway that local authorities were not color blind in dispensing justice, hence the reason for his guarded caution.[6]

4. New Orleans *Tribune*, June 28, 1865; Petition of Citizens of Monroe to J. Madison Wells, October 13, 1865, in Letters Received, Assistant Commissioner, Louisiana, BRFAL; *Daily Southern Star*, February 13, 1866; Caddo Parish PJM, July 2, 1866; St. John B. Liddell to his son, in Liddell Papers, LSU; New Orleans *Weekly Crescent*, November 18, 1865.

5. Conway to J. Madison Wells, September 6, 30, 1865, Governor J. Madison Wells to Conway, September 27, 1865, John Brownlee, *et al.*, response to Circular No. 15, September–October, 1865, all in Letters Received, Assistant Commissioner, Louisiana, BRFAL.

6. E. Ehrlich to Fenno, September 30, 1865, J. S. Clark to Conway, August 13, 1865, both in Letters Received, Assistant Commissioner, Louisiana, BRFAL; W. H. Van Arnam to Starring, April 27, 1865, in Letters Received, Provost Mar-

While the local court system proved troublesome to Conway, the bureau, and Louisiana blacks, local white hostility, particularly to black education, was also an increasing source of concern during the summer and early fall of 1865. The problem of finances was the main irritant. The Board of Education for Freedmen transferred to the Freedmen's Bureau a growing and substantial school system, but it also transferred a considerable debt. From the outset, financial difficulties plagued the military system. General Order 38, which created the board, provided for a tax on real and personal property to finance black education, but the tax never supported the black school system. One source claimed that only $31,247.10 was ever collected, Orleans Parish paying all but $1,358 of that. Local economic difficulties account in part for the low collection, although planter refusal to pay was also significant. In many instances provost marshals failed to initiate proceedings against offenders. The lack of funds was one reason for Banks's insistence that teachers be supplied room and board at local expense. It was estimated that such a plan would save the board $2,000 a month.[7]

The Board of Education operated on borrowed money throughout its tenure. The Corps d'Afrique fund was tapped for almost $7,000, but the Quartermaster Department bore the brunt of the expenses with funding in excess of $139,000. There is some question whether the latter amount represented a loan, per se. The Quartermaster Department probably derived the money from the sale of confiscated cotton and from its brief control of confiscated property. It is doubtful that Banks considered that a debt of the board. Whatever the circumstances, the school system was not self-sufficient, and with the transfer of control to the Freedmen's Bureau those sources of revenue were lost. General O. O. Howard,

---

shal General, DGR(U). By November, 1865, the bureau agent in Opelousas reported that the troops had left and it was unsafe for him to remain.

7. H. R. Pease to D. G. Fenno, October 26, 1865, in Letters Received, Assistant Commissioner, Louisiana, BRFAL. E. M. Wheelock to Banks, April 1, 1864, Letters Received, Bureau of Civil Affairs; James Bowen to H. J. Foster, May 26, 1864, Letters Received, Provost Marshal Lafourche, both in DGR(U). Deer Range Plantation Journal III (in White Papers, UNC), October 16, 1865; E. M. Wheelock to Banks, August 16, 1864, in Banks Papers, LC.

commissioner of the bureau, was concerned specifically about the $21,361.08 in outstanding bills he inherited from the board. He did not want his poorly financed agency saddled with debts.[8]

Black education in Louisiana faced a financial crisis in the summer and fall of 1865. Newly appointed bureau commissioner of education for Louisiana, H. R. Pease, proposed an annual capitation tax of $2 on all male freedmen over twenty-one years old in every parish that had schools. This, according to the education commissioner, would yield $150,000 yearly, leaving a deficit of only $30,000, which could be supplied by northern benevolent societies. Pease confidently reported that "Freedmen will pay this tax cheerfully and promptly." Despite Pease's optimism, the plan was not adopted.[9]

To stave off financial collapse and destruction of the school system Conway announced that the original school tax would henceforth be collected; if necessary, property would be seized and sold to meet the obligations. He was assured by General Canby of military assistance if needed. It was estimated that collection would yield over $200,000.

Conway's actions as bureau commissioner, particularly concerning the school tax, were resented by white residents of the state generally and Wells and his administration specifically, and they made their displeasure known in Washington. Wells claimed Conway was not fit to hold a governmental post: "He is a radical negro suffrage man—thinks the black better than the white man and is an active political speaker and agitator for negro suffrage and equality." Dr. Hugh Kennedy, Wells's conservative mayor of New

---

8. Banks to S. B. Holabird, August 9, 1864, in Banks Papers, LC; Banks to Holabird, June 9, 1864, Report of Funds Received by the Office of Superintendent of Education, April, 1864–December, 1865, James Taggard to Conway, July 21, 1865, all in Letters Received, Assistant Commissioner, Louisiana, BRFAL. The question of who paid for what as related to the Board of Education is confused. Conway wrote Charles Sumner in May, 1864, that the expenses for running New Orleans' black school for the preceding nine months had been paid for by the sale of cotton which had been confiscated at Port Hudson and cleaned by contraband blacks. See Conway to Charles Sumner, May 23, 1864, in Sumner Papers, HLHU.

9. H. P. Pease to D. G. Fenno, October 28, 1865 in Letters Received, Assistant Commissioner, Louisiana, BRFAL.

Orleans, described Conway's efforts to preserve the black school system and to protect black civil liberties as "attempts to provoke me upon the most rideculous [*sic*] pretences." The bureau, Conway, and his agents "seem to have studied only how they could give trouble and cause vexation," claimed Wells. All those remarks were directed to President Andrew Johnson.[10]

The complaints against Conway and the threatened confiscation and sale of property to finance black schools reached Howard via President Johnson. The national commissioner responded by sending bureau agent J. Scott Fullerton to Louisiana in October, 1865. Fullerton was instructed to investigate the situation in Louisiana, particularly Conway's activities. Although apparently dispatched by Howard, Fullerton kept Johnson informed of his observations and reactions. His basic attitude was reflected in an early report concerning Salmon P. Chase's speeches to freedmen supporting black suffrage: "[The speeches] are likely to make them discontent and to lead them to think that unless they get certain imaginary 'rights' they are not free." When Fullerton arrived in Louisiana he reported to Howard that "Conway will bring us . . . trouble." The latter's open endorsement of civil rights for blacks and his attempt to use the bureau "for carrying out certain political designs" contrary to the president's would hurt the bureau, he warned.[11] A few weeks later when Conway wrote Howard requesting a raise in salary, it was not only denied but was used as an excuse to ease him out of the bureau.

Concerning black education, Fullerton was quick to advise that the school tax should not be collected because of the weak economic situation in Louisiana: "The people are oppressed greatly now, and they are little able to bear it." Johnson responded with a telegram authorizing Fullerton to stop the collection. The following day Fullerton issued a circular in the name of the bureau that suspended the tax. He reported to Johnson that the suspension

10. J. Madison Wells to Johnson, July 29, September 23, 1865, Hugh Kennedy to Johnson, July 21, 1865, all in Andrew Johnson Papers, LC.

11. J. S. Fullerton to My Dear General, July 20, August 18, 1865, in Oliver Otis Howard Papers, Bowdoin College.

"will have a good effect" because continued collection would have "necessitated seizing property by force for some did not wish to pay as they thought it illegal." Fullerton further reported that members of the state legislature had assured him that school taxes paid by blacks would be used for black schools in the future. But he was also aware that the estimated legislative appropriation would not meet one quarter of the financial needs of the state's black educational system.[12]

Compounding the education problem, the bureau was losing many of the buildings it used as schoolhouses. In some parishes structures which had been white schools prior to the war were returned to the state Board of Education (white). Moreover, southern whites were petitioning for the return of their confiscated property, and increasingly their requests were being granted. The black system lost not only its source of sustaining revenue but also the buildings and the money spent on repairs. The Bureau lacked the resources to build new schools of its own.[13]

Throughout the Reconstruction period the Freedmen's Bureau tried various methods to raise revenue, but with limited success. The bureau also turned to northern aid societies with greater suc-

12. New Orleans *Tribune*, August 10, 1865; J. S. Fullerton to Johnson, October 28, November 1, 9, 1865, in Andrew Johnson Papers, LC; *House Executive Documents*, 39th Cong., 1st Sess., No. 70, p. 30. The Tax collection was the subject of an investigation. The results were inconclusive except for affirming that records were poorly kept and little money had been collected; see Report of the Commission Created to Investigate Records of the Collectors of the Tax for Colored Schools Levied by General Order 38, Department of the Gulf, December 19, 1865, in Miscellaneous Records, Assistant Commissioner, Louisiana, BRFAL; *Official Journal of the Proceedings of the Convention for the Revision and Amendment of the Constitution of the State of Louisiana* (New Orleans, 1864), 23–24.

13. John McNair to Banks, August 26, 1864, in Banks Papers, LC. John McNair to Board of Education for Freedmen, September 10, 1864; [B. Rush Plumly] to John McNair, November 28, 1864, both Letters Received, Superintendent of Education; M. J. Sheridan to Conway, October 2, 1865, Miscellaneous Records, Assistant Commissioner, Louisiana, all in BRFAL. E. M. Wheelock to C. H. Newton, May 25, 1865, in Letters Received, Provost Marshal Ascension, DGR(U). The attempt to reopen and maintain rural schools for whites was termed a failure in 1866. Needless to say, the schools were not offered to the Freedmen's Bureau. See address by Robert M. Lusher, July 30, 1866, in Robert M. Lusher Papers, LSU.

cess. Nevertheless, the system created by the wartime Board of Education could not be maintained except in New Orleans. In the fall of 1865 black students in Louisiana represented 28 percent of all black students in eleven southern states and the District of Columbia. By January, 1867, enrollment in bureau schools in Louisiana had dropped to 2,547 from a high of over 13,000 at the end of the war. The most substantial system of black education the country had witnessed to that time was effectively destroyed by Johnson and Fullerton.[14]

With Conway eased out of the bureau, Fullerton assumed the role of acting assistant commissioner in the state, and continued to chip away at the wartime programs: the school system was destroyed; an oppressive apprenticeship program replaced federally supported black orphanages and home colonies; land Conway had hoped to divide for freedmen was returned to white owners as were plantations worked by black lessees; a more militant antivagrancy campaign was instituted; and freedmen courts were abolished.[15]

Fullerton initiated the dismantling of the wartime work by issuing a statement to the freedmen. He informed them that he was replacing Conway and that things would be different. The essence of his lengthy address was that as free men they were on their own and that the bureau was not going to coddle them. They were free and had civil courts for redress. "For what more can you ask?" Commissioner Howard, the Christian soldier, announced that "General Fullerton performed his duties in accordance with his instructions."[16]

Fullerton's directives had immediate and negative effects on Louisiana's black population. On October 30, he issued a bureau circular which opened the way for stronger civil enforcement of vagrancy and apprenticeship laws, for increased violence, and for passage of the black codes. Because Louisiana law allowed freed-

14. *Report of the Joint Committee on Reconstruction*, 82; White, *Freedmen's Bureau*, 78; *House Reports*, 42nd Cong., 2nd Sess., No. 22, Pt. 1, p. 229.
15. See McFeely, *Yankee Stepfather*, 177–79, for an excellent study on that phase of the bureau's activities.
16. Shreveport *Caddo Gazette*, November 3, 1865; *House Executive Documents*, 39th Cong., 1st Sess., No. 11, p. 29.

men to testify in court and because "there [were] no legal disabilities resting upon them by reason of color," Fullerton saw no reason to continue the provost courts or bureau tribunals. Both were abolished, all pending cases were transferred to civil courts, and Conway's worst fears were realized. Throughout the fall of 1865 and into 1866, reports poured in describing discriminatory treatment of blacks in civil courts.[17] Powerless and without authority, bureau agents were able to do little to ease the troubled situation.

Continuing the process of returning the supervision of freedmen to local whites, Fullerton also sanctioned vagrancy and apprenticeship laws. In simple terms the vagrancy law allowed police to arrest unemployed blacks and then lease their services to planters to pay the fine. The apprenticeship law allowed black minors to be indentured to whites to "faithfully . . . serve and honestly and obediently do all things that a good servant ought to do . . . [in return for] . . . good and sufficient clothing, board, washing, lodging and schooling." In early October Conway had received a statement from Howard authorizing and endorsing such laws, but he did not act on it. Fullerton was not as timid. On October 31, he issued a circular which activated the state laws.[18] An unemployed black could thus be arrested for vagrancy and, while he awaited trial or served a lengthy sentence, have his children apprenticed to whites until they were eighteen to twenty-one years old.

White intimidation and violence increased significantly once the restraint provided by vigorous military agencies and federal troops was gone. The bureau was unable to curb it. Typically, the agent in Iberville Parish reported abuses by blacks and whites but concluded: "I have no power to deal with them."[19] The trend was

17. *House Executive Documents*, 39th Cong., 1st Sess., No. 70, p. 27; Reese Report, October 31, 1865, Butler to Fenno, November 6, 1865, Corrigan to Hayden, December 31, 1865, Osburn Report, April, 1866, Garretty to Gregg, April 30, 1866; Rollins Report, April 30, 1866, all in Letters Received, Assistant Commissioner, Louisiana, BRFAL.
18. Circular letter from O. O. Howard, October 4, 1865, in Letters Received, Assistant Commissioner, Louisiana; see also CXXXIV, both Louisiana, BRFAL. *House Executive Documents*, 39th Cong., 1st Sess., No. 70, p. 28.
19. F. A. Osburn Report, April 30, 1866, in Letters Received, Assistant Commissioner, Louisiana, BRFAL.

unmistakable, starting in early fall of 1865. Frequently one of the first acts of the rejuvenated parish police juries was the passage of black codes. Many times the slave codes were taken in toto except for replacing the word *slave* with *Negro* or *freedman*. The West Baton Rouge Police Jury acknowledged the abolition of slavery but emphasized the needs for "laws relative to the black population for the control of labor, [and] the punishment of crimes." It looked to the state legislature to pass the necessary acts but reported that local laws were necessary to keep the labor force in the parish. Blacks would have little say in the regulations which were "left to those who are better able to judge . . . their wants and who have a better knowledge of their character and habits from long experience and observation." Not only were blacks excluded from the process, but "emissaries and missionaries" who attempted to "create dissatisfaction and discontent among the colored population" were warned they would meet local resistance. Some parishes outlawed the sale of weapons or ammunition to blacks. Passes from "masters" again became obligatory. On Thanksgiving Day, 1865, a parish bureau agent wrote of the new laws: "Slavery is reestablished."[20]

Supplementing the parish regulations were municipal and state laws. The town of Monroe, Louisiana, prohibited blacks from entering the city limits without a pass from an employer; violators were arrested as vagrants and forced to labor ten hours without pay on the public works. All blacks were required to register their names, occupations, and employers. False registration, vagrancy, and being fired from a job were also offenses which sent blacks to the public works. The capstone of the new controls was provided by the state legislature. Acts were passed to regulate labor contracts, to prohibit blacks from carrying weapons, to prevent trespassing (designed to keep blacks on plantations), and to define and prohibit vagrancy. Any persons "tampering with, persuading, or inticing [*sic*] away, harboring, feeding, or secreting laborers,

20. West Baton Rouge PJM, August 10, 1865; W. Feleciana PJM, November 25, 1865; Frisbie to Conway, August 27, 1865, in Letters Received, Assistant Commissioner, Louisiana, BRFAL.

servants or apprentices" were liable under the new statutes. Public officials were bound to see that all females under eighteen years of age and all males under twenty-one years of age "under certain conditions" were apprenticed. In practice, the "certain conditions" translated into being black, without working parents.[21]

The New Orleans *Tribune* paid particular attention to the codes passed in Opelousas, probably the first in the state. No black was allowed within the city limits without a pass giving the reason for the visit and the time needed to complete it. Nor were blacks allowed to rent a house in town or live inside the city limits (unless a servant), to be on the streets after 10 P.M., to hold public meetings or preach without permission from the mayor, to carry fire arms, to drink alcohol or sell, barter, or exchange goods without written permission from employer or mayor. With the irony which characterized many of its editorials, the *Tribune* credited the town with an enlightened policy: allowing blacks to remain on the streets until 10 P.M., one hour later than in slavery. "This additional hour is the fruit of our victories in the field," claimed the newspaper. For some time the Creole voice had trumpeted for "one country— one law." To those who claimed the need for two sets of laws the *Tribune* prophetically warned that a united country required one set of laws for all and that having "the black law and the white law . . . will be no less than a reminiscence of slavery."[22]

A revival of the parish patrols accompanied the new laws and regulations. Active prior to occupation, the patrols were largely replaced by Federal troops during the war. As Union patrols withdrew, the night riders came to new life, and in some parishes they were more vigorous than they had been during slavery. Terrebonne Parish appropriated $3,000 to raise, equip, and pay a permanent force of twenty men and one commissioned officer. Other parishes also funded full-time patrols rather than relying on the antebellum volunteer system.[23]

21. Monroe *Intelligencer*, July 22, 1865; Michael Hahn, *Ex-Governor Hahn on Legislation Relating to Freedmen* (Washington, D.C., 1866), 1–3.

22. New Orleans *Tribune*, July 15, 19, February 23, 1865.

23. Terrebonne Parish PJM, December 9, 23, 1865; W. Feleciana Parish PJM, August 23, September 4, 1865; Jefferson Parish PJM, March 7, 1865; Militia

"The Southerners were fighting to keep the negro in his proper place," wrote a minister from Franklin. The patrols systematically disarmed freedmen in some parishes. Beatings, whippings, and murders became commonplace—by the end of 1866, over three hundred cases were reported to bureau agents in the state, a number which only suggests how widespread the violence was, since numerous cases were never reported.[24] Bureau agents in the field were overwhelmed by the changed race relations. The agent in Claiborne Parish wrote that his previous favorable reports should be disregarded—things were bad there. Incidents of abuse and ill treatment of freedmen were rising. Although his investigations frequently produced the guilty parties, the civil authorities, while promising justice for freedmen, did nothing. By late August, 1865, Caddo Parish had sixty cases of white assaults against blacks, five of them fatal. The agent complained that without troops he was powerless and that civil courts were unresponsive. Reports of fatalities came from St. Helena, Concordia, Sabine, and Natchitoches parishes, and reports of unpunished whippings and beatings were even more common.[25]

Blacks were unsafe in all their activities. In the rural parishes they were frequently harassed by patrols still in Confederate uniforms; in the cities the police were their tormentors. In New Orleans the guardians of public law broke up black religious meetings. Protests were made to an unresponsive chief of police. Twice in less than two weeks meetings of the "Society of Infant Jesus" were disrupted. In St. James Parish twenty-eight freedmen complained of being prohibited from attending church services by the patrol;

Documents, October, November, 1865, in Liddell Papers, LSU.

24. Hilton Diary (TU), September 9, 1865. Ehrlich Report, January 31, 1866; Reports of Murders, Assaults, etc., Committed on freedmen to February 20, 1867 in the State of Louisiana, both in Miscellaneous Records, Assistant Commissioner, Louisiana, BRFAL.

25. Stickney to Conway, July 2, August 26, 1865, Ehrlich to Fenno, December 19, 20, 1865, Ehrlich to Hayden, December 23, 1865, Emory to Conway, July 7, 1865, Hawes to Conway, September 5, 1865, all in Letters Received; Garretty to Gregg, April 30, 1866, Brown Report, April 30, 1866, Cromie to Mahnken, April 30, 1866, Clark to Hayden, May 30, 1866, Rollins Report, May 30, 1866, all in Letters Received, Assistant Commissioner, Louisiana, BRFAL.

the local bureau agent was asked to look into the matter but was also warned that "if this state of things continues there will be much danger of a serious disturbance here."[26]

The setbacks experienced in education and civil liberties were accompanied by similar problems in land and labor. Conway's initial announcement concerning land for 1866 did not specifically state that it would be deeded to the applicants *at that time.* Still to be worked out was the knotty question of the constitutionality of land confiscation. The 1866 agreements would be leases. It was widely understood, however, that eventually the claimants would own the land. The bureau had authority to sell it, and Howard intended it to go to blacks. But before purchases could be finalized, owners of the confiscated land had to be contacted, and those who could show "undeniable loyalty" (Howard's term) would have their property restored. Under those conditions considerable land would have been retained for distribution, and for that reason black expectations were high.

President Johnson rejected Howard's criterion. He ordered the bureau commissioner to return confiscated property to any southerner who received a pardon or took the oath of allegiance. That was a long way from "undeniable loyalty," which could have been interpreted as meaning never having aided, supported, or fought for the Confederacy. Johnson's order was transmitted to Louisiana on September 15, and by the end of the month property worth $800,000 was returned in New Orleans alone.[27] At that time freedmen had already applied for thousands of acres which they never

26. Conway to Hugh Kennedy, July 12, 1865, in Andrew Johnson Papers, LC; New Orleans *Tribune*, July 30, 1865; Pas Shepard and Twenty Seven Other Freedmen Petition to Headquarters, Freedmen's Bureau, December 25, 1865, in Letters Received, Assistant Commissioner, Louisiana, BRFAL.

27. *House Executive Documents*, 39th Cong., 1st Sess., No. 11, pp. 4–5; *House Executive Documents*, 39th Cong., 1st Sess., No. 19, pp. 1–2. Both documents are by Commissioner Howard; see also Roger Shugg, "Survival of the Plantation System in Louisiana," *Journal of Southern History*, III, 311–25 and William E. Highsmith, "Louisiana Landholding During War and Reconstruction," *Louisiana Historical Journal*, XXXVIII, 39–54 for sound evidence on how and to what extent the large plantations survived.

received. All that remained was the actual restoration. Four weeks later Fullerton arrived in Louisiana and restored almost all the plantation lands Conway had set aside for freedmen. The matter was finished.

Black expectations of developing an economic community based on agriculture were dashed by Johnson and the passive bureau. The refusal to allow freedmen to obtain land and to assist them in becoming economically secure was perhaps the greatest failure of Reconstruction. Without economic security, political power and personal liberty could never be guaranteed. During the war and immediately following it former slaves successfully leased and farmed land. They proved that individually, collectively, and at times with the aid of Creoles, they were capable of managing their lives and their land. But these efforts, too, were lost in the land restoration proclamation. A majority of the land leased by freedmen had been bureau-controlled. No doubt the same was true of the enterprises of the Freedmen's Aid Association. Funds and improvements achieved through months of hard work were gone, as was faith in the bureau and the government. Particularly in southern Louisiana, the bureau was considered a "conservative machine" after the land fiasco and Conway's removal.

The ascendancy of the Freedmen's Bureau, Governor Wells, and President Johnson also neutralized the limited gains made by plantation laborers. Governor Wells accused Conway and the bureau of being the major obstacle in restoring "order, industry and prosperity." Wells objected when Conway did away with Banks's wartime pass system, for it allowed blacks to leave plantations. Conway's bureau, charged Wells, prejudiced freedmen against their former masters. The same could not be said for Fullerton's bureau. Planters responded favorably to Fullerton's directives and circulars: "You will see by the orders from the freedman's [*sic*] bureau here that Genl. Fullerton plans for Sambo a different sorts . . . than what has been. . . . Much good must result from it." Another planter, after meeting and talking with Fullerton, reported that he "tells me that everything will be done by him . . . to help . . . with

the labor system." Planters generally acknowledged that "the change
. . . in the Freedman's Bureau gives us some hope."[28]

Without the active protection of Federal officials, the condition
of plantation laborers deteriorated. Some bureau agents attempted
to supervise contracts fairly, but they lacked the vigor and enforcement mechanisms which were available during the war. Planters,
who attempted to defraud laborers of wages under the watchful
eye of the military agencies, certainly continued trying under the
less powerful bureau.[29] It is doubtful that local white civilian courts
protected black wages in the same manner as had the bureau of
labor. The changes following Conway's removal tended also to
bring a decline in the wage system and a corresponding upsurge
of the share system. With southern whites again in control dissatis-
fied laborers lost their means of expressing grievances—in time
there were no forts, posts, picket stations, or labor depots to go to.
A mediating force in the form of Federal troops was rapidly becoming unavailable to blacks. Even when freedmen attempted the
old style agitation, local whites had authority to return them to
the plantations.

Starting with contracts for 1867, shares became the standard
means of payment, not because blacks preferred it, but because
planters did. The increase in gang sharecropping was accompanied
by the rise of plantation stores. Under the military a 10 percent
ceiling on profits discouraged the stores. Not so with the bureau,
and in 1866 planters started venturing into that lucrative field.
Illustrating the new system is the correspondence between a large
planter and his factor. The planter confided that his laborers were
dependent on him to provide them certain necessities during the
year, the costs of which would be deducted from their share of the

28. H. M. Waterson to Johnson, October 14, 1865, in Andrew Johnson Pa-
pers, LC; M. Gillis to St. J. R. Liddell, October 28, November 14, 1865; St. J. B.
Liddell to his son, November 11, 1865, all in Liddell Papers, LSU.
29. See, for examples, W. W. Tyler to L. Hayden, December 2, 1866, William
McCook to Captain Sterling, December 29, 1866, Thomas to Captain Sterling,
December 31, 1866; Sterling to O. J. Flagg, March 18, 1867, W. W. Howe to
Sterling, March 25, 1867, Fairex to Sterling, March 30, 1867, L. Corrigan to
A. F. Hayden, December 31, 1865, all in Miscellaneous Records, Assistant Com-
missioner, Louisiana, BRFAL.

crop. He acknowledged that "even if I had to borrow money to purchase these articles it would be profitable . . . as I can make twenty-five to fifty per cent on them." He was most anxious for the goods to be delivered, for "if I do not get them in my debt they will be too well off to commence work . . . until it is too late."[30]

The trend continued through the rest of the 1860s. The bureau supervised labor contracts and shares for the last time in 1868. Plantation stores and debt peonage increasingly became the order of the day for black plantation laborers in Louisiana.

The postwar Freedmen's Bureau in Louisiana did not meet even the modest standard set by the wartime military agencies. Under the direction of the bureau the incomplete and insecure advances made in the Department of the Gulf were modified, lessened, and in some instances eliminated. Although responsibility for those failures must be shared by the Freedmen's Bureau, they were, to an extent, a product of the immediate postwar political atmosphere. When authority was transferred from the Federal military to the conservative Unionist civil government of J. Madison Wells, setbacks were inevitable. Andrew Johnson's presidency had a similar effect. There was little any bureau agent could have done to prevent the loss of black leased land once Johnson decided upon restoration. Nor could the bureau have retained the school tax once Johnson decided it was not to be collected; Conway, had he remained, could not have forced its collection over objections by the president. Yet Howard, and thus the bureau, seemed to be a willing partner in many of these exercises, as William McFeely has eloquently pointed out.[31]

30. Conway supervised some of 1866's contracts, and the old system predominated in the Union parishes that year. See White, *The Freedmen's Bureau in Louisiana*, 121, on shares in 1867. See, for examples, Josiah C. Patrick to William Edwards and Co., June 6, 1866, Miscellaneous Document, both in Gay Papers, LSU; J. R. Liddell Contract with Freedmen, 1866, in Liddell Papers, LSU; Daybook, II, in Marshall Papers, LSU; Plantation Journals, VII, VIII, in McCollam Papers, UNC; Plantation Journal, XXVIII, in Thomas Butler Family Papers, LSU; Avoca Plantation Account, January–July, 1867, in J. Y. Sanders Papers, LSU, for the increase in shares and the rise of plantation stores.
31. McFeely, *Yankee Stepfather*, 289–328.

It is true that the bureau was relatively powerless in some areas and lacked the authority enjoyed by the military agencies; some of the postwar problems were thus unavoidable. But Fullerton's actions were beyond the question of inadequate authority and power—they were obvious attempts to court native whites at the expense of blacks. An agent of Conway's persuasion would have worked to save and improve, not dismantle, the imperfect military programs and policies and could have mitigated against harsher vagrancy and apprenticeship laws, infringements upon civil liberties, enforcement of black codes, and greed of dishonest employers. It is unclear how well he could have protected laborers' contracts without the use of Federal troops and the support of the national bureau, but it is doubtful that he would have become an accomplice of the planters as Fullerton did. The planters and former confederates alone gained from Conway's departure, and Howard must be faulted for Conway's removal and for Fullerton's destructive work in Louisiana.

By Christmas day, 1865, many of the broader issues concerning black Reconstruction in Louisiana were resolved. Blacks did not own the land most had hoped for and many had fought for; rather, they could look forward to little more than annual labor contracts, sharecropping, and plantation stores. Most rural blacks were living in segregated plantation cabins under the watchful eye of the white population. And, though a substantial black school system was still functioning, it would not survive another year. Creoles and freedmen had turned away from the state government, the Freedmen's Bureau, and the Johnson administration; they looked to Congress as their last potential ally. But neither "radical Reconstruction" nor its benefits—citizenship and temporary civil rights—allowed black Louisianians to move far beyond the terms set by the wartime experiment.

XI

Tragedy Revisited

c∕ͻ

In 1929, Claude Bowers labeled Reconstruction a "tragic era."[1] For Bowers, that tragedy was experienced almost exclusively by the white population of the defeated South, who allegedly suffered the oppression of subjection to northerners and former slaves. Modern Reconstruction historiography, by contrast, emphasizes how successfully postwar southern white leadership repulsed all challenges to its hegemony. The stillborn efforts to create a more democratic social and political order in the Reconstruction South, based on equal treatment of blacks, now appears to constitute the true tragedy of Reconstruction.

Nowhere was the tragedy more clearly played out—or at an earlier time—than in Civil War Louisiana. Despite the availability of land, labor, and financial resources sufficient to create a showplace of black achievement and a model for Reconstruction, Louisiana evolved in a very different manner. Federal policy there did not secure for the freedmen an equitable place in postwar southern society. It sought instead to win support of the white planter lead-

1. Claude Bowers, *The Tragic Era* (Cambridge, Mass., 1929).

ership. White accommodation—between planters and the Union military at first and between planters and Johnsonian politicians later—thwarted black aspirations and needs in wartime Louisiana and prefigured the nation's failure to meet similar needs and aspirations throughout the postwar Reconstruction South.

The old labor system had collapsed by the fall of 1862. Events and activities in Confederate Louisiana weakened the basis of the structure, and the fabric was threadbare and patched. Control of the labor force increasingly demanded the attention of rebels and Yankees alike. Slaves on Magnolia Plantation deserted the fields and erected a gallows in the quarters, while bondsmen near Shreveport feasted on roast pork, imprisoned a Confederate soldier in the stocks, and had a "perfect jubilee" despite their presence in rebel territory; black violence and theft of horses and arms increased, and runaways covered the state. Growing black assertiveness, congressional confiscation acts of the spring and summer of 1862, and Butler's wage-contract system of early fall were bench marks for changes yet to come.

The collapsed labor system only hints at the extent of wartime dislocation. Few if any parish police juries operated in the Federal part of the state. Reckless Confederate fiscal policy, military devastation, and inflated Confederate currency crippled the economy. Rebel soldiers, whose superiors insisted that no crops fall into Union hands, torched cotton and cane fields representing a year's resources. Abandoned plantations dotted the countryside, often void of both planters and slaves, who frequently left together as part of a refugee army moving westward to Texas; more often slaves joined Federal columns or worked their way to Union lines. Federal authorities confronted a chaotic situation.

Yet this chaos provided Lincoln and Union officials an opportunity to shape a new social and economic order. Particularly after emancipation, the military possessed wide authority in the Department of the Gulf, for only in purely political matters was the president an authoritative counselor. Louisiana also offered Union officials a bounty of resources: thousands of acres of confiscated cotton and cane land, over one million dollars worth of property, and 100,000 to 150,000 former slaves. The tragedy of black Reconstruction in occupied Louisiana evolved from the use and misuse of Louisiana resources and Federal authority by Banks, Lincoln, Johnson, Howard, Fullerton, and Congress.

Inadequate Federal policies clashed with black expectations for the future. Of the issues critical to the freedmen—freedom and family security, land and economic security, suffrage and equality before the law, education and social justice—only in emancipation and education did Federal actions even approximate black aspirations.

Louisiana freedmen, adamant in their desire for schools and education, if not for themselves, then certainly for their children, gave land, donated labor and materials to build necessary structures, raised funds, and purchased their own "freedmen libraries." Black children rapidly filled each newly opened school; the average student-teacher ratio in the Department reached sixty to one. With equal enthusiasm, some white military officials and civilians supported black education despite local objections and resistance. Banks converted confiscated buildings into schools, gave the Board of Education for Freedmen taxing power, helped finance the system from the Cotton and Corps d'Afrique Funds, and insisted that whites house rural teachers. The blend of black aspirations and Federal authority and resources left upwards of 50,000 black Louisianians reading and writing by the end of the war.

The educational successes accentuate the failures in land and labor. Black agricultural enterprises (both individual and communal) demonstrated the freedmen's desire and ability to work the land without white supervision, and the former slaves' response to Conway's land circular of August, 1865, clearly defined black aspiration for land ownership. Freedmen Aid Association programs might have encouraged Union officials to endorse those and similar ventures if Union policy genuinely sought to aid the freedmen. Had Banks and Conway followed the initiative of Louisiana's black leaders and agricultural laborers, the state could well have been a model for black economic independence in the new South.

But few Union officials favored such fundamental economic

changes. In general, they strove to limit the extensive economic rearrangements sure to result from emancipation. More often than not they worked to preserve and restore systems of property holding and agricultural production based on the economic subordination of blacks. Certainly, neither military nor civilian officials displayed any inclination to revolutionize the defeated South.

The Civil War was expensive, and the Federal government, eager to defray costs whenever possible, considered abandoned and confiscated plantations as sources of revenue, not opportunities for agricultural or social experimentation. Louisiana blacks seldom had access to those plantation lands, for they lacked the resources necessary to convince Treasury officials they could work them profitably. Because restoration of the plantation system demanded cheap, abundant labor—which in wartime Louisiana meant the freedmen—widespread black land ownership or leasing would have hampered if not prevented the rejuvenation of white-owned plantations by draining the labor supply and producing dissatisfaction among those workers remaining on white plantations. Black response to the land circular suggests that most freedmen preferred working the land for their own benefit, rather than working under Banks's labor system. Lacking that alternative, and given the central position cheap labor played in reviving the plantation economy, Louisiana freedmen reluctantly were incorporated into the contract-labor system.

Political Reconstruction was closely bound to economic recovery and the contract-labor system. In a planter-controlled state such as Louisiana, bringing the state back into the republic meant accommodating the planter leadership; that was particularly true after 1863. There was little possibility of successfully courting the planters without a concerted effort at restoring the economic basis of their power. Political Reconstruction demanded conservative economic policies.

While the failure to reconstruct Louisiana resulted primarily from economic and political policies designed to accommodate planter leadership, the venality, self-aggrandizement, and racism of some Union officials provided additional obstacles to reform. A number of individuals gained personally from their work in the Department of the Gulf. Probably Hubbs and possibly George Hanks and some provost marshals accepted bribes, kickbacks, and embezzled funds. Flanders used his position and the situation to obtain greater authority, influence, and political power. Banks, timid and cautious, kept one eye on opinions in the North and one on his political future and hesitated to do anything to ruffle either.

The radical attitudes of men like Butler, Banks, Fullerton, Johnson, and even Conway and Phelps substantially predetermined the tragedy of wartime Louisiana. There is no evidence to suggest that any of the major white protagonists in the Department of the Gulf related to the freedmen on a basis of equality. Most believed the former slaves incapable of functioning independently in a free, white society. Butler proposed that runaways usually were "vicious and unthrifty types" and that blacks feared firearms. Phelps, despite his early perceptions on the future of the war and slavery and his overt abolitionist actions, saw no place for blacks in America, thought their continued presence harmful to the nation, and supported African colonization while opposing the Fourteenth Amendment. Butler and Phelps only haltingly supported black liberation in any form beyond emancipation.

Banks and Conway, closer to the focus of power, authority, and the decision-making apparatus, were similarly troubled. The Massachusetts general initially believed that black troops should serve as laborers, not as line soldiers, and he gradually pushed black officers out of the service. His defense of the free-labor system abounds with paternalism and racism. Although he paid lip service to blacks eventually owning land, he refused to acknowledge objections to the contract program and repeatedly emphasized, without qualification, the advantages of his system over slavery: emancipation, wages, education, family security, and access to the courts. Banks rejected suggestions that those advances were incomplete or insecure or that the compulsory labor program left blacks somewhat short of full freedom.

Conway, like Banks, failed to understand that emancipation from bondage did not in fact make the former slaves free men and women; he too seemed willing to let black Louisianians linger somewhere between the two stations. When first coming to the labor bureau, Conway doubted the former slaves' abilities to govern their own lives. His 1864 *Report of the Condition of Freedmen in the Department of the Gulf* warned that "idleness would have resulted in their ruin. . . . Therefore it became necessary to manage them." Describing the labor program as "strict and even severe . . . in keeping them at their places of employment and in closely regulating their conduct," Conway assumed that the freedmen could not or would not work except in a supervised environment structured by whites.

By mid-1865, Conway changed many of his attitudes. His close association with the freedmen and the persuasion of the *Tribune* —which came to view the portly New York minister as a friend, albeit a friend who needed constant watching, cajoling, and sometimes harsh criticism—turned his head. Conway now considered the free-labor system temporary (as had most of the black leadership from the start); he recommended abolition of the pass system and publicly endorsed black suffrage. Convinced that the landholding pattern of large plantations would soon disappear, Conway believed that blacks should benefit from the change. He energetically worked for black land leases for 1866. Belatedly, the "business-like preacher" became aware of the possibilities for reform in Louisiana.

Conway's conversion and subsequent ousting from the Freedmen's Bureau (the two were closely related) reflected his deviation from the direction of Federal policy. Under the impetus of Andrew Johnson that policy had become even more conservative. It encompassed the transfer of the military bureau of labor to the Freedmen's Bureau, the weak leadership of O. O. Howard, and the return of Louisiana to the civilian government of J. Madison Wells. Fullerton's trip marked the implementation of Johnsonian policies in Louisiana. In a few short days he dulled the edges of the wartime programs in an attempt to appease Wells and Louisiana planters.

This policy of accommodation had serious consequences for Louisiana blacks. The alliance between Louisiana planters and

Washington politicians of the Johnsonian persuasion endangered the limited gains made by blacks despite native white opposition. Changes which accompanied the Johnsonian reaction in Louisiana demonstrated ably—and early—the danger which white reconciliation posed for the freedmen. The limited achievements of the wartime programs—although incomplete and insecure and unsupported by a forceful Union policy for black advances—look impressive when juxtaposed with the civil programs which emerged during Wells's administration. Military tribunals provided more justice for blacks than did southern white courts; scattered and underfinanced military orphanages and home colonies administered more sensitive social services to idle, ill, and underaged blacks than did state apprenticeship and vagrancy laws; military-regulated labor contracts commanded more economic security than did those which followed; the military education program disintegrated when transferred to the state government.

The policy of reconciliation was not, of course, the exclusive handiwork of Johnson and Wells. White accommodation at black expense began with occupation (when Butler vowed to protect all rights of property) and continued throughout the war and Reconstruction. Louisiana programs and policies which controlled free labor, revived the plantation economy, and sought political reunion were canopied by blue and gray cooperation.

The utility of Louisiana programs and policies was recognized outside the state even before the war ended. When Major General Lorenzo Thomas issued regulations for the "leasing of plantations . . . and the management of the Freedmen thereon" in the rich plantation area of the Mississippi Valley in March, 1864, he looked down the Mississippi River for guidance—"The rules adopted by Major-General Banks, in the Department of the Gulf, have . . . been taken as a basis." The Louisiana model permeated the Mississippi regulations: army recruiters could not enlist agricultural laborers, black soldiers needed passes to visit plantations, provost marshals mediated between management and labor while sitting as judges in freedmen courts; and regulations governing annual labor contracts, clothing, food, housing, wages, garden plots, corporal punishment, and black education duplicated Banks's free-labor program. Thomas aped General Order 23 down to and including the pass system.[2] One scholar has suggested that Banks's program was at work not only in Mississippi but also in parts of Alabama, Florida, and Georgia during the interim period from the end of the war to the time Freedmen's Bureau agents assumed local control.[3]

Federal policy makers (such as Thomas) looked to the Pelican State because the Louisiana experiment met postwar needs and realities. The Department of the Gulf, more than any other southern point controlled by the Union during the war, provided a realistic environment to devise Reconstruction policy and programs. The Louisiana situation was not the most amiable, however. In the Sea Islands of South Carolina, by contrast, the absence of southern whites (who fled before occupation), facilitated social and economic experimentation but made wartime Reconstruction there a somewhat artificial endeavor. White accommodation and reunion politics, without southern planters, were muted affairs. The rehearsal for Reconstruction in the Sea Islands so splendidly portrayed by Willie Lee Rose, offered few clues about regaining the loyalty of southern whites, especially the planter class. It therefore held less relevance for postwar policy makers than the Louisiana experiment, which caught southern planters, former slaves, Federal agencies, and politicians (black, blue, and gray) playing out Reconstruction roles.

Reconstruction in the fallen Confederacy has deja vu qualities when compared to Banks's Louisiana. The policies, the machinery, and the cast of characters at work throughout the Reconstruction South are familiar from occupied Louisiana. During the war, Louisiana planters wheedled concessions for controlling laborers and reviving plantations—they helped shape the contraband policy, the free-labor system, the black educational system, and the draft ex-

2. General Order 9, Military Division of Mississippi, March 11, 1864, Mississippi, BRFAL.
3. John B. Myers, "Black Human Capital: The Freedmen and the Reconstruction of Labor in Alabama, 1860–1880" (Ph.D. dissertation, Florida State University, 1974), 81–85.

emptions for plantation laborers—and similar accommodations emerged throughout the South by the end of Reconstruction. Lincoln tested his Reconstruction policy in Louisiana where native white southerners, military officers, and Federal officials struggled to bring the state back into the Union, a process which consumed the South for a decade. In wartime Louisiana, Federal agencies mediated social and economic race relations, established black schools, administered labor contracts and supervised freedmen courts, all predating the work of the Freedmen's Bureau.

But the severe limits on black advancements and liberties in wartime Louisiana demonstrated early the conservative predisposition of Federal Reconstruction policy makers. Only the subsequent quarrel between a northern Congress and a southern president, which originated from power rivalry more than an abstract Republican commitment to black rights, prompted the abortive effort to align blue and black at the expense of gray, known as Radical Reconstruction. Arranged on the basis of expediency more than principle, and entered into rather halfheartedly by the more powerful partner, the frail alliance of Radical Reconstruction proved ephemeral. Its originators compromised it from the start by continuing to woo southern whites in the hopes of voluntary cooperation and support. Radical Reconstruction, while promising black political and civil rights, actually contemplated no fundamental change in the economic role played by blacks. Accommodation between blue and gray at the expense of black—following the tragic script first acted out in wartime Louisiana—became the pattern in the South by the end of Reconstruction.

An Essay on Sources

This is not an all-inclusive essay on the sources used in preparing this study. Rather, it is a selective note referring predominantly to secondary works which covered some of the same historical ground that I have or provided significant background or peripheral material. It also provides an opportunity to discuss the relationship of this study to available secondary works, and occasionally to note which manuscript sources suggested a reevaluation of prevailing interpretations.

Literature on black labor in Louisiana from slavery through Reconstruction is readily available. Most satisfying in this aspect, as in others, are two classic studies deserving special mention: W. E. B. DuBois' *Black Reconstruction in America, 1860–1880* (New York, 1935) and Bell I. Wiley's *Southern Negroes, 1861–1865* (New Haven, 1938). Wiley's perceptive analysis of the war years and DuBois' emphasis on Louisiana and the freedmen in Reconstruction started my thinking on the topic. Their influence is evident throughout.

Louisiana slaves as laborers are best discussed by Joe Gray Taylor, *Negro Slavery in Louisiana* (Baton Rouge, 1963). Taylor can be supplemented by V. Alton Moody, *Slavery on Louisiana Sugar Plantations* (New Orleans, 1924), which has helpful discussions on the mechanics of sugar production and the labor requirements of that phase of plantation life. Any discussion of Louisiana slavery must include Henry Bibb's *Narrative of the Life*

209

of Henry Bibb, an American Slave (New York, 1849) and the magnificent slave narrative of Soloman Northrup, *Twelve Years a Slave* (Baton Rouge, 1968), edited by Sue Eakin and Joseph Logsdon.

New Orleans slavery is best treated by Charles Herman Woessner, "New Orleans, 1840–1860: A Study of Urban Slavery" (M.A. thesis, Louisiana State University, 1967). Woessner's thesis is an impressive reevaluation of Richard Wade's *Slavery in the Cities: The South, 1820–1860* (New York, 1964). Continuing on the city, black life during war and Reconstruction is superbly represented by John W. Blassingame, *Black New Orleans, 1860–1880* (Chicago, 1973). Rich in its treatment of social, economic, and intellectual life, as well as race relations, that study unravels many of the mysteries and myths surrounding the Crescent City and its residents. This study touches base with *Black New Orleans* on a number of significant issues.

Several books and articles carry black labor through the war years and into early Reconstruction. Charles P. Roland has two pieces—"Difficulties of Civil War Sugar Planting in Louisiana," *Louisiana Historical Quarterly*, XXXVIII, 40–62, and *Louisiana Sugar Plantations During the American Civil War* (Leiden, Netherlands, 1957)—in which the author insists that the problem of free labor and economic recovery was due largely to the refusal of blacks to work "efficiently."

J. Carlyle Sitterson in his *Sugar Country: The Cane Sugar Industry in the South, 1753–1950* (Lexington, 1953) and in "The Transition from Slave to Free Economy on the William J. Minor Plantations," *Agricultural History*, XVII, 216–24, also proposes that "the refusal of the freedmen to work with prewar efficiency further reduced the productivity of the labor force." And whereas Sitterson does discuss other problems hampering agricultural recovery, free-black labor gets some tough press from him as well as from Roland and others such as Joe Gray Taylor. In "Slavery in Louisiana during the Civil War " *Louisiana History*, VIII, 27–33, Taylor suggests that slavery disintegrated during the war but insists that black labor continued to be "disorganized and inefficient" throughout Reconstruction.

A number of M.A. theses—Gladys Stella Bringer, "Transition from Slave to Free Labor in Louisiana after the Civil War" (Tulane University, 1927); R. R. Constantine, "The Louisiana 'Black Code' Legislation of 1865" (Louisiana State University, 1956); Dorothy M. Baker, "An Economic Survey of New Orleans During the Civil War and Reconstruction" (Tulane University, 1942); Isabella Dorothy Lois Ellis, "The Transition from Slave Labor to Free Labor with Special Reference to Louisiana" (Louisiana State University, 1932)—generally find little value in free-black labor.

The contradiction between the conclusions of this study and those of many of the sources discussed above are as real as they appear to be. They are not, however, without some basis for explanation. Most of the available secondary works relied heavily on southern white sources. For example, Sitterson, Roland, and Wiley (particularly in his "Vicissitudes of Early Reconstruction Farming in the Lower Mississippi Valley," *Journal of Southern History*, III, 441–52), essentially depend upon two sets of plantation records for their conclusions about free-labor efficiency: the William J. Minor Papers and the William T. Palfrey Family Papers, both at the Louisiana State University Archives. And well they should use these plantation records, for they are extensive and complete; this study likewise profited from them. But they, like other plantation sources, however exceptional, describe events from the planters' side of the veranda. They tell the story from the particular perspective of the slaveholders who during the occupation period saw their way of life disappearing.

A different type of agricultural society emerges from reading the voluminous records of the Department of the Gulf and those of the Bureau of Refugees, Freedmen and Abandoned Lands, both in the National Archives. Moreover, the New Orleans *Tribune*, which clearly stands as an extraordinary document of nineteenth-century Afro-American history, tells of a different free-labor population. And if I have tended to rely upon the *Tribune* in instances of conflicting testimony that is because the newspaper's editors said one hundred years ago what many historians have started to say in recent years about the black experience in Civil War and Reconstruction.

A number of more current studies deal in whole, or part, with Louisiana's black labor population. Most significant and thorough is Louis S. Gerteis' *From Contraband to Freedmen: Federal Policy toward Southern Blacks, 1861–1865* (Westport, Conn., 1973). In his study of labor policies of the Union army in the occupied South, Gerteis found Banks's system the most restrictive. We are in agreement that Federal policy preempted the possibilities of any real reform. James McPherson, *The Struggle for Equality: The Abolitionist and the Negro in the Civil War and Reconstruction* (Princeton, 1964), treats the free-labor system and details its divisive effect among northern abolitionists. Gerteis and McPherson also suggest that the free-labor system was not quite what the planters or the military said it was.

Closely tied to the quality of labor was the debate over land for the freedmen. Roger W. Shugg, "Survival of the Plantation System in Louisiana," *Journal of Southern History*, III, 311–25, and William E. Highsmith, "Louisiana Landholding During War and Reconstruction," *Louisiana Historical Quarterly*, XXXVIII, 39–54, both document statistically not only the survival of the plantation system but the 100 percent increase of 100 to 500-acre places from 1860 to 1880. More significantly, Shugg concludes that the plantations survived only after a long and bitter struggle and that they were able to survive only through "the subordination of freedmen to peonage."

Since LaWanda Cox's pioneer work, "The Promise of Land for the Freedmen," *Mississippi Valley Historical Review*, XLV, 413–40, many scholars have looked toward the unobtained land as the ultimate failure of black Reconstruction. More recently Herman Belz, "The New Orthodoxy in Reconstruction Historiography," *Reviews in American History*, I, 106–13, and Richard O. Curry, "The Civil War and Reconstruction, 1861–1877: A Critical Overview of Recent Trends and Interpretations," *Civil War History*,

XXX, 215–38, have suggested that the land confiscation issue is overplayed by historians. Belz concludes that it is "unhistorical" to believe that land redistribution would have produced a solution to the problems of Reconstruction. While certainly not prepared to argue that land would take on such magical qualities, I propose, upon the evidence of the *Tribune* and the black response to Conway's Land Circular, that blacks' land expectations were high, that the traditional argument of blacks' needing economic security to guarantee social and political security is still valid, and that independent land ownership was necessary to assist in the formation of a black community in which homes, families, schools, and jobs —as well as land—might better withstand white tamperings.

The free-labor system, the survival of large plantations, and the failure of the freedmen to get land were equal legs of a tripod. The concerted effort made by military types and later by planters to revive and maintain the plantation economy preempted any real possibility of black land ownership. For a sure way of losing the peon-laborers (described as so essential by Shugg) would have been to make land of their own available to them.

The role of the Freedmen's Bureau in Louisiana can be surveyed from three perspectives. An adequate factual overview, but troubled by aged and aggressive stereotypes, is John Cornelius Englesman, "The Freedmen's Bureau of Louisiana," *Louisiana Historical Quarterly*, XXXII, 145–224. More thorough but only slightly more satisfying in his treatment of the freedmen and black aspirations and contributions, is Howard A. White, *The Freedmen's Bureau in Louisiana* (Baton Rouge, 1970). The best study on the bureau as it relates to the tragedy in Louisiana is William McFeely, *Yankee Stepfather: General O. O. Howard and the Freedmen* (New York, 1970). Stressing the failure of Howard and the bureau as the failure of the nation, he tells a provocative and indispensable story.

The smooth transition from the wartime bureaus of Conway and Banks to the peacetime Freedmen's Bureau is touched upon by Thomas May, "Continuity and Change in the Labor Program of the Union Army and the Freedmen's Bureau," *Civil War History*,

XVII, 245–54. May also suggests the inability, or reluctance, or both, of local bureau agents to significantly assist the freedmen beyond annual labor contracts in his article "The Freedmen's Bureau at the Local Level: A Study of a Louisiana Agent," *Louisiana History*, IX, 5–20. The present study, of course, concurs with May's suggestion of continuity between the military and the bureau agencies in Louisiana and looks to McFeely's work for support in the contention that the bureau was even less responsive to black needs than were the wartime agencies.

Wiley, White, and Englesman give the outlines of black education during war and early Reconstruction, but the struggles during the war period can best be seen in the Department of the Gulf Records and in the American Missionary Association Papers. The Association papers are crucial to understanding the friction and hostility between civilian teachers and the military in Louisiana. The best general study of the AMA is Richard Bryant Drake, "The American Missionary Association and the Southern Negro, 1861–1868" (Ph.D. dissertation, Emory University, 1957), although Drake is sparse on this aspect of the Association's troubles. Blassingame's *Black New Orleans* covers wartime education and is the best source for following that topic through Reconstruction. Helpful for the prewar period is Betty Potter, "The History of Negro Education in Louisiana," *Louisiana Historical Quarterly*, XXV, 728–821.

Blassingame and Wiley also treat the black military experience in Louisiana. And nothing can touch Mary F. Berry's "Negro Troops in Blue and Gray: The Louisiana Native Guard, 1861–1863," *Louisiana History*, VIII, 165–90, for information on who the free-black soldiers were. Donald E. Everett, "Ben Butler and the Louisiana Native Guards, 1861–1862," *Journal of Southern History*, XXIV, 202–17, delineates that stormy relationship. "The Union Army as an Educational Institution for Negroes, 1862–1865," *Journal of Negro Education*, XXXIV, 152–59, and Dudley T. Cornish, "The Union Army as a Training School for Negroes," *Journal of Negro History*, XXXVII, 368–82, discuss that aspect of black army life. The Freedmen's Bureau Records, the

Department of the Gulf Records, and the AMA Papers have additional information on military education. Those collections and the *Tribune* provide information on the harsh recruitment methods, the problems of military families, and the essentially ambivalent relationship between Louisiana's blacks and the military.

A number of pieces deal with free blacks in Louisiana: James E. Winston, "The Free Negro in New Orleans, 1803–1860," *Louisiana Historical Quarterly*, XXI, 1075–85; Annie Lee Stahl, "The Free Negro in Ante-Bellum Louisiana," *Louisiana Historical Quarterly*, XXV, 300–396; and, most thorough, H. E. Sterkx, *The Free Negro in Ante-Bellum Louisiana* (Rutherford, N.J., 1972). Three sources provide some biographical information: Rodolphe L. Desdunes, *Nos hommes et notre histoire* (Montreal, 1911) and A. E. Perkins (ed.), *Who's Who in Colored Louisiana* (New Orleans, 1930). Particularly impressive is David Rankin's "The Origins of Black Leadership in New Orleans During Reconstruction," *Journal of Southern History*, XL, 417–40.

Louisiana politics has received considerable attention from Willie M. Caskey, *Secession and Restoration of Louisiana* (Baton Rouge, 1938), John Rose Ficklen, *History of Reconstruction in Louisiana Through 1868* (Gloucester, Mass., 1910), and Ella Lonn, *Reconstruction in Louisiana After 1868* (New York, 1918). Although hampered by conservative antinorthern and antiblack attitudes, these studies are helpful for the general outline of politics. For different reasons our overall assessment of Lincoln's and Banks's roles are compatible. Standing alone as a source for black involvement in wartime politics is Donald E. Everett, "Demands of the New Orleans Free Colored Population for Political Equality, 1862–1865," *Louisiana Historical Quarterly*, XXXVIII, 43–64, and his "Free Persons of Color in New Orleans, 1803–1865" (Ph.D. dissertation, Tulane University, 1952).

Amos E. Simpson and Vaughn Baker, "Michael Hahn: Steady Patriot," *Louisiana History*, XIII, 229–52, has helpful but adoring information on Banks's gubernatorial candidate; and Francis Byers Hams, "Henry Clay Warmoth, Reconstruction Governor of Louisiana," *Louisiana Historical Quarterly*, XXX, 521–53, provides similar information, with considerably less adoration, on the controversial Warmoth. More helpful is Philip D. Uzee, "The Beginnings of the Lousiana Republican Party," *Louisiana History,* XII, 197–211, but Uzee misunderstands the crucial 1863 phase which ends in December with Lincoln and Banks abandoning the radicals, black and white. Ludwell H. Johnson's "Lincoln and Equal Rights: A Reply," *Civil War History,* XIII, 66–73, is a provocative piece which correctly proposes that the Hahn government was Banks's creation, and that Lincoln's acts in Louisiana were, first and last, politically motivated. Louis Gerteis, "Salmon P. Chase, Radicalism and the Politics of Emancipation, 1861–1864," *Journal of American History,* LX, 42–62, is essential to understanding crucial Washington events.

James Peyton McCrary's study, "Moderation in a Revolutionary World: Lincoln and the Failure of Reconstruction in Louisiana" (Ph.D. dissertation, Princeton University, 1972), splendidly details the political failure in Louisiana. Covering the same manuscript sources—Lincoln, Banks, Chase, and Butler Papers in the Library of Congress, the Chase Papers in the Historical Society of Pennsylvania, the Thomas J. Durant Papers and the Minutes of Union Association of Jefferson and Orleans Parish in the New York Historical Society—the present study and McCrary's depart from the traditional interpretation of wartime politics by reappraising the radicals (particularly Durant) and by viewing Lincoln's and Banks's involvement as a conservative influence, rather than radical. Essential also are the George F. Shepley Papers at the Maine Historical Society, which provide information not found elsewhere, and the New Orleans *Tribune,* which has important information of the black political reaction.

Bibliography

MANUSCRIPTS

BOWDOIN COLLEGE LIBRARY, BRUNSWICK, MAINE

Howard, Oliver Otis. Papers.

DILLARD UNIVERSITY, AMISTAD RESEARCH CENTER, NEW ORLEANS

American Missionary Association Papers.

HARVARD UNIVERSITY, HOUGHTON LIBRARY, CAMBRIDGE, MASS.

Sumner, Charles. Papers.

HISTORICAL SOCIETY OF PENNSYLVANIA, PHILADELPHIA

Chase, Salmon P. Papers.

LIBRARY OF CONGRESS, WASHINGTON, D.C.

Ayers, George R. Papers.
Banks, Nathaniel P. Papers.
Bennett, James Gordon. Papers.
Butler, Benjamin F. Papers.
Chase, Salmon P. Papers.
Covode, John. Papers.
Dawes, Henry L. Papers.
Denison, George. Papers.

Johnson, Andrew. Papers.
Limongi, Felix. Papers.
Reid, Whitlaw. Papers.
Stanton, Edwin M. Papers.
Stevens, Thaddeus. Papers.
Wade, Benjamin. Papers.

LOUISIANA STATE UNIVERSITY DEPARTMENT OF ARCHIVES,
BATON ROUGE

Banks, Nathaniel P. Papers.
Batchler, Albert. Papers.
Bond, Priscilla M. Papers.
Bowman, James P., and Family. Papers.
Brent, Rosella Kenner. Papers.
Bringier, Louis A., and Family. Papers.
Buhler Family Papers.
Butler, Thomas, and Family. Papers.
Causey, R. J. Papers.
Church Archives. Historical Records Survey, Works Project
    Administration.
Comstock, Cyrus B. Papers.
Cousinard, E. Papers.
Evens, Nathaniel, and Family. Papers.
Flanders, Benjamin F. Papers.
Gay, Edward J., and Family. Papers.
Guess, George W. Papers.
Gurley, John W. Papers.
Hahn, Michael. Papers.
Hale, William George. Papers.
Harding, S. Diary.
Heard, A. J. Papers.
Hepzibah Baptist Church Papers.
Jarrard, Simon G. Papers.
Johnson, Henry. Papers.
King, William F. Papers.
Landry, Severin. Papers
Lauve, Gustave. Diary.
LeBlanc Family Papers.
Liddell, Moses and St. John Richardson. Papers.

Lusher, Robert M. Papers.
Marshall, George, and Family. Papers.
Marston, Henry W., and Family. Papers.
Miller, Thomas D. Papers.
Minor, William J. Papers.
Moore, Thomas O. Papers.
Morse, E. A. Papers.
Newell, Robert. Papers.
Palfrey Family Papers.
Palfrey, William T. Papers.
Polk, H. W. Papers.
Pugh, Alexander F. Papers.
Pugh, William W. Papers.
Risley, Alice Cary. Diary.
Robinson, Henri. Papers.
Sanders, Jared Y., and Family. Papers.
Slauson, Daniel D. Papers.
Soloman, Clara. Diary.
Smith, J. D. Papers.
Spears, Ann E. Papers.
Stone, Kate. Diary.
Taliaferro, James G. Papers.
Tyson, Robert A. Diary.
Weeks, David, and Family. Papers.
Wharton, E. C. Papers.
Whitney, William H. Papers.
Zackman, William. Papers.

MAINE HISTORICAL SOCIETY LIBRARY, PORTLAND

Barnard, Charles. Papers.
Calderwood, Eben S. Papers.
Joyce, Lawrence P. Papers.
Shepley, George F. Papers.

NATIONAL ARCHIVES, WASHINGTON, D.C.

Bureau of Refugees, Freedmen and Abandoned Lands Records. Record
    Group 105.

Civil War Special Agents Treasury Department Records. Record Group 366.
Customs Bureau Special Agents Records. Record Group 36.
Department of the Gulf Records (Union). Record Group 393.
General Papers, Adjutant General Office Records. Record Group 94.
Inspector General Office Records. Record Group 159.

NEW ORLEANS PUBLIC LIBRARY, NEW ORLEANS

Register of Free Colored Persons Entitled to Remain in the State, 1840–1864.

NEW YORK HISTORICAL SOCIETY LIBRARY, NEW YORK

Durant, Thomas. Papers.
Journal of a Louisiana Rebel.
Reports of the General Committee of the Union Association in New Orleans and Jefferson, Louisiana.
Rider, Claudius W. Diary.
Sentell, Edward H. Diary.
Sentell Family Papers.
Ullman, Daniel. Papers.
Wright, Howard D. Papers.

NEW YORK PUBLIC LIBRARY, NEW YORK

Phelps, John W. Papers.

TULANE UNIVERSITY, HOWARD-TILTON MEMORIAL LIBRARY, NEW ORLEANS

Acklen Family Papers.
Baker, Jacob. Papers.
Bell, George. Papers.
Breaux, G. A. Diary.
Cummings-Black Family Papers.
Department of the Gulf Records (Confederate).
Ferry, Alexis. Papers.
Gammons, T. E. Papers.
Hilton, The Reverend Charles Whitehorn. Diary.
McCall, Henry. Papers.

Ogden, Henry D. Papers.
Remington, Ambert O. Papers.
Shepley, George F. Papers.

UNIVERSITY OF NORTH CAROLINA,
SOUTHERN HISTORICAL COLLECTION, CHAPEL HILL

Bayside Plantation Papers.
Carmouche, Annie Jeter. Papers.
Cheatham, Benjamin F. Papers.
Fales, Silas Everett. Papers.
Gibson-Humphreys Family Papers.
Guion Family Papers.
Hawes, Maria Southgate. Diary.
Howard, Charles, and Family. Papers.
Johnson, Sarah. Papers.
Kean-Prescott Family Papers.
Kirby-Smith, Edmund. Papers.
Logan, George. Papers.
McCollam, Andrew. Papers.
Perkins, John Jr. Papers.
Power, Louise Ellen. Diary.
Prudhomme, Phanor. Papers.
Raymond, Clara Compton. Papers.
Rivers, Mary E. Diary.
Rost Hermitage Plantation Papers.
St. Rosalia Plantation Records.
Stark, Theodore O. Papers.
Thompson, Lewis. Papers.
Wadley, Sarah L. Diary.
Warmoth, Henry Clay. Papers.
White, Munsel. Papers.

NEWSPAPERS

Alexandria *Constitutional*
Baton Rouge *Daily News*
Boston *Journal*
Caddo *Gazette*
Greensburg *Imperial*

Liberator
Monroe *Intelligencer*
Monroe *Weekly Telegraph*
Natchitoches *Union*
National Anti-Slavery Standard
New Orleans *Bee*
New Orleans *Black Republican*
New Orleans *Daily Southern Star*
New Orleans *L'Union*
New Orleans *National Advocate*
New Orleans *Times*
New Orleans *Daily Picayune*
New Orleans *Tribune*
New Orleans *Weekly Crescent*
Opelousas *Patriot*
Pointe Coupee *Democrat*
Shreveport *News*
Shreveport *Semi-Weekly News*
West Baton Rouge *Sugar Planter*

JOURNALS

American Missionary Magazine, 1862–1864
De Bow's Review, 1859–1867

DOCUMENTS

FEDERAL

U.S. Bureau of the Census, *Eighth Return.*
U.S. *House Executive Documents.* 39th Congress, 1st Session, No. 11. *Report of the Commissioner of the Bureau of Refugees, Freedmen and Abandoned Lands, November, 1865.*
U.S. *House Executive Documents.* 39th Congress, 1st Session, No. 19.
U.S. *House Executive Documents.* 39th Congress, 1st Session, No. 70.
U.S. *House Reports.* 39th Congress, 2nd Session, No. 16.
U.S. *House Reports.* 39th Congress, 1st Session, No. 30. *Report of the Joint Committee on Reconstruction.*

U.S. House Reports. 42nd Congress, 2nd Session, No. 22, Part 1. *Report of the Joint Select Committee to Inquire into the Condition of Affairs in the Late Insurrectionary States.*

STATE

Acts Passed by the Twenty-Seventh Legislature of the State of Louisiana in Extra Session at Opelousas, December, 1862–January, 1863. Natchitoches, 1864.
Acts Passed by the Sixth Legislature of the State of Louisiana at Its Extra Session Held in the City of Shreveport on the 4th of May, 1863. Shreveport, 1863.
Annual Message of Governor Henry Watkins Allen to the Legislature of the State of Louisiana, January, 1865. Shreveport, 1865.
Annual Report of the Auditor of Public Accounts of the Legislature of the State of Louisiana, January, 1860. Baton Rouge, 1860.
Annual Report of the Auditor of Public Accounts to the General Assembly of the State of Louisiana. Baton Rouge, 1861.
Official Journal of the Proceedings of the Convention for the Revision and Amendment of the Constitution of the State of Louisiana. New Orleans, 1864.
Rapport Annull de l'Auditeur des Comptes Publics, a le Legislature l'Etate de la Louisiane, Janvier, 1861. Baton Rouge, 1861.
Report to the Board of Control of the Louisiana Penitentiary to the General Assembly. Baton Rouge, 1859.

PARISH

Avoyelles Parish Police Jury Minutes
Bienville Parish Police Jury Minutes
Caddo Parish Police Jury Minutes
Caldwell Parish Police Jury Minutes
Franklin Parish Police Jury Minutes
Iberville Parish Police Jury Minutes
Lafayette Parish Police Jury Minutes
Pointe Coupee Parish Police Jury Minutes
St. Charles Parish Police Jury Minutes
West Baton Rouge Parish Police Jury Minutes
West Feleciana Parish Police Jury Minutes

PAMPHLETS

Adderman, J. M. *Reminiscences of Two Years*. Providence, 1866.
Banks, Nathaniel P. *Emancipated Labor in Louisiana*. New York, 1865.
Chickering, Thomas E. *Diary of Forty-First Regiment Infantry Massachusetts Volunteers*. Boston, 1863.
Conway, Thomas W. *Final Report of the Bureau of Negro Labor*. New Orleans, 1865.
————. *Report of the Condition of Freedmen in the Department of the Gulf in 1864*. New Orleans, 1864.
Cutler, R. King. *Address of Hon. R. King Cutler, United States Senator of Louisiana to the Citizens of the State of Louisiana*. Np., n.d.
Douglas, Frederick. *Equality of All Men Before the Law and Defended*. Boston, 1865.
General Orders of the United States Army, Department of the Gulf, 1863–1864. N.p., n.d.
Hahn, Michael. *Ex-Governor Hahn on Louisiana Legislation Relating to Freedmen*. Washington, D.C., 1866.
————. *Inaugural Address of Michael Hahn, Governor of the State of Louisiana, Delivered at New Orleans, March 4, 1864*. N.p., n.d.
Hayes, D. E. *A Thrilling Narrative of the Suffering of Union Refugees and the Massacre of the Martyrs of Liberty of Western Louisiana*. Washington, D.C., 1866.
Luber, Francis. *Memoir of the Military Use of Colored Persons that Come to Our Armies for Support or Protection*. N.p., n.d.
Observations on the Present Condition of Louisiana. N.p., n.d.
Proceedings of the Convention of the Republican Party of Louisiana, New Orleans, 1865.
Wheelock, Edwin Miller. *Special Report of the Board of Education for Freedmen*. New Orleans, 1864.

ARTICLES

PRIMARY

Collins, Robert. "Essay on the Management of Slaves." *De Bow's Review*, XXXIII, 154–57.
Fitzhugh, George. "The Negro Imbroglia." *De Bow's Review*, III, 518–22.
"Journal of the War." *De Bow's Review*, XXXVI, 95–108.
[Willey, Nathan.] "Education of the Colored Population of Louisiana." *Harper's News Weekly Magazine*, XXXIII, 246–50.

SECONDARY

Belz, Herman. "The New Orthodoxy in Reconstruction Historiography." *Reviews in American History*, I, 106–113.

Berry, Mary F. "Negro Troops in Blue and Gray: The Louisiana Native Guard, 1861–1863." *Louisiana History*, VIII, 165–90.

Blassingame, John. "The Union Army as an Educational Institution for Negroes, 1862–1865." *Journal of Negro Education*, XXXIV (Spring, 1965), 152–59.

Cornish, Dudley T. "The Union Army as a Training School for Negroes." *Journal of Negro History*, XXXVII (October, 1952), 368–82.

Cox, LaWanda. "The Promise of Land for the Freedmen." *Mississippi Valley Historical Review*, XLV, 413–40.

Curry, Richard O. "The Civil War and Reconstruction, 1861–1877: A Critical Overview of Recent Trends and Interpretations." *Civil War History*, XXX, 215–38.

Everett, Donald E. "Demands of the New Orleans Free Colored Population for Political Equality, 1862–1865." *Louisiana Historical Quarterly*, XXXVIII, 43–64.

———. "Ben Butler and the Louisiana Native Guards, 1861–1862." *Journal of Southern History*, XXIV, 202–17.

Frazier, E. Franklin. "The Negro Slave Family." *Journal of Negro History*, XV, 198–259.

Gerteis, Louis S. "Salmon P. Chase, Radicalism, and the Politics of Emancipation, 1861–1964." *Journal of American History*, LX, 42–62.

Harlan, Louis R. "Desegregation in New Orleans' Public Schools During Reconstruction." *American Historical Review*, LXVII, 663–75.

Highsmith, William E. "Louisiana Landholding During War and Reconstruction." *Louisiana Historical Quarterly*, XXXVIII, 39–54.

Johnson, Ludwell H. "Lincoln and Equal Rights: A Reply." *Civil War History*, XIII, 66–73.

Kessel, Charles. "Educating the Slaves—A Forgotten Chapter of Civil War History." *Open Court*, XXXXI (April, 1927), 239–56.

———. "Edwin Miller Wheelock." *Open Court*, XXXIV, 562–69.

May, J. Thomas. "The Freedmen's Bureau at the Local Level: A Study of a Louisiana Agent." *Louisiana History*, IX, 5–20.

———. "Continuity and Change in the Labor Program of the Union Army and the Freedmen's Bureau." *Civil War History*, XVII, 245–54.

Potter, Betty. "The History of Negro Education in Louisiana." *Louisiana Historical Quarterly*, XXV (July, 1942), 728–821.

Rankin, David C. "The Origins of Black Leadership in New Orleans During Reconstruction." *Journal of Southern History*, XL, 417–40.

Shugg, Roger W. "Survival of the Plantation System in Louisiana." *Journal of Southern History*, III, 311–25.

Simpson, Amos E. and Vaughn Baker. "Michael Hahn: Steady Patriot." *Louisiana History*, XIII, 229–52.

Sitterson, J. Carlyle. "The William J. Minor Plantation: A Study in Ante-Bellum Absentee Ownership." *Journal of Southern History*, IX, 59–74.

Stahl, Annie Lee. "The Free Negro in Ante-Bellum Louisiana." *Louisiana Historical Quarterly*, XXV (January, 1942), 300–396.

Taylor, Joe Gray. "Slavery in Louisiana During the Civil War." *Louisiana History*, VIII, 27–33.

Uzee, Philip D. "The Beginnings of the Louisiana Republican Party." *Louisiana History*, XII, 197–211.

Wiley, Bell I. "Vicissitudes of Early Reconstruction Farming in the Lower Mississippi Valley." *Journal of Southern History*, III, 441–52.

Winston, James E. "The Free Negro in New Orleans, 1803–1860." *Louisiana Historical Quarterly*, XXI, 1074–85.

BOOKS

PRIMARY

Bacon, Edward. *Among the Cotton Thieves*. Detroit, 1867.

Basler, Roy P., ed. *The Collected Works of Abraham Lincoln*. 8 vols. New Brunswick, N.J., 1953.

Beecher, Harris H. *Record of the 114th Regiment N.Y.S.V.* Norwich, N.Y., 1866.

Bibb, Henry. *Narrative of the Life and Adventures of Henry Bibb, an American Slave*. New York, 1849.

Bosson, Charles. *History of the Forty-Second Regiment Infantry Massachusetts, 1862, 1863, 1864*. New York, 1866.

Butler, Benjamin F. *Butler's Book: Autobiography and Personal Reminiscences of Major-General Benjamin F. Butler*. Boston, 1892.

———. *Private and Official Correspondence of General Benjamin F. Butler During the Period of the Civil War*. 5 vols. Norwood, Mass., 1917.

Carpenter, George H. *History of the Eighth Regiment Vermont Volunteers.* Boston, 1866.

Chenery, William H. *The Fourteenth Regiment Rhode Island Heavy Artillery (Colored) in the War to Preserve the Union, 1861–1865.* Providence, 1898.

Clare, Josephine. *Narrative of the Adventures and Experiences of Mrs. Josephine Clare.* Lancaster, Pa., 1865.

Corsan, W. C. *Two Months in the Confederate States Including a Visit to New Orleans under the Domination of General Butler.* London, 1863.

Duganne, Augustine Joseph Hickey. *Camps and Prisons: Twenty Months in the Department of the Gulf.* New York, 1865.

Flinn, Frank M. *Campaigning with Banks in Louisiana in '63 and '64 and with Sheridan in the Shenandoah Valley in '64 and '65.* Lynn, Mass., 1887.

Fremantle, Sir Arthur J. *Three Months in the Southern States.* New York, 1864.

Hepworth, George H. *The Whip, Hoe and Sword: Or the Gulf Department in '63.* Boston, 1864.

Hosmer, James K. *The Color-Guard: Being a Corporal's Notes of Military Service in the Nineteenth Army Corps.* Boston, 1864.

Johns, Henry T. *Life with the Forty-ninth Massachusetts Volunteers.* Pittsfield, Mass., 1864.

Johnson, Charles B. *Muskets and Medicine: Or Army Life in the Sixties.* Philadelphia, 1917.

Lufkin, Edwin B. *The Story of the Maine Thirteenth.* Bridgton, Maine, 1898.

Marshall, Albert O. *Army Life, 1861–1864.* Joliet, Ill., 1886.

Moore, J. F. *History of the Fifty-Second Regiment Massachusetts Volunteers.* Boston, 1893.

Northrup, Soloman. *Twelve Years a Slave.* Sue Eakin and Joseph Logsdon, eds. Baton Rouge, 1968.

Powers, George W. *The Story of the Thirty-eighth Regiment of Massachusetts Volunteers.* Cambridge, Mass., 1866.

Smith, George Gilbert. *Leaves from a Soldier's Diary.* Putnam, Conn., 1906.

Sprague, Homer B. *History of the 13th Infantry Regiment Connecticut Volunteers During the Great Rebellion.* Hartford, Conn., 1867.

Stevens, William B. *History of the 50th Regiment of Infantry Massachusetts Volunteer Militia in the Late War of the Rebellion.* Boston, 1907.

Stevenson, Benjamin F. *Letters from the War.* Cincinnati, 1884.

Tiemann, William F. *The 159th Regiment New York State Volunteers in the War of the Rebellion, 1862–1865.* Brooklyn, New York, 1891.

Van Alstyne, Lawrence. *Diary of an Enlisted Man.* New Haven, Conn., 1910.

United States Department of War. *The War of the Rebellion: A Compilation of the Official Records of the Union and Confederate Armies.* 129 vols. Washington, D.C., 1880–1901.

SECONDARY

Belz, Herman. *Reconstructing the Union: Theory and Policy during the Civil War.* Ithaca, N.Y., 1969.

Blassingame, John W. *Black New Orleans, 1860–1880.* Chicago, 1973.
———. *The Slave Community: Plantation Life in the Antebellum South.* New York, 1972.

Bowers, Claude. *The Tragic Era.* Cambridge, Mass., 1929.

Capers, Gerald M. *Occupied City: New Orleans under the Federals, 1862–1865.* Lexington, 1965.

Caskey, Willie M. *Secession and Restoration of Louisiana.* Baton Rouge, 1938.

Desdunes, Rodolphe L. *Nos hommes et notre histoire.* Montreal, 1911.

DuBois, W. E. B. *Black Reconstruction in America, 1860–1880.* New York, 1935.

Ficklen, John Rose. *History of Reconstruction in Louisiana (Through 1868).* Originally published 1910; Baltimore, 1966.

Fogel, Robert William and Stanley Engerman. *Time on the Cross: The Economics of American Negro Slavery.* New York, 1974.

Genovese, Eugene. *Roll, Jordan, Roll: The World the Slaves Made.* New York, 1975.

Gerteis, Louis S. *From Contraband to Freedmen: Federal Policy toward Southern Blacks, 1861–1865.* Westport, Conn., 1973.

Harrington, Fred Harvey. *Fighting Politician: Major General N. P. Banks.* Philadelphia, 1948.

Hesseltine, William B. *Lincoln's Plan of Reconstruction.* Chicago, 1967.

Lonn, Ella. *Reconstruction in Louisiana after 1868.* New York, 1918.

McFeely, William. *Yankee Stepfather: General O. O. Howard and the Freedmen.* New York, 1970.

McPherson, James M. *The Struggle for Equality: The Abolitionist and the Negro in the Civil War and Reconstruction.* Princeton, 1964.

Moody, V. Alton. *Slavery on Louisiana Sugar Plantations.* New Orleans, 1924.

Parton, James. *General Butler in New Orleans.* Boston, 1871.

Perkins, A. E., ed. *Who's Who in Colored Louisiana.* New Orleans, 1930.

Phillips, Ulrich Bonnell. *American Negro Slavery. A Survey of the Supply, Employment, and Control of Negro Labor as Determined by the Plantation Regime.* Baton Rouge, 1966.

Randall, James G., and David Donald. *The Civil War and Reconstruction.* Lexington, Mass., 1969.

Roland, Charles P. *Louisiana Sugar Plantations During the Civil War.* Leiden, Netherlands, 1957.

Rose, Willie Lee. *Rehearsal for Reconstruction: The Port Royal Experiment.* New York, 1964.

Sandburg, Carl. *Abraham Lincoln: The War Years.* 4 vols. New York, 1939.

Shugg, Roger. *Origins of the Class Struggle in Louisiana.* Baton Rouge, 1939.

Stampp, Kenneth. *The Peculiar Institution: Slavery in the Ante-Bellum South.* New York, 1956.

Sitterson, J. Carlyle. *Sugar Country: The Cane Sugar Industry in the South, 1753–1950.* Lexington, 1953.

Sterkx, H. E. *The Free Negro in Ante-Bellum Louisiana.* Rutherford, N.J., 1972.

Taylor, Joe Gray. *Negro Slavery in Louisiana.* Baton Rouge, 1963.

Trefousse, Hans Louis. *Ben Butler: The South Called Him Beast!* New York, 1957.

Wade, Richard. *Slavery in the Cities: The South 1820–1860.* New York, 1964.

West, Richard S., Jr. *Lincoln's Scapegoat General: A Life of Benjamin F. Butler, 1818–1893.* Boston, 1965.

White, Howard A. *The Freedmen's Bureau in Louisiana.* Baton Rouge, 1970.

Wiley, Bell I. *Southern Negroes, 1861–1865.* New Haven, 1938.

Winters, John D. *The Civil War in Louisiana.* Baton Rouge, 1963.

THESES AND DISSERTATIONS

Baker, Dorothy M. "An Economic Survey of New Orleans During the Civil War and Reconstruction." M.A. thesis, Tulane University, 1942.

Bahney, Robert Stanley. "Generals and Negroes: Education of Negroes by the Union Army, 1861–1865." Ph.D. dissertation, University of Michigan, 1965.

Bringer, Gladys Stella. "Transition from Slave to Free Labor in Louisiana after the Civil War." M.A. thesis, Tulane University, 1927.

Constantine, R. R. "The Louisiana 'Black Code' Legislation of 1865." M.A. thesis, Louisiana State University, 1956.

DiMartino, Mary. "Education in New Orleans During Reconstruction." M.A. thesis, Tulane University, 1935.

Drake, Richard Bryant. "The American Missionary Association and Southern Negroes, 1861–1868." Ph.D. dissertation, Emory University, 1957.

Dubroca, Isabelle Christina. "A Study of Negro Emancipation in Louisiana, 1803–1865." M.A. thesis, Tulane University, 1924.

Ellis, Isabella Dorothy Lois. "The Transition from Slave Labor to Free Labor with Special Reference to Louisiana." M.A. thesis, Louisiana State University, 1932.

Everett, Donald E. "Free Persons of Color in New Orleans, 1803–1865." Ph.D. dissertation, Tulane University, 1952.

Fisher, Robert A. "The Segregation Struggle in Louisiana, 1850–1890." Ph.D. dissertation, Tulane University, 1967.

Luke, Josephine. "From Slavery to Freedom in Louisiana, 1862–1865." M.A. thesis, Tulane University, 1939.

McCrary, James Peyton. "Moderation in a Revolutionary World: Lincoln and the Failure of Reconstruction in Louisiana." Ph.D. dissertation, Princeton University, 1972.

Myers, John B. "Black Human Capital: The Freedmen and the Reconstruction of Labor in Alabama, 1860–1880." Ph.D. dissertation, Florida State University, 1974.

Sterkx, Herbert E. "Free Negro in Ante-Bellum Louisiana, 1724–1860." Ph.D. dissertation, University of Alabama, 1954.

Woessner, Charles Herman. "New Orleans, 1840–1860: A Study of Urban Slavery." M.A. thesis, Louisiana State University, 1967.

Index

231